7.10

COLONY AND CONFEDERATION

Canadian Literature Series

George Woodcock, general editor

COLONY
AND CONFEDERATION

Early Canadian Poets
and Their Background

edited by
GEORGE WOODCOCK

with an introduction by
ROY DANIELLS

University of British Columbia Press
Vancouver

COLONY AND CONFEDERATION:
Early Canadian Poets and Their Background

© 1974 by the University of British Columbia

International Standard Book Number: 0-7748-0031-3

Printed in Canada by
The Morriss Printing Company Ltd.
Victoria, British Columbia

CONTENTS

NOTE ON THE TEXT

Most of the essays included in this volume have been published in *Canadian Literature*. In these cases, with one exception, the contributions have been left as they were originally published, but the date of publication has been added at the end of each so that the reader will be able to establish the perspective in time from which it was written. The exception is Norman Newton's "Classical Canadian Poetry and the Public Muse", where the author added material which he felt was strongly relevant to his argument, strengthening rather than changing it.

In addition to the Introduction, five previously unpublished pieces have been written for this volume to add greater comprehensiveness to the field of study. They are "The Journey of Discovery" by George Woodcock, "Charles Sangster" by Donald Stephens, "A Choice of Worlds" by W. J. Keith, "The Wound under the Feathers" by Glenys Stow and "Bliss Carman" by John Robert Sorfleet. We thank the authors of the reprinted essays who have given us permission to print them here.

G.W.

INTRODUCTION

Roy Daniells

Tに HE PECULIAR VIRTUE of the essays which make up this
book is that they encourage us to look beyond the confines of their ostensible
subject matter, Victorian and Edwardian poetry in Canada, as well as to look
at the poems themselves with a sharper gaze, a more critical and, at the same
time, more appreciative eye.

We shall inevitably begin by looking back, seeking to achieve historical perspective. We face once more the enigma of colonialism, the peculiar willingness of
Canadians to be amenable to and proud of a colonial status until such time as it
developed into the concept of the Dominion and this, in turn, became a concept
of greater independence without hostility to what went before.

We have been accustomed to think of certain salient groupings of Canadians
who provided a high and dramatic tension to the political situation: Empire
Loyalists whose aversion from the America of the Revolution had its counterpart
in adherence to the British crown, or Québecois whose culture and religion
offered so many points of contrast to American republicanism as to make a tie
with Britain the lesser of two evils. To such central and salient elements of the
population, historians have been adding others, smaller and more remote but
each decisive in its own region and capable of a literary voice. The inhabitants
of the Pacific coast did not need to be told that their only sure shield against
eventual Americanization was the British Navy.

The thoughtful Canadian of liberal views can ponder the paradox that British
Imperialism, now suffering so bad a press, and the Navy whose vessels could be
hell afloat for the ordinary seaman — the boatswains' right to strike men arbi-
trarily persisted into the nineteenth century — that these criminal abuses of
power, whether international or personal, were inextricably intertwined with the
preservation of Canada's independence.

At every point in the picture and at every stage of the argument, regardless

I

of what is being depicted or asserted concerning Canada, the reader of our poetry or student of our history becomes aware of the role played by the sheer extent of the terrain, four thousand miles from east to west. The obvious problems of communication and transport overlay political issues; e.g., the town-meeting of the American states, so powerful a factor in the formation of democracy south of the border, did not and could not develop. At a deeper level, distances foster personal isolation and terrify the individual consciousness, as so much recorded experience of the prairies testifies. It is distance, moreover, that keeps the twin problems of national unity and national identity circling about each other without coming to grips. A certain blandness and tentativeness, which make themselves felt in the poetry, may be attributed to the Canadian's enforced willingness to subsume distant and disparate communities within his national purview without any pressing desire to unify their customs and regularize their attitudes. The longest coastline in the world provides, among other things, innumerable nooks and crannies.

The fifteen critical essays that follow present the same pattern of diversities which decline to be regularized yet neighbour one another without too much reluctance. They do not present a natural ideological or chronological sequence. They do not set up opposing schools or academies of poets. The world peopled by Canadian poems is singularly unstructured. There is not in the period under review a poet of agreed pre-eminence. There are few irreconcilable differences of class or religion, of education or temperament — such as make for dramatic clashes. There is even an absence of enmity and of scandal. We have nothing comparable to the critics who so vigorously attacked and defended Hardy, after his death.

The reader of the essays which follow will find the historical reasons for this state of affairs suggested and implied in many of contexts. He may ruminate, in the manner of C. P. Snow, on the tide in the affairs of men that, taken at the flood, leads on to great works of literature. Or on the attendant phenomenon, that nationalists, at the peak of their country's political or military success, tend to overrate its literary productions, while nationals of a country feeling its way toward self-realization and self-justification tend, conversely, to underrate its works of literature. As we move into an unknowable future, it is anybody's guess as to what role, moral or material, creative or diplomatic, intellectual or humanitarian, Canada must enact if literary production is to leap to a high and internationally applauded level. It will, nevertheless, be for many Canadians a matter of profound concern.

Though the reader with an historical sense may at some point doubt that the late Victorian heritage of Roberts, Carman, Lampman and company can possess any relevance to our own problems, he will discover, upon reflection, that problems parallel to our own traverse the whole body of their writing. Landscape is as vital to us as to them, though our own engagement is more likely to lead to concern than to euphoria; an uncoordinated search for myths and symbols which will serve to embody national experience engrosses us no less, though our bent is away from the cosmic and toward the psychological; the Indian and the Eskimo are as visible now as at the turn of the century, though it is less often their immemorial past than their viable future that comes into focus.

In addition to the history of Canada as a political or social entity, we find in these papers *une tranche de vie* of our literary history. Its centre can be conveniently located in the work of Isabella Crawford. In the words of George Woodcock: "Crawford retained within a precarious balance her warring inclinations towards socially-oriented narrative and inwardly-oriented lyrical verse." He demonstrates her dilemma between the requirements of poetry using traditional devices to record the emergence of new social forms and, on the other hand, the demands of the individual voice which, reflecting individual sensibility, achieves an original tone..

It is Crawford and D. C. Scott who have benefited most from our revived interest in high colonialism. New works, hitherto lying in manuscript, or new evaluations of known poems have broadened, thanks to some energetic critics, the base itself of our appreciation. If one is not in entire accord with Gary Geddes as regards the merits of Scott's "Piper of Arll", one does become aware of a deeper significance than has customarily been credited to the poem.

Certain large themes have also benefited from re-examination in the context of a Victorian or Edwardian ethos. Lampman's sense of a divine spirit in the world, to be reached through meditation or "dream"; Crawford's brave attempt to project the substance of myth; Roberts' perception, as he worked through his tales of animals, of links between animal, human and divine: these, we can now see, are in some sense period pieces, perfectly at home in the context of a prevailing ethos between, say, the Crimean War and the War of 1914-1918, a period when doctrinal religion was at a discount but when faith and aspiration proved vital and ever striving upward.

Some readers of the essays which follow may dispense completely with historical considerations and ask, instead, how the poets under review deal with timeless problems of life and death. These numinous issues lift their heads in all periods

3

and in landscapes of many kinds. *Monte Cristo* is as palpably an affirmation of resurrection as Bunyan's allegory is an exposition of pilgrimage; both hit the mark because of the simple and radical nature of the image and the sustained intensity of its presentation. The capacity of our Victorian and Edwardian poets to express ultimate truths of this kind should perhaps be viewed, if only momentarily, against a general background of Canadian writing. Our religious writing *per se* tends to be defensively expository; our novelists, however well they expound the human condition, tend to settle for a secular solution; few of our poets speak effectively to the reader who despairs of life. Is it too harsh to suggest that scarcely any Canadian literary image of regeneration, of pilgrimage to an attained goal, of forgiveness and power to reconcile, of the eternal city, has as yet impressed itself upon the world's imagination? Or should we rather say that this is the wrong question, public recognition being the last thing the possessor of true powers of vision desires or needs?

If, ranging the broad spectrum of Canadian poetry, we keep our eyes open for significant myth cogently presented, we are likely to find it between covers that bear the names of women, inconspicuous as a flower in a garden with winding paths. Here is Jay Macpherson:

> Cold Pastoral: The shepherd under the snow
> Sleeps circled with his sheep.
> Above them though successive winters heap
> Rigors, and wailing weathers go
> Like beasts about, time only rocks their sleep,
> An ark upon a deep,
> And drowsy care, to keep the world from death,
> Maintains his steady heartbeat and warm breath.

If such is the pattern, we might expect Crawford, among the poets dealt with in this present volume, to strike myth's authentic note of simplicity, mystery and rapture. Such, indeed, is the case:

> My masters twain their camp-soul lit,
> Streamed incense from the hissing cones,
> Large, crimson flashes grew and whirl'd
> Thin, golden nerves of sly light curl'd
> Round the dun camp, and rose faint zones....
> The darkness built its wigwam walls
> Close round the camp, and at its curtain
> Press'd shapes, thin woven and uncertain
> As white locks of tall waterfalls.

4

Writing in *Canadian Literature*, Ann Yeoman commended Crawford's imaginative perspicacity: she "has understood this need for a unifying and identifying language of symbols as necessary to the development of a native culture and literature — and this alone makes her an important literary figure in Canadian art."

Likenesses and differences between Canadian and British poets of the Victorian-Edwardian period are continually in evidence. Wordsworthian meditative observation is very common in Canadian poetry; the commonplace is a starting point for philosophical reflection. But we do not find "home thoughts from abroad" in any quantity. It is hard for the Canadian poet to conceive of some corner of a foreign field that is for ever Canada. It is equally difficult for him to alternate, as Kipling did so naturally, between the assured sights, sounds and customs of the Motherland and the exotic habits and strange scenes of lands abroad. If the Canadian poet expands in any quarter and takes cognizance of the strangeness of its scenes, it is likely to be within his own country. When Roberts speaks of Canadian soldiers fallen in Egypt and buried there, the really mysterious and evocative lines of his poem concern the landscape of Canada:

> On soft Pacific slopes, — beside
> Strange floods that northward rave and fall, —
> Where chafes Acadia's chainless tide —
> Thy sons await thy call.

The modern reader must bear in mind that poets of the period we are now considering did not enjoy the advantages of air travel and that this lack coloured their imaginative grasps of the Canadian terrain without limiting its scope. Their types of two-dimensional travel were such that ideas of vastness, of endlessness, of hardship in travelling and of the sheer extent of the unknown or unreachable were a permanent source of wonder, of outreach imaginative rather than cartographic.

When all is said and done and criticism has stretched to its full extent, nothing will keep the appreciative reader of our literature from cherishing the handful of poems that most appeal to him personally. These will not be confined to poems of social or national significance; nor will they consist only of expressions of intense private emotion. They may depict "the animal man in his warmth and vigour, sound and hard and complete"; they may catch the diurnal round: "Glittering and still shall come the awful night" or the annual cycle: "Pale season, watcher in unvexed suspense". They will sometimes achieve their special resonance, as do many of the most memorable lines penned in England, from circumstances, permanent or immediate, in which they took shape. For myself, the most poignant set of personal surroundings in the period we are considering were those of Isabella Crawford, living over a store in Toronto, she and her mother in cramped quarters and close to poverty. From all of which she rose into regions of the imagination: "Love's solid land is everywhere!"

Our appreciation of individual lines and passages will be sharpened by insights furnished in the following pages. We are shown that poetry in the service of a public image is less likely to succeed than poems of private sensibility; that the search for fundamental myth related to life in Canada never ceases; that religious aspiration, a desire to come to some rapport with the absolute, lifts its gaze unwearied; that ready access to Canada's unique beauties and unrestrained natural forces is a powerful poetic motive. Even the limitations of poets such as Carman, Lampman and Service become significant and illuminating.

This book should be kept on an accessible shelf. It does not yield its full meaning at one perusal; its usefulness is not bounded by the critical arguments it applies to particular poets. It will be taken down, reread and pondered in the context of many cultural problems. The writers it introduces us to coped with doubts and difficulties that, in altered forms, still confront us. And they were, without exception, undismayed.

CLASSICAL CANADIAN POETRY AND THE PUBLIC MUSE

Norman Newton

EVERYBODY SEEMS TO BELIEVE that classical Canadian poetry is mediocre; the question is not whether, but why. Various explanations have been advanced. At times this mediocrity has even been treated as its chief quality, an expression of the national virtues of sobriety and reasonableness. In this article, I propose to look into one aspect of the mediocrity of classical Canadian poetry, and to offer some explanations of my own, in the hope of stimulating discussion.

"Mediocre" means "of middling quality", not "bad". There is no doubt that some classical Canadian poetry is quite bad. But what we have, it seems, is a poetic landscape mediocre in the best sense, possessing few outstanding features, but rich in pleasant fields and wooded hills. Indeed, when one considers English and French poetry together, one discovers a body of work which is surprisingly solid for a country with so short a literary history and, until recently, so small a population. It compares very favourably with that produced over the same period of time by countries with much older literary traditions — nineteenth-century Spain, for example. Nevertheless, it is, even if in the best sense of the word, mediocre. One may apply to the Canadian poetic tradition the judgment Lampman applied, with great good sense, to himself: "There never was any great poet, but simply a rather superior minor one who sometimes hit upon a thing which comes uncommonly near to being very excellent."

Canadian poetry is also distinctive. Nothing better indicates a national identity than the fact that our traditional French and English poets, in spite of mutual ignorance, had a great deal in common. In this, they no doubt reflected a certain similarity between the two cultures. As John Porter recently pointed out in an article in *Cultural Affairs*, "English and French Canadians are more alike in their conservatism, traditionalism, religiosity, authoritarianism, and elitist values than the spokesmen of either group are prepared to admit." The poetry, for its part, reflects a conservatism closer to that of pre-industrial society than to the capitalist conservatism of the United States: a very strong sense of the ties of orthodox Christianity even when these ties were rebelled against, a sense of the heroic, a strong attachment to place (usually expressing itself as an idealization of the village and rural life of the poet's boyhood), a fondness for ornate and colourful language, a tendency to personify nature which went beyond the poetic conventions of the age and approached mythogenesis — and, on the negative side, a lack of wit (Canadian wit tended, and tends, to be annoyingly simple-minded), an inability to sustain intellectual argument on a high level of subtlety, and a lack of that daring which makes the poet an inventor as well as a singer and craftsman. Clearly these positive and negative elements were related to each other.

Simple definitions are often false ones, and I am not oblivious of nuance when I say that traditional Canadian poetry in both English and French seems to me very conservative even in the political sense, and that this quality is closely bound up with the Canadian character as it expressed itself in our formative years. The two most important factors in the history of this country have been the English-Canadian rejection of the American Revolution and the French-Canadian rejection of the French Revolution, rejections which were related even as these two revolutions were. Conservatism as such does not make for mediocrity; but a particular kind of conservatism does, and this particular kind of conservatism was strong in nineteenth-century Canada. It was most evident in what one might call "public poetry" — hence my title. It is in public poetry that the poet most clearly expresses what he conceives to be his role in society. My contention is that the peculiar qualities of nineteenth-century Canadian poetry, both the good and the bad ones, arose out of the poetic community's conception of its own role. This in fact was a misconception, but one which developed very naturally out of the confusions of the age itself, in which the aristocratic idea of art was dying.

I first became fully aware of this when I was working on a radio production of Heavysege's *Count Filippo*. There has always been a clash of opinions about the value of Heavysege's work. Smith has compared his Malzah to Ariel or Caliban, and has referred to *Count Filippo* as "brilliantly written and well-constructed . . . in the manner of Beaumont and Fletcher". Others have come to the conclusion that he is very nearly the worst poet who has ever lived.

8

I have, at times, almost inclined to the latter opinion. There is no doubt that Heavysege could write lines of incomparable grotesqueness. But his sonnets are good; and when, many years ago, I came across a copy of *Count Filippo* in the Toronto Public Library, my first impression was that it is a curious mixture of utter banality and originality, with some moments of great power and others of unexpected subtlety. Certainly, it seemed no mere "closet drama", but a truly imaginative if ludicrously uneven poetic drama, which I felt then would probably work in performance.

A few years ago I had a chance to look at it again. Since I was producing radio drama for the CBC, I decided to commission a radio version from Peter Haworth. Mr. Haworth prepared a sensitive and intelligent adaptation, and the play was presented on a programme called Midweek Theatre. As it turned out, the play did indeed "work", in spite of great flaws which no editing could eliminate.

The qualified success of *Count Filippo* gave me the confidence to commission, again from Mr. Haworth, a radio adaptation of *Saul*. This was prepared from a conflation of two of the printed editions of the play. In 1974 it was presented on CBC Tuesday Night. *Saul* is huge, of course, and even Mr. Haworth's fine two-hour version left most of it out. The actors found it very playable, and, indeed, served the text splendidly. Once again, there were unavoidable stretches of bathos; nevertheless, *Saul* proved to be a unified work of art, epic in feeling and encompassing heaven, earth and hell with superb audacity. Some of its scenes — Saul's encounter with Malzah, his mad scenes, the scene with the witch of Endor — were seen to be as powerful as anything in English drama outside the best of the Elizabethans and Jacobeans. The scenes with the spirits, which at first had struck me as inept because I was expecting dark Miltonic grandeurs, suddenly came clear: Heavysege, like Massinger in *The Virgin Martyr*, was treating his evil spirits as types of loathsome inanity or vulgar cunning and vengefulness; they are wicked as human beings are wicked.

The experience of directing the play, while it increased my respect for A. J. M. Smith's intellectual courage in championing a work which most Canadian literati still scorn, forced me to opinions rather different from his. He had seen it as "a huge closet drama in blank verse, interspersed with lyrical interludes" and had compared it with Beddoes' imitations of Webster and Tourneur. In production it emerged as an effective theatrical work, strong in situation and characterization. It seemed to owe little to Webster and Tourneur, and nothing to Beddoes. The debt to Shakespeare was less than I had expected and was largely a matter of

9

obvious verbal echoes, easily detached from context. Many of the speeches were more Miltonic than Shakespearian, quite in the tradition of the late eighteenth-century poetic drama of England, with its neoclassical tendencies. A strong Byronic influence was apparent, though Heavysege's dramatic diction was superior to Byron's. Indeed, it was at its best superior to that of any of Heavy-sege's contemporaries or immediate predecessors, including Shelley, though only as long as he kept his eye on the subject: his lyrical divagations were comparatively weak. I came to the conclusion that Heavysege had chosen his masters carefully. He was seeking a way back to an idealized literary past and had learned from his contemporaries only those points of style which had seemed to him to be in the "true tradition".

He might profitably be compared with Charles Doughty, whose epic poem, *The Dawn in Britain*, is almost as little-known as *Saul*, and for similar reasons. Doughty was also an archaizer. Both belonged to a now-dead tradition of Protestant Christian epic with a theological bias, never precisely defined, towards a heroic Arianism. Its God was a god of battles and its cosmos was a basically pre-Copernican one, in which both Hell and Heaven may be located in space, thus making it possible for angels and demons to engage in aerial wars. It favoured a craggy, grandiose and consciously archaic style. The presence of Milton brooded over this school, and even when its exponents consciously rejected his influence (as Doughty did), they considered themselves to be in competition with him. If *The Dawn in Britain*, a work of real splendour in its narrow way, is more successful than *Saul*, it is because Doughty went all the way and created a towering artificial diction which excluded all nuances irrelevant to his subject.

Doughty went to Arabia to find the fierce world of tribal monotheism which his imagination needed. Heavysege came to Canada, and it cannot be doubted that he came for artistic as well as money-making reasons, even if they were unconscious and will always remain unknown: a man with his sense of poetic vocation would not emigrate simply "to better his position".

Canada has been a refuge for folk and archaic elements which have died in Europe. Folklorists have discovered medieval ballads and seventeenth-century court songs magically preserved, though in an altered and countrified form, in the folk-music of Quebec; they have discovered Elizabethan slang in the dialect of Newfoundland; the tradition of classical bagpipe playing, "pibroch", survived in the Maritimes long after the Scots themselves had lost interest in it. In Heavysege we have something more remarkable: a Jacobean sensibility transplanted whole, though with some damage in transit, into the nineteenth century.

Perhaps the circumstances of his life help to explain the anomaly. He was a Yorkshireman and a member of the artisan class, a cabinet-maker and carpenter. His parents were strict in their religious views, and rigidly moralistic. He was largely self-educated; he met few writers of even moderate distinction, and his intellectual and artistic life was largely a solitary one.

In other words, Heavysege was born into a provincial and hence archaic sector of English society. When he was a child, his parents determinedly kept him "unspotted from the world". He escaped the conformity-inducing influences of formal education and entered young into a trade which had maintained longer than many others the old handicraft traditions. True, he did leave provincial Huddersfield, but he did so only to go to even more provincial Montreal, ruled by an elite consisting of merchants, true-blue English Tories, descendants of French seigneurs, and a few annexationists.

We do not know why Heavysege came to Canada, but it is clear that he did not realize how deeply inimical nineteenth-century Canadian society was to the poetic spirit. His gigantic chronicle play was completely irrelevant, so far as the life of his time was concerned. We know that he was saddened by lack of recognition; we also know that he bore the uncertainty and drudgery of his daily life with Christian patience, but not without the very natural hope that he would be "discovered". After all, he had given very powerful poetic form to ideas which were being expressed, though in feeble and woolly form, from most Canadian Protestant pulpits; *Saul* was unorthodox, and, in spite of its flaws, it was the only significant religious drama written in English since *Samson Agonistes*. Why, since Canada was a Christian country, was nobody interested? (Doughty must have been similarly puzzled: had he not described, in new-minted words and with a ruggedness and power of style unknown since Anglo-Saxon times, the coming of Christianity to Britain?) But the orthodox were not interested and perhaps they were even repelled. There is a sense in which poetry cannot lie, and when they saw what they professed to be their world embodied in a work of the imagination they did not like it. They preferred banality, since orthodoxy was to them a source not of challenge, but of mindless comfort. They ignored the book or praised it and did not read it. Some of Heavysege's fellow poets in Britain or the United States, notably Coventry Patmore, praised the poem highly; but epics are like great public buildings and are not created for a select circle. The theatre, of course, ignored the play; Heavysege prepared an acting version, but it was never presented and has since disappeared.

Most of the criticism he received from Canadians — whether it was intended well or ill — did him more harm than good. *Jephtha's Daughter* which, unlike his other works, he carefully revised along lines suggested by well-meaning friends whose taste represented the norm of his time and place, is dull and conventional; and here we find another anomaly, since it is the most polished and self-consistent of his productions. Apparently Heavysege's genius and his lack of taste were inseparably related; he could write "correctly", but only by writing dully.

Let us revert, after what must seem a long digression, to our main theme. Do we not find, in many classical Canadian poets, the same combination of talent and miscalculation? Is not this unfortunate combination most apparent in their public poems? This phenomenon is precisely due, I believe, to the fact that their poetic talents could only operate when they wrote in a state of illusion — an illusion, I have suggested, as to their social role. They could still deceive themselves, though not consistently, into the belief that their society valued their contribution to the spiritual life of the age, that they were as poets a functional part of the social body. Society was willing to aid them, though half-contemptuously, in this self-deception and politely applauded the odes, political sonnets, and lyrics in which they expounded what they conceived to be the national ethos. From time to time the poets became aware of their true position, that of outsiders who were tolerated rather than loved or respected, and their tendency was then to retreat into a defensive subjectivity. Even in their most confident moments, however, the doubt as to their role was present, though hidden. The result was an uncertainty of intonation in the poetic voice, which might manifest itself as bluster, over-insistence on the obvious, vulgar and fumbling attempts to capture the sentimental popular imagination, and other features of bad style.

Thus a kind of universal schizophrenia is apparent. There is the real Charles Sangster, a playful, minor poet of springtime, with a pleasant taste for country girls. Then there is the Sangster who wrote *Brock*, with its marvellously comic closing lines —

> Briareus-limbed, they sweep along,
> The Typhons of the time.

The thought of Brock as Typhon is an image of horror worthy of Blake; but Sangster did not mean it that way.

There is Isabella Crawford, who could have written fine personal lyrics with a gnomic force, but chose to waste her talents writing about men with axes, whom she did not understand. There is Charles Mair, an autumnal sensibility, a quiet lazy dreamer after the manner of James Thomson, who trickled his gentle talent away into the vast dusty mould of a chronicle drama about Tecumseh. There is Sir Charles G. D. Roberts, who should have written nothing but regional pastorals, but tried to write hymns of empire. Bliss Carman ruined his talent, as Desmond Pacey has pointed out, trying to be the spokesman of a crudely vigorous optimism which was alien to his sensuous, feminine and melancholy temperament. In Archibald Lampman and D. C. Scott, who came nearest to realizing themselves in their work, there is often an annoying split between impulse and diction.

Here we come a bit closer to our quarry, which is an elusive one, and must be surrounded: it cannot be dispatched cleanly and at first sight. As has been implied, every time our classical poets tried to fulfil a social function, to perform their public "use" as poets, which is to say, every time they tried to write a patriotic poem, a historical epic, or a serious theatrical work, the result was in some way embarrassing. On the other hand, when they described a personal experience, or responded to a landscape they loved, the result was often beautiful. Clearly, unlike the contemporary poet, they did feel they had a use, and so did their society. Poets were still expected to write ceremonial odes for the visits of noble or royal persons, for example, and were expected to give utterance to the great religious and political truths. Society did indeed demand poetry, and it demanded poetry on the same themes that poets of earlier ages had treated. For some reason, though, it seemed to demand bad poetry.

It is a curious fact that in nineteenth-century Canada literature became connected with the civil service in a way it has never been, one is inclined to think, in any other country outside Tsarist Russia. Sangster, Mair, Lampman, W. W. Campbell, D. C. Scott and Tom MacInnes were all civil servants, and Sir Charles G. D. Roberts was one of the official historians of the First World War. There was also a strong connection with the clergy: Campbell was a clergyman before he entered the civil service, F. G. Scott was an Anglican priest, and Roberts, D. C. Scott and Lampman were the sons of clergymen. Most of the other poets in the "canon" seem to have been involved in, or related to people involved in high-level journalism, medicine or the law. They were an elite group, obviously: they were to a very large extent dependent upon public institutions for their living, and most of them came from "good families" of the old-fashioned kind. There was little connection with the world of business.

A similar though not identical pattern may be discerned in the Quebec of the nineteenth and early twentieth centuries. Pamphile Le May, Louis-Honoré Fréchette, Gonsalve Desaulniers, Jean Charbonneau, Lionel Léveillé and Paul Morin were lawyers, judges, or combined law with public service; William Chapman, Albert Ferland and Edouard Chauvin were civil servants with the federal or provincial governments; Nerée Beauchemin and Guy Delabaye were doctors; René Chopin was a notary. Most of the other poets of the period were journalists; some were priests or abbés.

Compare this situation with that in the United States, where, at least between the Civil War and the New Deal era, national and state governments ignored the arts on the whole. A few United States poets were civil servants; but most were employed by universities or worked as journalists. On the other hand, there has been, in the United States, enlightened private patronage of a type very rare in Canada. Usually this patronage was offered, in the days before the great tax-exempt foundations, by members of an immigrant financial or capitalist elite, who patronized the arts in the manner of the European haute bourgeoisie. But they were much more interested in painting and music than in poetry. It is not surprising that nineteenth-century United States writers tended to be more "individualist" than their Canadian counterparts, and that they felt less identity with the aims of their governments. The great classics of United States literature are all seditious, as has been pointed out more than once, and United States poets who have consciously identified themselves with the political establishment, such as Archibald MacLeish, have found their poetic stock plummeting as a result. In Canada, one suspects, a MacLeish would have been "Dean of Canadian Poetry" several times over.

From the days of de Tocqueville on, visitors to or natives of the United States have been pointing out that it is a profoundly anti-poetic society. However, de Tocqueville, in his inspired and penetrating simplicity, appears to have come closest to the truth, namely, that United States society is anti-poetic because it is anti-aristocratic and anti-monarchical, as such an archetypically capitalist society must inevitably be. The intellectual life of the United States after the Revolution and before the Civil War had, on its upper levels, elements of a refinement — though a thin, attenuated and provincial refinement — of essentially European and aristocratic or pseudo-aristocratic type, and the farmers and frontiersmen were producing a folk culture of real vigour. It is from such societies, when they mature, that poetry springs. But this society was not allowed to develop; it was cut down in the Civil War and was finally obliterated by the rise of industrial big business in the latter half of the nineteenth century. One of the profound and tragic beauties of Whitman's work is that he was glorifying a world which was disappearing, though he thought it the world of the future — the world of the farmer, the pioneer, the sailor, and the free, independent artisan. The America he heard singing was dying as it sang, and this gives his poems the heroic beauty of a great elegy, a beauty he could sense in the already half-mythical and archaic figure of Abraham Lincoln.

IN CANADA, THOUGH, the social effect of the Age of Business was delayed. Right through the Second World War we were still presenting an image of ourselves in our propaganda films as a nation of wheat-farmers, fishermen, sailors, trappers and dwellers in small country towns. French Canada, producing spokesmen like the Abbé Groulx, a clerical pamphleteer and historian who could have fitted very comfortably into the France of Charles X (I do not intend this to be taken as condemnatory of the Abbé) was even more archaic. Indeed, in the seigneurs, Canada had had a land-owning hereditary aristocracy up to 1854, and the habitants were not fully relieved of their "feudal" obligations until 1940. Our Governors-General, right up to the end of the Second World War, were English noblemen. Even our political radicalism — the agrarian socialism of the C.C.F. and the petty-bourgeois anti-capitalism of early Social Credit — had a piquantly old-fashioned quality.

Furthermore, many of the social ideals upheld by the "Establishment" up to the end of the Second World War were aristocratic ones. We were loyal to the monarch and to the land: Americans fought for Mom's apple pie, that symbol of happy consumption, but we fought for those waving fields of wheat. We considered ourselves (though mistakenly) a specifically Christian country, and thought it more important to be law-abiding than to be clever. Our propaganda media extolled the dignity of agricultural labour and idealized the simple homely virtues. Our official symbols, and the persons who embodied the ceremonial life of the state, were aristocratic in tone. Of all American states, only Canada could have produced such a figure as our late Governor-General, General Georges Vanier. In his nobility and his extraordinary public presence, he represented a type — and I mean this as a tribute to his memory — not found elsewhere outside historical films. He was a poetic figure. Our Houses of Parliament have on them carvings of all the animals and birds to be found in Canada. What could be more poetically archaic than that? One is reminded of the garden outside the

Temple of the Sun in Incaic Cuzco, which contained gold and silver images of all the birds and animals of the empire.

The following passage, from a sermon preached in Upper Canada in 1824, must be one of the last statements, from an "Establishment" source at any rate, of the doctrine of degree.

> One is formed to rule and another to obey. Subordination in the Moral World is manifest.... The beauty and advantages of this arrangement are obvious and universally acknowledged.... The various relations of individuals and societies require a mutual exchange of good offices.... The Magistrate requires the aid of his people, the Master of his servant. They are all dependent upon one another.... The lowest order enjoys its peculiar comforts and privileges, and contributes equally with the highest to the support and dignity of Society.... All discontent and murmuring at the inferiority of our Station is [therefore] most unreasonable.

Such ideas were echoed again and again by the spokesmen of what has been called "The Family Compact", in their disputes with radicals and liberals.

In times long past, attitudes and ideas such as this gave birth to great buildings of state, cathedrals, epic poems and verse dramas. They did not in Canada, because the tradition was dying, almost dead. But if one can personify a tradition, it kept trying, even in its dying hours, to do what it had done all its life. It was this tradition which continued, with the automatism of the moribund, to produce cathedrals and buildings of state in the Gothic style, epic poems in the Roman style, and verse dramas in the Jacobean style. No poet of the United States could address his country as "O Child of Nations, giant-limbed", or refer to one of his national heroes as Sangster referred to Brock, as one who "in his lofty sphere sublime / Sits crowned above the common throng". The nearest they came to such classical personification and apotheosis was in the Revolutionary period, when some popular broadsheets and ballads spoke of Washington in terms suitable to the eighteenth-century military aristocrat, with his code of honour —

> Great Washington he led us on,
> Whose streaming flag, in storm or sun,
> Had never known disgrace.

We have now to examine why a tradition which was certainly a noble one, and which, since it answers certain needs that seem to be part of the intrinsic nature of man, is an inherently vital one, did not produce work of more value. The answer seems to be that we are dealing here with an official "Establishment" ideology which, while it was largely respected by the people of the country, did not rise from their common life, and did not rest upon an economic and political base consistent with its aims.

Official Canada, aristocratic Canada, was by no means alien or exotic: it was as native as the world of the logger and the wheat-farmer. But the concessions made after the Mackenzie and Papineau rebellions, which stifled what was a developing indigenous French and English aristocracy and nipped Church Establishment in the bud, prevented it from establishing roots in the economic, political and social soil of the country. Had we been at that time an independent country, this quiet liberal-capitalist revolution would probably have produced a society similar to that of the United States, which we would then have joined. (Indeed, as is well known, the Rebellion Losses Bill of 1849 strengthened the annexationists' cause immensely.) Fortunately we were not independent at the time: the United States dared not intervene, for fear of war with Britain. What happened instead was that the aristocratic idea, deprived of its local roots, became more firmly attached to the metropolitan centre. Those who belonged to the elite, or aspired to enter it, cultivated modified English accents and entered their children in schools modelled after the English type. Sometimes, as is usually the case with those who pursue refinement and taste as canonical virtues rather than graces of everyday life, the result was somewhat artificial. Brian Moore, in the book he wrote on Canada for Time Inc., tells of a remark made by an English earl about Vincent Massey. "Fine chap, Vincent", he said, "but he does make one feel a bit of a savage."

Beneath the level of the official elite, there was developing an economic life very similar to that of the United States, though less sophisticated and less cruel. Effective power was in the hands of businessmen, and what is virtue to the aristocratic mind is to the business mind either folly or obscurantism. Because the United States was above all the Land of Business, Canadian businessmen tended to become "Americanized". Indeed, in our conflicts with the United States in the late eighteenth and the nineteenth centuries, many members of the mercantile community played a treasonable or near-treasonable role, though there is no doubt that they would have been fiercely and violently nationalistic if that had been the profitable stance.

Nevertheless, to them, the virtues inculcated by the official elite were matters of convenience only. The monarch was a kind of hereditary president or a means of preserving social stability, thus a mere convenience. Love of the land made sense only if agriculture were more profitable than other forms of economic activity; thus, those waving fields of wheat were merely sources of income, and had no mystical beauty. Labour had no dignity, only a price. The law was to be respected only if it encouraged business growth; if it hampered the expansion of business, it was to be changed. Christianity, to steal a phrase from a man who understood capitalism well, was the opium of the people, and thus of value, but only if one did not insist on a Christian business ethic. As to art, it was a diversion or an intellectual consumer product. Thus the businessmen, who were and are the effective rulers of the country, had no use for odes, epics or verse dramas. The poets were serving an idea which was, in terms of the everyday life of the country, completely hollow.

From time to time this struck home. In his sonnet, *The Modern Politician,* Archibald Lampman indicates how close he came to understanding the situation.

> What manner of soul is his to whom high truth
> Is but the plaything of a feverish hour,
> A dangling ladder to the ghost of power?
> Gone are the grandeurs of the world's iron youth,
> When kings were mighty, being made with swords.
> Now comes the transit age, the age of brass,
> When clowns into the vacant empires pass,
> Blinding the multitude with specious words.
> To them faith, kinship, truth and verity,
> Man's sacred rights and very holiest thing,
> Are but the counters at a desperate play,
> Flippant and reckless what the end may be,
> So that they glitter, each his little day,
> The little mimic of a vanished king.

The thought in this sonnet is at once deeply traditional and savagely acute. But the diction is Victorian Synthetic, that grandiose and magniloquent substitute for true grandeur and magnificence which was as much a product of the "age of brass" as Lampman's politician himself. Lampman has adopted an aristocratic voice to express an aristocratic sentiment, but the voice of the Victorian aristocrat was that of a dog who is all bark and no bite, and is only waiting for the burglar to toss him a bone. I do not want to be misunderstood; Lampman is no hypocrite; he feels all he is saying; but his muddled idea both of his role and of his relationship to aristocratic ideals has led him into writing his poem in such a manner that it is almost rendered ineffectual.

Had the poets realized what was going on, they might have produced work of great value. One of the advantages possessed by French writers of the nineteenth and early twentieth centuries, for example, was the fact that aristocratic and capitalist-democratic ideas had been fighting openly, and on a high intellectual level, ever since the Revolution. Later socialism, the child of capitalism, had entered the battle. Thus, Claudel, Péguy and Bernanos knew they were being "reactionary". Writers in the United States, too, acquired a social consciousness; and it is interesting that this consciousness showed itself in its most refined form in New England and the Southern States, where the traditions of eighteenth-century British America had retained a vestigial life. James, Eliot and many Southern writers also knew they were being "reactionary", though in many cases they had to visit Europe to acquire an understanding of their role. Some French-Canadian writers also achieved this awareness.

In English Canada this did not happen, and the reason it did not happen, it seems to me, is that here the aristocratic tradition kept an appearance of vitality well into this century, just as it did in Britain. By a series of most astute compromises, British aristocracy and the monarchy had lasted through the revolutionary violence of the late eighteenth century, and the more subtle pressures of the nineteenth. But there is no doubt that one of these compromises was accommodation to the business ethic. It was the sort of thing that was never talked about when one was wearing one's ermine; but in the process man discovered a new kind of hypocrisy, a new combination of mean calculation with high and pompous speech. The aristocratic ideal of the Victorian elite was largely a matter of "keeping up appearances".

Now the essence of keeping up appearances is that the appearances must be entered into with just the right degree of irony and inner detachment. If one allows the pretended motives to become real ones, then one becomes an anomaly. An aristocrat may keep up the old house and perform all his ceremonial functions. But if he begins to think like an aristocrat, he will begin to scorn the capitalist ethic. Thus, since the world is dominated by capitalism, he will cease to be effective. He will fail. If he has enough power or money to avoid failure, he will probably be attacked in the press as a spokesman for obscurantism, or an enemy of the people. Nor can he afford a spokesman (poets have usually been, in their public character, spokesmen for aristocratic ideals if not aristocratic practice) who gives his game away by setting up standards he cannot meet. Therefore he favours in literature a certain hollowness, pomposity and lack of reality which will correspond to his own nature. An aristocratic elite which has made this fatal compromise will tend to support an official idea of culture and morality which is at once empty, affected and pretentious. This was the character of Victorian art at its worst. In Britain, it was carried into our own century by the old *Times*, the

BBC at its stuffiest, and certain aspects of the Anglican church. It is in this manner that avant truths become clichés.

The HEROIC, EPIC, ARISTOCRATIC VIEW of Canada was just such a "truth", and it was made into a cliché in just the same way. For Canadian history *is* epic and heroic. Something of it comes through, for me, in Fréchette's *La Decouverte du Mississippi*. I am naive enough to be thrilled by the confidence of a stanza like:

> Jolliet! Jolliet! deux siècles de conquêtes,
> Deux siècles sans rivaux ont passé sur nos têtes,
> Depuis l'heure sublime où, de ta propre main,
> Tu jetas, d'un seul trait, sur la carte du monde
> Ces vastes régions, zone immense et féconde,
> Futur grenier du genre humain!

The same heroic quality is to be found in Cremazie's *Le Drapeau de Carillon*, D. C. Scott's Indian poems, and parts of Pratt's *Brébeuf and His Brethren*, which has moments of real nobility. I do not claim that any of these are "great poems". The heroic quality I speak of is a matter of temperament, not talent; it is flawed by obvious stupidities; and I put it down to a certain archaism in the Canadian temperament. There is nothing similar in the poetry of the United States. There is a hidden sadness and disillusion even in Whitman. Indeed, there is nothing quite the same in any poetry I have read, except perhaps in André Chènier's sketch for *Le Chant d'Alonzo*, which was to have been part of a projected epic, *L'Amérique*, and begins, "Salut, o belle nuit, étincelante et sombre . . . ." Perhaps it is significant that Chènier never wrote the epic; perhaps it is also significant that this great poet, who had once thought himself a liberal revolutionary, discovered, at the very foot of the guillotine, that his sympathies were aristocratic.

Curiously enough, we have never understood the ideological basis of this heroic quality — a quality which, though I do not profess to be very sensitive to painting, I seem to find also in the paintings of the Group of Seven and Emily Carr. We have always thought of it as a response to the Canadian landscape, which is certainly very large. But this is almost to take a naive environmentalist view, and in any case, if the size of the landscape explained it, we would expect to find the same quality in the poetry of the United States.

I would say that the mediocrity of our classical public verse, at its dull average, is very closely linked to the virtues it has at its best, and that both its mediocrity and distinction are closely related to the archaic and anomalous quality of nineteenth- and early twentieth-century Canadian society, which was in many respects as "backward" a society as Ireland and Spain are today. To illustrate more clearly what I mean, I will quote some lines which indicate these two qualities, so closely related.

Sangster's *The Soldier of the Plough* begins thus:

> No maiden dream, nor fancy theme,
> Brown Labour's muse would sing;
> Her stately mien and russet sheen
> Demand a stronger wing.
> Long ages since, the sage, the prince,
> The man of lordly brow,
> All honour gave that army brave,
> The Soldiers of the Plough.
> Kind heaven speed the Plough!
> And bless the hands that guide it;
> God gives the seed —
> The bread we need,
> Man's labour must provide it.

This stanza is a real museum of anomalies. The first quatrain is a model of Victorian ineptitude, a crown of coal in which the phrase "fancy theme" is perhaps the sootiest gem. The line, "Long ages since, the sage, the prince", has, in its balancing of images of traditional wisdom and inherited power, a truly archaic ring, almost a folkish dignity; but it is followed immediately by "the man of lordly brow", which is a line suited to a poet of the Romantic Revival, such as Sir Walter Scott, looking back at the Middle Ages. "The Soldiers of the Plough" is the kind of image Victorian journalists loved to use when they were feeling sentimental about farmers. "Kind heaven speed the Plough; / And bless the hands that guide it" reminds one of *Hymns Ancient and Modern*. Yet the stanza ends with three lines ("God gives the seed . . ." etc.) which are absolutely medieval in feeling.

In other words, we have in this one stanza a poet whose mind is moving from a truly medieval, rather peasanty sensibility to a Victorian counterfeit of that sensibility. Obviously he does not know the difference; there is no irony or deliberate contrast here.

Or let us consider Frederick George Scott's *The Wayside Cross*.

> A wayside cross at set of day
> Unto my spirit thus did say —
>
> "O soul, my branching arms you see

> Point four ways to infinity.
>
> One points to infinite above,
> To show the height of heavenly love.
>
> Two point to infinite width, which shows
> That heavenly love no limit knows.
>
> One points to infinite beneath,
> To show God's love is under death.
>
> The four arms join, an emblem sweet
> That in God's heart all loves will meet."
>
> I thanked the cross as I turned away
> For such sweet thoughts in the twilight grey.

The first couplet is a conventional little prelude in the Victorian manner, a couplet which Archdeacon Scott might well have used to help him get into the poem, but which he should then have thrown away or rewritten. Well satisfied with it, he went on. And went on to what? Four couplets which might have been written by a contemporary — a minor contemporary, certainly — of George Herbert. These images have an emblematic sharpness and intellectual clarity, showing great things imaged in familiar and homely things, which is metaphysical, not simply influenced by metaphysical verse, as are so many other early twentieth-century poems. (Archdeacon Scott died in 1944.)

But then the poet, as if somehow embarrassed by the reality of the poetic experience, begins to drift back into a Victorian facsimile of piety. In intellectual content, the next couplet is still metaphysical, but in style it is sweet and sickly. The concluding couplet is utterly banal, and the last line, which ought to climax the poem, is the weakest of all. Once again, we find the genuinely poetic and the falsely poetic side by side, and it appears the poet does not know the difference.

IN THE POETRY OF Duncan Campbell Scott we find a dark, fierce and direct poet living in the same body with a gentle and dreamy "sweet singer" of rather feminine temperament. In this case the personality is not divided between true poet and false poet, but between major poet and minor poet. Yet here again Scott is not aware of his two-sided personality. In fact, each poet keeps intruding into the other's verses. Both are at their best in such poems as *Night Hymns on Lake Nipigon*, but their mutual presence is just what keeps this poem, which has extraordinary moments, from being the great poem it almost is.

It is my contention that we are dealing here, not with a form of mental illness, but with a cultural phenomenon —a phenomenon which is certainly present in much nineteenth-century verse, but is apparent with particular obviousness in English-Canadian nineteenth-century verse, for reasons which I have tried, in a necessarily circuitous manner, to examine. Many of the classical Canadian poets thought of poetry as a public as well as a private art, and they shared this view with their readers and the elite which sponsored them, or into which they had been born. The social ideas they sought to embody in their poems were, to a large extent, conservative ones — more conservative, perhaps, than many of them realized. But they did not understand, at least they did not understand clearly, the real ambiguity of their position in relation to society, a society which demanded that it be reflected and expressed in poetry because this was still, to those who spoke English, the noblest of the arts. However, this society had in reality a deep-seated contempt for poetry. Thus the relationship between the Canadian poet and society was a false and even a poisonous one, which vitiated the poetic impulse at its source, and resulted in a body of poetry notable for its vacillation between the truly poetic and the pseudo-poetic.

For the reason indicated at the beginning of this article, I have confined myself largely to a consideration of this situation as it affected English-language poets in this country. That French-Canadian poets found themselves in a similar position is indicated by the following lines from *La Patrie au Poète*, by Albert Ferland, whose dates are 1872-1943.

> Rêveur, pourquoi m'aimer comme on aime une femme?
> Tes yeux se sont mouillés d'avoir vu ma beauté;
> Pour comprendre ton coeur et vivre ta fierte,
> Poète, mon enfant, il me faudrait une âme!
>
> Les noms des fiers Aïeux dont l'honneur et la foi
> Font pensif l'étranger qui traverse mes plaines,
> Chante-les, plein d'orgueil, dans tes strophes hautaines;
> Poète, ces grands Morts ne revivent qu'en toi.
>
> Va, Barde primitif des vierges Laurentides,
> Va t'en pleurer ton coeur comme un fou dans les bois,
> Fidèle au souvenir des héros d'autrefois,
> Tandis que l'or vainqueur fait les hommes avides!
>
> Poète, mon enfant, tu me chantes en vain,
> Je suis la Terre ingrate où rêva Crémazie;
> Célèbre si tu veux ma grave poésie,
> Mais pour toi, mon enfant, je n'aura pas de pain!   (1972)

23

THE JOURNEY OF DISCOVERY

Nineteenth-Century Narrative Poets

George Woodcock

I<small>T IS POSSIBLE</small> that if Canada has any epics, they are, with the exception of certain poems by E. J. Pratt, in prose. Indeed, outside the dramatic genre — which includes the poetic closet plays of Mair, Hunter-Duvar and Heavysege in the nineteenth century and an interesting variety of verse plays for radio and stage about a century later — long poems of any kind and quality have been rare except in a limited period of the early Victorian era and the years immediately preceding it. In the present century one can cite, outside the Pratt canon, only a few isolated examples that have any significance: Birney's "David", Philip Child's *The Wood of Nightingales*, a couple of poetic travelogues by Louis Dudek, and perhaps Reaney's *A Suit of Nettles*. And even if the decades from the end of the Napoleonic wars to Confederation do offer a weighty-looking list of narrative or at least long discursive poems, only a few are of lasting interest, and only two — I suggest — are outstanding in literary terms. What strikes one most indeed is not, among the long poems of that period, a noticeable variation of approach or quality, but rather a peculiar monotony of theme and matter. The two poems I have noted as "outstanding", Isabella Valancy Crawford's "Malcolm's Katie" and Charles Heavysege's *Jezebel*, are so at least partly because in varying ways they stand *aside* from the rest.

Until recently it was not easy to study any of the representative works of Canada's most prolific period in long poems. Verse was written then for even smaller audiences than today, and usually published in small editions which were not reprinted. Charles Sangster's "The St. Lawrence and the Saguenay" did not appear again for 116 years after its first printing in 1856, though then it was printed on two separate occasions in one year, 1972. Howe's "Acadia" has never

24

been published in full; even the incomplete version appearing in 1874 had to wait 98 years for second printing. Heavysege's *Jezebel* did not find its way into a volume during the poet's life; it had to wait 104 years after its original appearance in the January, 1868, issue of the *New Dominion Monthly* before it finally appeared within covers in a slender pamphlet presented by the Golden Dog Press of Montreal, also in 1972. Indeed, so rare have been copies of early Canadian long poems that until the 1970's, unless we had access to one of a small number of well-endowed libraries, most of us have had to gain our impressions of such works — including the verse plays of the period as well as narrative poems — from brief extracts printed in anthologies.

Within the last three or four years, however, a fair number of Canada's Victorian and pre-Victorian long poems have become available to readers. David Sinclair's collection of *Nineteenth Century Narrative Poems*, which appeared in the New Canadian Library, included *The Rising Village* by Oliver Goldsmith the younger, Joseph Howe's "Acadia", Sangster's "The St. Lawrence and the Saguenay", Alexander McLachlan's *The Emigrant* and Isabella Valancy Crawford's "Malcolm's Katie", all as they were originally published, together with lengthy extracts from William Kirby's rambling 178-page poem, *The U.E.: A Tale of Upper Canada*. *Nineteenth Century Narrative Poems* appeared in 1972, which was something of an *annus mirabilis* in revivals, since not only did Sangster's "The St. Lawrence and the Saguenay" have its second reprinting then in a collection of his poems which appeared in the University of Toronto Press's Literature of Canada series, but in the same series and the same year "Malcolm's Katie" also appeared in a facsimile reproduction of the 1905 edition of Isabella Valancy Crawford's *Collected Poems*.

A number of much-mentioned if not much-read long poems of the same period remain to be reprinted. Fragments of Standish O'Grady's *The Emigrant* and of John Hunter-Duvar's *The Emigration of the Fairies* appear in A. J. M. Smith's *Book of Canadian Poetry*, but such works as Peter Fisher's *The Lay of the Wilderness* and John Richardson's ponderous *Tecumseh* remain out of print; their unavailability is perhaps less regrettable than the fact that several of the longer poems of that strange half-genius Charles Heavysege (as well as his plays) are still unreproduced. His *Jephtha's Daughter* should certainly be revived. However, given the present tendency to reprint any work of Canadian literature that has the least academic interest, it seems likely that these gaps will soon be filled.

But the reasons why we are interested enough in such poems as I have mentioned to read them again after a century of neglect goes beyond a mere academic concern. It is true that the expansion of studies in Canadian literature at most universities, particularly at the graduate level, has created a demand for works from our past that even a decade ago were familiar only to a few literary historians and anthologists. It is true also that the rise of nationalist sentiment has tempted us to place on such works an added value that is political in origin and sentimental in nature. Yet there are motives beyond either the academic or the political in our almost abrupt desire to read poems that so long have lain undisturbed on the remoter shelves of our libraries' special collections.

We read them because of our desire to find the roots of a culture that has at last grown apart from its parent cultures, and because we want to understand our ancestors and predecessors in the land. We read them, as we become conscious of our perilous relationship with the natural environment, because they depict in often vivid terms the life of a pristine Canada when the mechanical age was hardly beginning, and because most of their authors are closely preoccupied, though in a different way from us, with a concern for the environment that for them is expressed in a desire to tame and transform it. We also sense the irony implicit in the fact that the humanizing conquest of the wilderness they celebrate led inevitably to the destructive unbalancing of natural relations which we begin to fear may incur our own destruction.

As Roy Daniells has pointed out, in reading these mainly pre-Confederation poets:

> We sense ... one profound change of sensibility, now that pioneer days are past and gone. It is the loss of confidence, of cheerfulness, of joy, of eagerness. (*Canadian Literature* 56).

And we do so, uneasily aware of an ironic division in our own attitude towards such qualities. For if we envy the cheerfulness and joy of these poets, if we admire their confidence and eagerness, it is with the sense that such admirable traits, because they were united with a less admirable lack of prophetic insight, produced those very consequences in terms of the thoughtless exploitation of the natural world that have made our age one of anxiety rather than confidence, of apprehension rather than joy. The fullness of living they celebrated passed into the excess of living we lament, and so, when we read such poems as "The Rising Village" and even, despite its dark undertones, "Malcolm's Katie", we find ourselves torn between two emotions: a quasi-romantic nostalgia for a time that could produce what Roy Daniells has also called "this élan, this ineradicable optimism and abounding hopefulness, this chorus of testimony to the ultimate

26

goodness of life" (a testimony that runs even through the sombre horrors of Heavysege's *Jezebel* as evil beings are finally defeated and the balance of God's world is adjusted), and at the same time a certain knowing pity for a generation that did not recognize the threat of the "little cloud . . . like a man's hand" that came up out of the sea towards them.

When we turn from the phenomenon of our own interest in the narrative poems of early Canadian literature to the poems themselves, there are three questions that immediately confront us. Why was the long discursive poem with its narrative line so popular a form in the colonial period? Why is there a gap of almost fifty years after "Malcolm's Katie", the last of the long narrative poems of the earlier period, before the next significant poems of that kind were published by E. J. Pratt in the 1920's? And why were the narrative poems of any interest that appeared during that interlude the kind of spare and compact verse tales of which one finds good examples among the works of Charles G. D. Roberts and D. C. Scott or, on another level, among those of Robert W. Service?

I would suggest that the answer to the first question is that the long narrative poem was in fact an essential transitional form which reflected not only the efforts of Canadian poets to find a way of writing that expressed their experience in a raw, half-dependent society, but also the gradual and reluctant realization by men of taste and intelligence that their hopes of building in the New World a purified version of the society they had left behind in the Old World were doomed to frustration. They had to accept that what they were creating would be different, and one of the casualties of that acceptance, which was formalized by the fact of Confederation, was the long narrative poem.

Essentially, in the discursive and quasi-philosophic form that it most often assumed in nineteenth-century Canada, the long narrative poem was the close descendant of the kind of long reflective poem, with its essentially social orientation and its desire to project an ordered world in an ordered form, that flourished in Britain through most of the eighteenth century and, somewhat modified by the influences of Scott and Byron, survived in the works of writers like Hood and Praed and Samuel Rogers well into the nineteenth century. This was poetry characterized by bland sentiment rather than by the ordered rage of the Restoration poets or the ordered passion of the Romantics. Because of its stylized vocabulary and phrasing, its metrical regularity, and a selection of images and sentiments almost as formalized as Homer's, it was comparatively easy poetry to write, dependent on intent rather than inspiration; any man of letters with a sense of the sound of words could practise it reasonably well. By the same token, it became a form best written by poets of the second rank. Pope and Swift at the beginning, and Byron towards the end of the period, are marginal to the poetry of sentiment because of the idiosyncracy of genius, and it is significant that among the Canadian poets I have mentioned Isabella Valancy Crawford and Charles Heavysege also stand somewhat apart, idiosyncratic and, as poets, more ultimately interesting than the rest.

Originality and experimentation in literature are the features of a culture established and self-confident, of a tradition that is strong enough to accept and require transmutation. Pioneer cultures are inevitably conservative; the continuity of values and forms must be preserved precisely because experience is changing, and in the case of writers working within such a culture, their very isolation makes them seek the security of accepted forms rather than the adventure of new ones; the adventures find their place in the content of the narrative.

The Rising Village, first published in 1825, more than half a century after the elder Oliver Goldsmith's *The Deserted Village*, and thus the first Canadian narrative poem of any distinction, displays these characteristics in an extreme degree. Oliver Goldsmith was not merely the great-nephew of the celebrated writer who was Dr. Johnson's friend. He was also the son of a man who had left the United States rather than accept a republican form of government, and he himself was born in the Loyalist pioneer town of St. Andrews, New Brunswick, not long after it was established. While it is true that his own life, spent mostly as a schoolboy and a colonial official in the city of Halifax, was somewhat remote from the pioneer past, he had heard from participants of the hardships involved in setting up a new community in the wilderness, and in writing of such a community — and of the development of the Maritime provinces in general, which occupies the latter pages of *The Rising Village* — he was taking a subject that lay near the hearts and memories of his fellow colonists.

Yet the colonial desire to proceed within a safe framework of conventions determined the form of his poem. Urged on, apparently, by his brother, he decided not only to write in the same form as *The Deserted Village*, down to the vocabulary and the rhyming iambic couplet, but also to make his poem specifically a counterpart to his great-uncle's work, contrasting the growth of Maritime rural society from the emigrant village of his infancy with the decline of Irish and English rural society from the pre-enclosure villages of the elder Oliver's infancy.

He makes the relationship specific when, in the early lines of *The Rising Village*, he remarks:

> If then adown your cheek a tear should flow
> For Auburn's village, and its speechless woe;
> If, while you weep, you think the "lowly train"
> Their early joys can never more regain,
> Come, turn with me where happier prospects rise,
> Beneath the sternness of Acadian skies.

And in his portrayal of the mainly happy outcome of settlement in the New World, there seems no doubt that he has in mind the passages in *The Deserted Village* where emigration is portrayed as a tragic end for those who have been displaced from the sufficient existence of the English cottager before he was deprived of his customary access to land for cultivation and grazing. It is a "dreary scene" indeed to which the elder Goldsmith takes his dispossessed peasants as he portrays them attempting to make their settlement beside the Altama River in Georgia.

> Far different there from all that charmed before,
> The various terrors of that horrid shore;
> Those blazing suns that dart a downward ray,
> And fiercely shed intolerable day;
> Those matted woods where birds forget to sing,
> But silent bats in drowsy clusters cling;
> Those poisonous fields with rank luxuriance crowned,
> Where the dark scorpion gathers death around;
> Where at each step the stranger fears to wake
> The rattling terrors of the vengeful snake;
> Where crouching tigers wait their hapless prey,
> And savage men more murderous still than they;
> While oft in whirls the mad tornado flies,
> Mingling the savaged landscape with the skies.

The wilderness of *The Rising Village* is by no means lacking in its terrors of wild beasts howling around the backwoods cottage, or of "savage tribes in wildest strain" who

> ... oft in sternest mood maintain
> Their right to rule the mountain and the plain

and who "doom the *white man's* instant death". North American experience was still too near the horrors of wars conducted by British and French with Indian

29

auxiliaries, of whole villages massacred on the marches of civilization, for the vision of settling the wilderness to be wholly without shadows. But they are shadows to be dispelled by "patient firmness and industrious toil", and in the end there emerges a new Auburn, though recognizably different from its English original, for while the Deserted Village represented the end of a tradition of long-matured skills and customs, the Rising Village has all the makeshift quality of pioneer life. Indeed, it is when the younger Oliver sets out to describe that make-shift life with ironic zest that his poem attains its greatest vigour, using the couplet to satiric effect in a manner that recalls Pope rather than the earlier Goldsmith.

For example, the pedlar who used to wander through the emergent settlements is shown assuming a "merchant's higher title", and there follows a sharply con-crete description of the contents of a backwoods store:

> Here, nails and blankets, side by side, are seen,
> There, horses' collars and a large tureen;
> Buttons and tumblers, fish-hooks, spoons and knives,
> Shawls for young damsels, flannel for old wives;
> Woolcards and stockings, hats for men and boys,
> Mill-saws and fenders, silks, and children's toys;
> All useful things, and joined with many more,
> Compose the well-assorted country store.

The "half-bred" Doctor arrives:

> No rival here disputes his doubtful skill,
> He cures, by chance, or ends each human ill;
> By turns he physics, or his patient bleeds,
> Uncertain in what case each best succeeds.

And when the schoolhouse is erected, there is no true master, "in every art refined",

> But some poor wanderer of the human race,
> Unequal to the task, supplies his place ...

while under his insufficient knowledge and discipline:

> The rugged urchins spurn at all control,
> Which cramps the movement of the free-born soul,
> Till, in their own conceit so wise they've grown,
> They think their knowledge far exceeds his own.

From this point, the poem loses its temporary grip on actuality. A tenuous pathetic love motif is introduced in the sad tale of poor Flora driven mad by wicked Albert's betrayal, and the poem ends in a celebration of the joys of contemporary Acadian life, with patriotic and pro-British invocations:

> Thy grateful thanks to Britain's care are due,
> Her power protects, her smiles past hopes renew,
> Her valour guides thee, and her councils guide,
> Then, may thy parent ever be thy pride! —

and with a vision of the apotheosis of Acadia as:

> ... the wonder of the Western skies ...
> Till empires rise and sink, on earth, no more.

IN OTHER EARLY CANADIAN narrative poems, with the theme of emigration and settlement in the wilderness remaining so popular as to be almost constant, one finds the same divergence as in *The Rising Village* between vast stretches of mere verse distinguished by no more than the trite thought and clichéd images made familiar by eighteenth-century sentimental poetasters, and the occasional passages whose actuality keeps them immediate even for us who read them a century or more afterwards. Often it is the writers less polished in a conventional sense who achieve this effect most frequently, so that while Standish O'Grady's *The Emigrant*, a poem projected in four cantos of which only the first was completed, seems as a whole a rambling and amateurish piece, yet on almost every page there are a few lines, at least a couplet, where a flash of sharp, original imagery opens a glimpse of the author's vigorous and independent mind. The climate of Canada seems especially to have obsessed O'Grady, and some of his best passages are about the grimness and extremity of its winter,

> Whose frozen air in one bleak winter's night
> Can metamorphose *dark brown hares into white.*

Pursuing his sardonic course, O'Grady seems to have realized, as the later nineteenth-century Canadian poets did, that the sharp condensed tale in verse is more effective among the necessities of a new society than the longueurs of the traditional discursive verse which, like his contemporaries, he was attempting in *The Emigrant*. As a consequence, one of the best fragments of early Canadian poetry is the Barhamesque passage, embedded in *The Emigrant*, on the discomfiture of the devil in frozen Quebec.

Old Nick took a fancy, as many men tell,
To come for a winter to live in Sorel,
Yet the snow fell so deep as he came in his sleigh,
That his fingers and toes were frost-nipt on the way.

In truth, said the demon, who'd ever suppose,
I must go back again with the loss of all those;
In either extreme, sure it matters me not,
If I freeze upon earth or at home I'm too hot;

So he put back his sleigh, for he thought it amiss,
His clime to compare to a climate like this;
And now 'tis resolved that this frightful new-comer
Will winter in hell and be here in the summer.

In Joseph Howe's *Acadia*, another incomplete and roughly constructed work (though composed by the most versatile of early Canadian men of letters), the natural vigour of the poet, his zestful interest in scenes of action, his sharp feeling for the physical beauties of his native Nova Scotia, emerge to redeem the poem's formal lameness and sameness.

There the smooth lake its glassy bosom shows,
Calm as the wearied spirit's last repose;
Here frowns the beetling rock high o'er the tide,
Fanned by the branches of the forest's pride;
Here gently sloping banks of emerald dye
Kiss the pure waves that on them softly lie,
While buoyant flowers, the lake's unsullied daughters,
Lift their bright leaves above the sparkling waters.
There foams the torrent down the rocky steep,
Rushing away to mingle with the deep,
Shaded by leaves and flowers of various hues;
Here the small rill its noiseless path pursues,
While in its waves wild buds as gently dip
As kisses fall on sleeping Beauty's lip.

The turns of phrases are often hackneyed, the conceits worn, as a language much used may be hackneyed and worn but carry genuine feeling, which this poem abundantly does as it continues with its identification of trees and flowers by specific tint and form, eventually creating in the mind's eye a landscape of Pre-Raphaelite brightness and immediacy, a landscape glowing from within like the magically perceived landscapes of adolescence. And indeed, reading Howe, and later reading Sangster and Crawford, one realizes what a splendid and pristine world the poets saw as their habitation; it was a perception proper to the youth of a people in a land yet incompletely possessed by either mind or hand.

An especially striking aspect of Howe's *Acadia* lies in its dichotomy of attitude towards the Indian. Considered in ideal terms, the Indian still appears in the poem as the "noble savage" invented and admired by eighteenth-century writers who had never left Europe, and Howe spends many lines, after he has described the wild landscape of Nova Scotia, telling of the life, simple in its appropriateness to such an environment, which the Indians led in their undisturbed past.

> But, when the white man landed on the shore,
> His dream of gods and spirits soon was o'er;
> He saw them rear their dwellings on the sod
> Where his free fathers had for ages trod;
> He saw them thoughtlessly remove the stones
> His hands had gathered o'er his parents' bones;
> He saw them fell the trees which they had spared,
> And war, eternal war, his soul declared.

At this point the noble savage of European invention is transformed by circumstance into the revengeful scourge of so much North American experience, and the most vigorous and best passage of *Acadia* is one that tends to contradict the generally bucolic nature of the rest of the poem: a vivid imaginative reconstruction in verse of the massacre of a settler and his family by Indians who attack by night. Howe pities the victims, yet there is obviously a part of the mind of this fierce fighter for rights and liberties that feels with the savage victors, and their inevitable and doomed resentments, as Goldsmith never did.

T HE EMIGRANT THEME is treated in a variety of ways by the early nineteenth-century Canadian poets, though the treatment is always to a large degree derivative from British masters. Alexander McLachlan, in another of many poems entitled *The Emigrant*, presented what was less a narrative poem than a suite of songs and poetic episodes, loosely woven around the record of a mythical emigrant settlement. McLachlan's models are numerous, though Scott and Burns were probably his closest masters, and he stands outside the tradition of eighteenth-century gentility to which Goldsmith and Howe belong. Coming of poor origins, he remembered old injustices more sharply than his contemporaries. His "Lean lank Tom, the politician" sings of England like a latter-day John Ball:

> "The squire's preserving his game.
>   He says that God gave it to him,
> And he'll banish the poor without shame
>   For touching a feather or limb.
>
> "The Justice he feels very big,
>   And boasts what the law can secure,
> But has two different laws in his wig,
>   Which he keeps for the rich and the poor.
>
> "The Bishop he preaches and prays,
>   And talks of a heavenly birth,
> But somehow for all that he says,
>   He grabs a good share of the earth...."

And there is the old Scots piper, Donald Ban, remembering the destruction of the habitations of the clansmen when they were dispossessed and forced to emigrate. For Donald emigration has brought no real betterment; old, blind and poor, he wanders in the settlements, playing the laments for people of other cultures who do not understand, and dying in loneliness. The fundamental difference between McLachlan's view of what had been achieved in Canada, and that of earlier poets like Goldsmith and Howe and even of contemporaries like Sangster, emerges when one contrasts with their essential optimism the suggestion McLachlan projects that at the time he wrote, with Canada changing from a collection of settlements into a nation, the simple goodness of the pioneering life, with its values of mutual aid and mutual trust, were fading fast.

> Much remains still to be told
> Of those men and times of old,
> Of the changes in our days
> From their simple, honest ways,
> Of the quacks on spoils intent,
> That flocked to our settlement,
> Of the swarms of public robbers,
> Speculators and land jobbers,
> Of the sorry set of teachers,
> Of the bogus tribe of preachers,
> Of the host of herb physicians,
> And of cunning politicians.

> But the sun has hid his face
> And the night draws on apace. . . .

It is a dark vision not absent from the last poet in the purview of this essay, Isabella Valancy Crawford.

The voyage that McLachlan's emigrants take to their Upper Canadian lands occupies a considerable part of his poem, and others among these nineteenth-century poets found the journey a convenient form to give shape to their discourse. William Kirby, in *The U.E.: A Tale of Upper Canada*, brings his English peasants, who flee from the hard times after the Napoleonic wars, up the Gulf and River of St. Lawrence, announcing the exotic and historic scenes along the way with outbursts of patriotic bombast and with frequent lapses into unconscious comedy, as when he introduces the adventures of Aeneas into an account of the chairs and sofas transported by the emigrant family, and ends a description of the Labrador coast and its teeming herds of walrus and seal with the lines:

> And dwarfish Esquimaux, with caution steal
> Their oily prey, and dress their nauseous meal.

John Hunter-Duvar, whose fancifulness and delicacy of technique places him in almost diametric opposition as a poet to the loud and witless Kirby, turned the device of the journey into a fine exercise in Byronic irony when, in his *Emigration of the Fairies*, he brought a company of elfin migrants across the Atlantic on a floating eyot and led them ashore on Prince Edward Island to establish their settlement. If charm were the sole criterion for poetic excellence, this delightful piece of rococo whimsicality would rank highest among the works I mention in this essay. For other reasons it does not, and they are reasons which to an even greater degree militate against one's acceptance of Sangster.

For the emigrant narrative, Sangster substitutes a tenuous and unnecessary love story as he takes his reader on a full-scale guided tour of the two rivers of his longest poem's title, "The St. Lawrence and the Saguenay". The inclination towards the journey as an element of narrative structure which Sangster showed in its most extreme form was linked with the rapid increase in the facility of travel in Canada round about the mid-nineteenth century. The railway, curiously, did not strike the imagination of these poets, perhaps because so much of early North American experience had oriented them towards the waterways as natural channels of communication; it was the steamboats, which made water transport quicker and even safer, that appealed to their imagination, and one senses genuine delight and wonder as Kirby says:

> But passing on, the rapid steamer glides
> Smooth as a swan upon the glassy tides ...

or as Sangster evokes

> ... the strong steamer, through the watery glade
> Ploughing, like a huge serpent from its ambuscade.

SANGSTER WAS PERHAPS the most facile versifier among early Canadian poets, and with the exception of Hunter-Duvar and Isabella Crawford, the most versatile poet in a merely technical sense. Yet, except for brief exceptional passages, "The St. Lawrence and the Saguenay" remains the least tangible and the least memorable of the poems I mention. This is partly because it lacks the strong thematic spinal structure that is needed to sustain a long discursive poem. But it is equally due to the level and enamelled quality of Sangster's verse, always smoothly running and usually consisting of a chain of familiar metaphors linked by banal thoughts. This level tone, combined with a scarcity of fresh and striking images, makes it hard for us actually to visualize what Sangster is trying to tell us, and there remains in the mind a luminous and rather misty image like those created by the Canadian academic painters of the same period, who found themselves defeated by the attempt to capture a vastness which they could never quite encompass, a harshness they could never quite admit.

Occasionally, Sangster jolts out of his even pace with some authentic perception, some original image, and one gets a fleeting sense of a different poet behind the conventional façade. As he describes the Thousand Islands, for instance, there is one moment when one seems fleetingly to be witnessing the emergence from this bland poet's unconscious of some harsh germ of myth.

> Here nature holds her Carnival of Isles.
> Steeped in warm sunlight all the merry day,
> Each nodding tree and floating greenwood smiles. . . .

So, in the usual Sangsterian manner a verse begins, and then the mood abruptly shifts:

> And moss-crowned monsters move in grim array;
> All night the Fisher spears his finny prey;
> The piney flambeaux reddening the deep,

> Past the dim shores, or up some mimic bay;
> Like grotesque banditti they boldly sweep
> Upon the startled prey, and stab them when they sleep.

Yet we return to conventionalized Indians and "their birchen fleet", to duck-hunters and picnickers, and the dread Fisher never repeats his startling emergence.

And then, when Sangster attempts to describe the Saguenay, his customary manner breaks down for three whole stanzas as he finds that what he has to portray is too divergent from his usual experience to submit to customary metaphors. All at once the scene springs into its peculiar life as he describes it with uncharacteristic starkness:

> ... Pile on pile
> The granite masses rise to left and right:
> Bald, stately bluffs that never wear a smile;
> Where vegetation fails to reconcile
> The parchèd shrubbery and stunted trees
> To the stern mercy of the flinted soil ...
>
> Here groan the mills, and there, the household fire
> Sends up its smoke above the straggling briar
> And dwarfish evergreens that grow between
> The stubborn rocks — that grow but to expire ...
>
> ... Trebly dun
> The shades of sullen loneliness that lie
> On rugged L'Ance l'Eau when no living thing is nigh.

There is a melancholy toughness in such lines that is unlike anything else in Sangster, but it is a quality too rarely shown to relieve his general failure, which lies in the absence of any inner urge powerful enough to give him the themes that would raise his work above the level of fairly accomplished verse.

Heavysege was a poet of quite a different tone and quite a different character. He had strength rather than accomplishment, passion rather than polish, inner urge rather than outer amenity. His efforts to express himself in the mid-Victorian age as if he were writing in the reign of James I had at times ludicrous consequences, particularly when he failed to remember how the connotations of words and phrases changed. Sangster, cautious and meticulous, would never have been trapped into a solecism like that which Heavysege unconsciously commits when he makes Ahab cry out to Jezebel: "Take back thy bloody vine-yard!" But Sangster, on the other hand, could never have made a story of the ancient world so passionately immediate as Heavysege made *Jezebel*, transforming the stern prose of the Bible into a poetic form that in no way diminishes it.

Jezebel, of course, provided an occasion to which Heavysege's approach was perfectly adapted. Such a story could never have been satisfactorily rendered in any kind of verse that was being written by other Canadian poets at that time. It needed the power and darkness of an archaic language spoken by a living man, and this is what Heavysege provided. Moreover, given the strongly religious cast of English-Canadian society in the Confederation age, when the Bible was by far the most familiar of all books, it could be argued that if the colonial situation demanded the use of borrowed styles, Heavysege's Jacobeanisms were less out of place than the Augustan gentility of Goldsmith or the neo-classicist fancies of Sangster.

But is there an element beyond the mere re-creation of long-dead passions that accounts for the peculiar tension one senses running through the poem? Is there an element that makes *Jezebel*, set in another place and time, nearer to the other narrative poems — with their settings in recent Canada — than at first sight appears? It seems to me there may have been.

Implicit in almost all the poems I have discussed is the sense of Acadia or Canada as a land with its own selfness, its own way of existence that must be preserved. The difference of this land from the republic to the south is sometimes only implied, as in "The St. Lawrence and the Saguenay", or is expressed indirectly through an emphasis on loyalist values, as in *The Rising Village* and *Acadia*. In Kirby the Canadianism is strongly and openly present, and the sense of the United States as a threat and an enemy is militantly expressed. The fort of Quebec is "England's assurance and Columbia's dread", and Glengarry reminds the poet of the time when "Columbia's routed hosts fled pale" before its warriors, while Ethwald, the poem's young hero, dies "foremost of the faithful band/Who quelled invasion and preserved the land".

Jezebel, of course, is not overtly about Canada and the United States, but it is about a land threatened with alien domination, represented by the foreign queen and the infidel and materialistic faith of Baal she seeks to impose. *Jezebel* was probably written in 1867 and appeared in 1868, the year after Confederation, in a Montreal magazine — the *New Dominion Monthly* — whose very title stresses its nationalist inclinations.

When one further considers the central role Heavysege gives to the episode of

38

Naboth's vineyard, which takes up the whole of the middle canto of the poem, the underlying parallels become even more interesting. Heavysege expands the Biblical version to represent Ahab wandering in his palace garden, enjoying sunlight after storm, forgetting the slaughter on Mount Horeb, and immediately coveting Naboth's vineyard; as soon as the strife in his kingdom ends, in other words, he becomes rapacious for the land of others, as American politicians did for Canadian land after the Civil War was over. And he significantly expands Naboth's Biblical answer ("The Lord forbid it me, that I should give the inheritance of my fathers unto thee") to read:

> I cannot yield thee that which is not mine,
> But was my father's, and must be my son's.
> Ask me not for it, then; yet beg aught else,
> And I will give it thee; but God forbid
> That I should yield thee mine inheritance.

There follows the sequence in which Naboth is falsely accused and then killed so that his land may pass into Ahab's hands.

Heavysege, it seems evident, was not expanding and elaborating the Biblical story of the king and the vineyard without a topical purpose, for during the years leading to Confederation the story of Naboth's fate was much in Canadian minds as a parable reflecting fears of invasion and annexation. In 1867 no less a figure than Sir John A. Macdonald declared: "A brilliant future would await us were it not for those wretched Yankees, who hunger and thirst for Naboth's field." One does not have to speculate outrageously to imagine the reading many Canadians must have given *Jezebel* when it appeared in 1868, particularly as they related Naboth's death by false accusation to the suggestion of certain American leaders that Canada be handed over to settle the *Alabama* claim, which was no concern of Canadians.

Roy Daniells has pointed out, in the review to which I have already referred, that "Isabella Crawford is in a somewhat different class, both in sensibility and in craftsmanship," from the other nineteenth-century narrative poets. "Malcolm's Katie", as he pointed out, has qualities that are both mythic and melodramatic, and these qualities have been adequately examined by other critics. But though there are passages in "Malcolm's Katie" of a lyrical intensity and excellence unattained by previous Canadian poets, they are combined with a powerful tale of love, jealousy and conflict welded on to a thematic structure not unlike that of

39

the earlier narrative poems, embracing the settlement and conquest of the wilderness, and ending in a patriotic invocation.

> I would not change these wild and rocking woods,
> Dotted by little homes of unbark'd trees,
> Where dwell the fleers from the waves of want,
> For the smooth sward of selfish Eden bowers. . . .

Yet even on the social level — and Crawford is openly conscious of this, describing her hero Max as "social-soul'd" — there is evident a sense that the Canadian world has moved irrevocably beyond the simplicities of the pioneer beginnings.

> Then came smooth-coated men with eager eyes
> And talk'd of steamers on the cliff-bound lakes,
> And iron tracks across the prairie lands,
> And mills to crush the quartz of wealthy hills,
> And mills to saw the great wide-arm'd trees,
> And mills to grind the singing stream of grain;
> And with such busy clamour mingled still
> The throbbing music of the bold, bright Axe —
> The steel tongue of the Present, and the wail
> Of falling forests — voices of the Past.

It is curious but significant that while Max rather simply boasts:

> My axe and I, we do immortal tasks;
> We build up nations — this my axe and I!

the long speech by the villain Alfred, exposing the mortality of nations as of men, is far more telling.

Here we may have a clue to the reason for the interlude, the half-century from Crawford to Pratt, in which no significant long narrative poems were written by Canadians. Crawford retained within a precarious balance her warring inclinations towards socially-oriented narrative and inwardly-oriented lyrical verse. Within herself she represented the conflict point that arises in any culture when the poetry which uses accepted means to chart the emergence of a new society becomes outmoded, because as society grows individual expression once again seeks a voice, and an original voice at that. The poets who followed her were concerned with the latter need, and even the narratives they wrote were no longer of social import; instead they narrowed individual experience, individual achievement and defeat, into their small compass. It was only when, after creating Canada, Canadians had to some degree identified themselves, that the social themes emerged again with Pratt in longer poems, raised often into myth and, at Pratt's best, distanced into the epic dimension which the earlier narrative poets never attained.

(1974)

HIGH COLONIALISM
IN CANADA

Roy Daniells

THERE ARE CANADIANS who regard our colonial beginnings with distaste and who consider filial gratitude from a young culture to an older one as sentimental at best and at worst degrading. I should like to advocate an entirely opposite view.

An examination of literary and critical writings in Canada between, say, 1870 and 1920 reveals a widespread belief in the value of continuing tradition to a nation beginning its independent course. The limits of this paper allow me to refer only to work in English. How deep Quebec's colonial roots reached down has recently been shown in W. J. Eccles' penetrating study, *Canada under Louis XIV*.

High colonial aspirations looked forward to political freedom but did not seek instantaneous total independence. Even the act of founding a new nation was in fact compatible with concern for tradition and loyalty to the Crown. Graeme Mercer Adam, editor of the *Canadian Monthly* and ardent nationalist, writes in 1872: "It is possible that the hour of Canadian nationality may be drawing near. If so, let us prepare to found the nation, not in ingratitude but in truth and honour." Truth and honour are words not much in current use but in this remote context they stir the heart, as Sidney said of the ballad of Chevy Chase.

In contending for the reality of a high colonial culture in Canada, let us quickly look for the image of it in the works of two poets, a novelist, an anthologist, a periodical editor and the compiler of a school reader. My examples are necessarily brief but not, I hope, inconclusive. A single stanza of Blake or Burns, a single paragraph of Addison or Arnold, may give us an insight into the man and his outlook on the world. Is not this also true of Canadian writers? The old notion of touchstones still has its uses.

Among high colonial poets, Roberts and Lampman are, I think, the most impressive: the first for his historical, representative and seminal qualities, the second for the intrinsic aesthetic quality of his verse. Let us confine ourselves for the moment to landscape; Roberts and Lampman are in the forefront of those who have tried to compose the Canadian scene. There is, of course, no landscape until we look at it. We choose what to regard and from what point of view, at what time and in what context. We import our own emphases, emotions and criteria. Roberts and Lampman proffer their help in this operation.

Could we reopen Roberts' *Orion?* You recall how Lampman was enchanted by the poem, like Keats looking into Chapman's Homer. I never walk up between Trinity College and the Royal Ontario Museum without seeing Lampman's shadowy form a little ahead, the small square volume of *Orion* in his hand and his heart full of rapture, that Canada at last had its own poetry. *Orion,* he said, "written by a Canadian, by a young man, one of ourselves... was like a voice from some new paradise of art, calling us to be up and doing". He was about nineteen at the time and Roberts a year or so older.

The actual texture of descriptive passages in the poem is of great interest.

> Where the slow swirls were swallowed in the tide,
> Some stone-throws from the stream's mouth, there the sward
> Stretched thick and starry from the ridge's foot
> Down to the waves' wet limits, scattering off
> Across the red sand level stunted tufts
> Of yellow beach-grass, whose brown panicles
> Wore garlands of blown foam. Amidst the slope
> Three sacred laurels drooped their dark-green boughs
> About a high-piled altar. There the king,
> Œnopion, to whose sceptre bowed with awe
> The people dwellers in the steep-shored Chios,
> Stood praying westward.

Now it is clear that King Œnopion, for all his vineyards and olive-groves (elsewhere described in the poem), his sacred laurels and his altar, is furnished with a New Brunswick beach. The thick sward down to the tidal limit, the red earth: I need not labour the point. You recall how the old photographers put their clients before a backdrop of distant castellation framed in flowery meadows, the hither edge of which neatly accommodated itself to the fur rug underfoot.

Let us see how, in a more subtle way, Lampman himself works, how in a poem like "April" Canada and Keats combine. If we listen to such lines as these:

> Pale season, watcher in unvexed suspense,
> Still priestess of the patient middle day. . . .
>
> Dreaming of summer and fruit-laden mirth.
>
>   . . . the brown bees
> Murmur faint dreams of summer harvestries.
>
> The faces of sweet flowers, and easeful dreams. . . .

we hear the echo, line after line, of well known harmonies from the great odes of Keats:

> Dance, and Provencal song, and sun-burnt mirth.
>
> For Summer has o'er-brimmed their clammy cells.
>
> I have been half in love with easeful death.

In the midst of these recollections, the authentic Canadian scene nevertheless appears:

> The old year's cloaking of brown leaves, that bind
> The forest floor-ways, plated close and true —
> The last love's labour of the autumn wind —
> Is broken with curled flower buds white and blue
> In all the matted hollows, and speared through
> With thousand serpent-spotted blades up-sprung,
> Yet bloomless, of the slender adder-tongue.
>
> In the warm noon the south wind creeps and cools,
> Where the red-budded stems of maples throw
> Still tangled etchings on the amber pools,
> Quite silent now, forgetful of the slow
> Drip of the taps, the troughs, and trampled snow.

But even here, among the Ontario sugar maples, there is heard the clear echo of a known ode of Keats:

> Or by a cider-press, with patient look,
> Thou watchest the last oozings, hours by hours.

It is both surprising and delightful to see how, in another familiar poem, "At the Ferry", Matthew Arnold is in attendance. To look again at some detached passages:

44

But under all to one quiet tune,
    A spirit in cool depths withdrawn,
With logs, and dust, and wrack bestrewn,
    The stately river journeys on.

Faint films of smoke that curl and wreathe;
    And upward with the like desire
The vast grey church that seems to breathe
    In heaven with its dreaming spire.

And still my thought goes on, and yields
    New vision and new joy to me,
Far peopled hills, and ancient fields,
    And cities by the crested sea.

Beyond the tumult of the mills,
    And all the city's sound and strife,
Beyond the waste, beyond the hills,
    I look far out and dream of life.

Arnold is with us, joining in, line after line:

But the majestic river floated on. . . .

And that sweet City, with her dreaming spires.

Roam on! the light we sought is shining still.

Then through the great town's harsh heart-wearying roar,
Let in thy voice a whisper often come,
To chase fatigue and fear. . . .

But, again, the authentic Canadian scene appears, this time as an old sawmill, and we hear the saw, engaging a log, change its tone:

At moments from the distant glare
    The murmur of a railway steals,
Round yonder jutting points the air
    Is beaten with the puff of wheels;
And here at hand an open mill,
    Strong clamour at perpetual drive,
With changing chant, now hoarse, now shrill
    Keeps dinning like a mighty hive.

Lampman, then, in a subtle and quiet masterly way, is using the viewpoint and technique of Keats (with whom he had a secret natural affinity), and Arnold,

45

and others in the English poetic tradition in order to interpret the Canadian scene. What helps us to identify it as high colonialism is that it is done consciously and with great delight.

Our concern is at the moment with the literary image of high colonialism but a passing reference to painting may be allowed. In our National Gallery hangs a painting by Lucius O'Brien, called "Sunrise on the Saguenay". O'Brien was born in Canada, the son of an army officer. He attended Upper Canada College, found a patron in the Marquis of Lorne and became President of the Royal Canadian Academy. The amateur who enjoys his picture, knowing nothing of the immediate influences on his style, can nevertheless enter pretty fully into O'Brien's sensibility. Across those calm waters and through those rising mists can be seen the smiling wraiths of many traditions. The fallen pine in the foreground barely conceals Salvator Rosa. It is a romantic view, giving a chance to every device of aerial perspective. The immense cliffs flanking the bay loom out of cloud with towering grandeur. Here is the real substance of the Canadian scene, harmonized by a carefully chosen atmosphere. The Saguenay "doth like a garment wear/The beauty of the morning. . . ." Not only harmonized, the scene is humanized, by the addition of a vessel in the offing, ready to sail, and in the middle distance a small craft near which a boat is being rowed. The human scale is preserved, against the stupendous background; this width of water and height of wooded cliff are neither strange nor inimical; they invite the viewer, like the landscape openings in "L'Allegro". I personally enjoy this picture, as a record of high colonial sensibility, because it brings traditional techniques to the service of an undistorted record of a *locus classicus* of Canadian scenery and because it breathes a cheerful confidence in man's ability to live in this our landscape. It is not in any sense a dull or superficial performance; it achieves assurance and serenity without forcing or falsifying the donné of the locale; it is a picture which the Marquis of Lorne, whose own portrait was painted by Millais, must have enjoyed, and the Canadian who cannot enjoy it today must be either totally insensitive or else in total rebellion against the past or else possessed by horrid antagonisms which vent themselves on whatever they encounter.

THE UNIQUE FLAVOUR of a wine derives not only from its datable vintage but also from the location of the vineyard, sometimes within very narrow limits. Charles Gordon (hereinafter referred to as Ralph Connor) was born within a few months of Lampman and knew the Ottawa River with the same loving familiarity. "A perfume and a wintry chill", wrote Lampman, "Breathe from the yellow lumber piles." It is a world familiar to the man from Glengarry.

Lampman, as we have seen, employs a mechanism of apprehension and expression derived from English poetry to encompass and record the Canadian scene. Connor, greatly aided by memories of childhood, projects with triumphant ease the perfect image of a Scottish colony. Glengarry, the most easterly of the Ontario counties, is peopled by Scots, not only from the patronymic Glengarry district just north of Pitlochry but from the Highlands and Islands generally. *The Man from Glengarry* embodies a whole ethos which takes in region, race and religion. The Ontario forest is made to serve this ethos by transformation into a magic, enclosed world as filled with absorption and emanation as Grimm's Schwartz-wald. It opens to disclose a scene of woodcutters and children, of giants and gentle princesses, of perils and deliverances. "The solid forests of Glengarry have vanished", begins Connor's preface, but in another sense they are as enduring as Sherwood or Arden.

The perfection of the colonial spirit in this Scottish Presbyterian community is shown by its refusal to adulterate the heritage. French, English, Irish, Americans and at least one Mexican appear, together with some account of Methodists, Baptists, Roman Catholics and atheists. These are not despised or rejected; they simply cannot meet the Scottish standards. If an Englishman has his leg crushed in the fury of a communal barn-raising, it gives an opportunity for the skill of a Scottish medical student. If Methodists unwisely agree to a public debate on theology, they retire after the Presbyterian minister's first denunciation. This question of an element of comedy in the high colonial record, of a mild absurdity so endearing that it must be the product of a retrospect upon what has been well loved, — this we must return to before leaving the subject.

The Canadian West is a good touchstone for true high colonialism. Connor shows us his hero making a speech in New Westminster at a moment when there is a wave of resentment against Confederation. "It was Ranald's speech, everyone said, that turned the tide. His calm logic made clear the folly of even considering separation; his knowledge of, and his unbounded faith in, the resources of the province, and more than all, his impassioned picturing of the future of the great Dominion reaching from ocean to ocean, knit together by ties of common interest, and a common loyalty that would become more vividly real when the provinces had been brought more closely together by the promised railway. 'Send him

47

East', cried a voice. 'Yes, yes, that's it. Send him to Ottawa to John A. It's the same clan!' "

The neatness with which the novelist links moral and political issues, expands the ethos of Glengarry to cover and preserve the entire community, and leaves us indebted to Scottish virtue for our very existence is beyond all praise. Added posthumously to Connor's autobiography is the line from Bunyan, "The trumpets sounded for him on the other side!" It is my belief that these were, in fact, bag-pipes.

T HE MOST EXPLICIT SPOKESMAN for high colonialism I have yet encountered is W. D. Lighthall, chiefly memorable as the editor of an anthology, *Songs of the Great Dominion*, which first appeared in 1889. Lighthall was then about thirty-two years of age, a lawyer living in Montreal. His introduction affects this reader, at least, as some Renaissance cartographical view, in perspective, of an Italian ducal city beside its rolling river, Apennines in the background, the four winds blowing vitality upon it from the cardinal points and a band of angels with their trumpets spreading wide its fame.

Lighthall's sentences have the true heroic quality of rhetoric; what sounds like hyperbole has a direct relation to fact. He speaks of Canada as having in her hands the solution of those problems of Empire which concern every true Briton, "proud and careful of the acquisitions of British discovery and conquest".

> She is Imperial in herself, we sons of her think, as the number, the extent and the lavish natural wealth of her Provinces, each not less than some empire of Europe, rise in our minds; as we picture her coasts and gulfs and kingdoms and islands, on the Atlantic on one side, and the Pacific on the other; her four-thousand-mile panorama of noble rivers, wild forests, ocean-like prairies; her towering snow-capped Rockies waking to the tints of sunrise in the West; in the East her hoary Laurentians, oldest of hills. She has by far the richest extent of fisheries, forests, wheat lands, and fur regions in the world; some of the greatest public works; some of the loftiest mountain-ranges, the vastest rivers, the healthiest and most beautifully varied seasons.... In losing the United States, Britain lost the *smaller* half of her American possessions: — the Colony of the Maple Leaf is about as large as Europe.

"But what", Lighthall continues, "would material resources be without a corresponding greatness in man?" He finds it in a concept of loyalty. The French in

Quebec are loyal to their own imperial tradition. The Loyalists withdrawing from the rebel Colonies have accomplished "the noblest epic migration the world has ever seen: — more loftily epic than the retirement of Pius Æneas from Ilion. . . . 'Why did you come here?' was asked of one of the first settlers of St. John, New Brunswick, a man whose life was without a stain; — 'Why did you come here, when you and your associates were almost certain to endure the sufferings and absolute want of shelter and food which you have narrated?' *Why did we come here?*' replied he, with emotion which brought tears: — *'For our loyalty.'* "

If greatness is equated to loyalty, we must ask, loyalty to what or to whom? The primary answer is, of course, to the Crown, but for Lighthall this has immense and all encompassing implications, like Tennyson's concept of loyalty to Arthur. Lighthall's expansion of British loyalty does not stop at the level of Canadian patriotism but broadens out to take in the world. The Empire will last only if it upholds an ideal that men will suffer and die for and "such an Ideal — worthy of long and patient endeavour — may be found in broad-minded advance toward the voluntary Federation of Mankind." It is difficult to match Lighthall for a buoyant, fresh, engaging confidence in our future; for the candour of his idealism; for the breadth of his historic and geographic grasp; for the clarity of his crystallization of high colonial faith and hope.

His limitations are also apparent, especially the one he shares with Ralph Connor, an inability to see the actual ideals of French Canadians in full perspective. It is, in the circumstances, venial. Connor can get as far as a cordial symbolic reconciliation between leaders of opposed gangs of Scottish and French or Irish loggers. Lighthall can produce a finely turned exemplary tale, *The Young Seigneur*, extolling the virtues of the habitant and of those of his countrymen who combine the old heroic qualities of authority with progressive ideas, and begging the French in Quebec to provide front-rank leadership for the whole country. But that is as far as they can go, in the closing years of the nineteenth century. We cannot ask more of them; their sin is one of omission rather than commission. For the latter we must await the report on Bilingualism and Biculturalism.

WE MUST INCLUDE IN OUR SURVEY a quick glance at some pages of *Rose-Belford's Canadian Monthly*, Volume I, published in 1878. It succeeded the *Canadian Monthly and National Review* which had just ceased publication and it retained the same remarkable editor, Graeme Mercer Adam.

Rose Belford rescued the operation and it went on into the 1880's. I have always seen her as a striking and for some reason dark-haired girl, with financial resources of her own, a taste in literature ranging from Homer and Horace to Wilkie Collins, a charmingly forthright manner, and — somewhat literally I admit — with a red rose in her raven tresses. Although further research revealed that these virtues, on the cultural side at least, appertained rather to Mr. Rose and Mr. Belford, two publishers who jointly supported the journal, the image of my own Rose Belford is still with me, more living than, say, Kathleen ni Houlihan or Laura Secord.

From this volume I choose one article, entitled "Canadian Nationality", by William Norris of Toronto. Norris believed that Canada might shortly sever the "slight link" binding her to Britain and the prospect did not trouble him.

> It, therefore, behoves all true Canadians to be prepared for whatever may occur. There is but little to be done. A Governor elected every seven years by both our houses of Parliament, the appointment of a small diplomatic body, and the adoption of a flag are all that is needful. Surely, a people who have an independent and final Supreme Court is equal to this. The flag may cause some difficulty, but not necessarily. We have the colours already — it is only necessary to place them. The red first, representing Englishmen and Scotchmen; the white, representing the French who first colonized Quebec and the French-Canadian people who now inhabit it; and the green, though questioned by some, is acknowledged by all to represent the Irish. These colours, placed vertically, with the Union in the upper corner as now, would make a good Canadian flag and attract the regard of a majority of the people who inhabit the Dominion. The green, especially, would be worth 100,000 men to the Dominion in case of any difficulty with our neighbours, and would effectually Canadianize the Irish.

Norris foresaw, also, the disintegration of the United States and the thought afforded him considerable satisfaction.

> Already she shows signs of dissolution. . . . A hot-bed progress among alien and half-assimilated people will surely accelerate the end. They are in a dilemma either horn of which is fatal. They must either submit to the mob and the commune, and see their cities blaze as they did three years ago, or to a standing army and a general who will destroy their institutions and make himself dictator. In either event, disintegration is sure to follow. As power steps from the disorganized grasp of the United States, it will fall to Canada as her natural right, making her the first nation on this continent, as she is now the second. United closely, as we shall be from the Atlantic to the Pacific by a common nationality, our country will go on, increasing from age to age in wealth, in power and in glory; and it may not be too much of a stretch of the imagination to think, that as it is the latest

developed portion of a new world ... it may be the country where a last great, and fully developed humanity may find its fitting habitation and abode.

Norris was not an altogether accurate prophet but he did put his finger on two problems that today trouble every thoughtful American; he did foresee in Canada independence, national growth and, as a condition for these, the need for unity; and he knew that we should have vertical red and white segments in our new flag. Like Lighthall he can rise into rhetoric without losing contact with the firm ground of fact and, again like Lighthall, he envisages wealth, power and glory in the context of a humane ideal. That he is genuinely high colonial in his suppositions one further sentence will demonstrate. "And, lastly, we shall have the good will of England and possibly her guarantee for our independence, as she guarantees that of Belgium, in starting our national career."

Our final reference, which I will make as succinct as possible, is to a school reader published in Toronto in 1901 and in use, at least as late as 1916, in high school classes in Victoria. It was a magnificent assemblage of great names, going back to Plato and coming down to Macdonald and Laurier. It had a range of material from Thomas à Kempis to Oliver Wendell Holmes. It dealt with the death of Socrates and with the Union Jack. It introduced one to the Ancient Mariner and to the Canadian Song Sparrow. In an appendix, the unnamed editor explained what he was attempting. The five and a half pages of small type cannot be summarized, they are so thronged with implications. But may I quote a few of the closing sentences, concerning his choice of patriotic pieces?

> Tennyson's "Hands all Round" belongs to the period of the revolution which left Napoleon III Emperor of France. The line "We likewise have our evil things" suggests comparison with Kipling's "Recessional", which was written on the occasion of Queen Victoria's Jubilee in 1897. The first two stanzas will be found in fac-simile on p.8 of this anthology; the remaining three are as follows ....

He then quotes them, to their conclusion, "For frantic boast and foolish word, Thy mercy on Thy people, Lord!" and he continues,

> If "that man's the best cosmopolite who loves his native country best", this group of selections should, in the hands of intelligent and patriotic teachers, prove an effective means of inculcating incidentally a spirit of rational patriotism. Its most striking characteristic is the absence of the glorification so common in this kind of literature.
>
> The last group is intended to bring pointedly into view the magnanimous spirit in which, during the past two and a half centuries, Great Britain has dealt with her colonies, especially in the way of conceding to them — "frankly" as Mr. Gladstone says — the right to manage their own domestic affairs. The latest outcome

51

of this policy is the formation of the "Commonwealth of Australia" in imitation of the "Dominion of Canada"; neither Canadians nor Australians would have taken part in the war in South Africa but for their belief that it would speedily lead to the establishment of a similar nationality there.

So we pass from Plato to à Kempis, to Tennyson and Mr. Gladstone, to Canadian volunteers in South Africa and to loving one's native country best, without frantic boast or foolish word. It is literature and appreciated as such, but it is also life and as such to be lived. It has the unmistakable accent of greatness, for all its simplicity, like Arthur among his knights though many of them in richer arms than he. It is Canadian colonialism in its high and palmy days.

What creates the aesthetic effect of organic unity in this ideology of high colonialism? It is the power of imagination to project a vision of Canada having its own logic and consistency. As in a time of miserable civil strife Milton could see England as a giant roused from sleep, or as Blake, among the dark mines and mills could view the rising walls of Jerusalem in England's green and pleasant land, so *mutatis mutandis* these Canadians attained a vision of their own country. In historical fact there were grave doubts and dangerous dissensions. In the pageant presented by Lighthall or Connor, these are performers of the anti-masque, soon driven into the wings by personifications of faith, hope and loyalty.

Appreciation and some laughter often mingle in a retrospect of colonial Canada. "Truth and honour", "the trumpets sounded for him", "a life without a stain": is it that we can no longer believe in such possibilities? Or do we smile as we would at a photograph of grandparents? Such outmoded clothes and conscious character; yet essential to our own existence and remembered with affection. This laughter can be salutary, self-revealing, free from denigration.

The end of high colonialism may conveniently be placed at the beginning of this century's third decade. Canadian veterans of the First World War had just returned; the *Canadian Forum* commenced publication in 1920; the old *University Magazine* ended the next year. Yet it goes without saying that high colonial emotions were not instantly extinguished in 1921. A few years ago there arose in my own home a slight problem of identification as the name of one Louis St. Laurent came up in conversation with my mother. St. Laurent is the prime minister, my wife explained. But my mother, who had not set foot in England for thirty years, replied very simply, "Winston Churchill will always be my prime minister."

In conclusion, here are eight lines of Lampman. They are sapphics; we know from one of his letters they pleased him. They show the chain of connection from

Sappho, to the metrical practice of English schoolboys, to Trinity College in
Toronto and to the flowers of the Ottawa countryside which Lampman loved.
And they tell us that, in spite of change and decay, the fragrance of what has
once been loved remains.

> Brief the span is, counting the years of mortals,
> Strange and sad; it passes, and then the bright earth,
> Careless mother, gleaming with gold and azure,
> > Lovely with blossoms —
> Shining white anemones, mixed with roses,
> Daisies mild-eyed, grasses and honeyed clover,
> You and me, and all of us, met and equal
> > Softly shall cover.

(1969)

CHARLES SANGSTER

The End of an Era

Donald Stephens

I
F A SINGLE DEVICE can be said to characterize modern literature, it is the interior monologue, directed not outward but towards itself.
Nineteenth-century poets are marked by their attempt at dialogue, usually with
others but sometimes only with themselves; even the "dramatic monologue"
involves the presence of a listener, aside from the reader. For Canadian poets,
writing in the mid-nineteenth century, there was little "inner world"; their reality
was the outer world, the world they could describe and record, not only for those
living in their own time, but also for those who would come after them. Though
theirs were often the voices of lonely men isolated in thought and fact from others,
the whole intention and concern of those voices was with the present world preparing itself for a future. The poet of that time in Canada was assured of his past,
of the roots from which he came; he often imitated consciously the thoughts and
forms of poety written before his time. Though he was alone in an alien world
— where people did not understand him, where the intellectual stimulus was
limited — he was aware of his potential audience; the listeners he hoped to reach
were never imaginary. He knew very well the time and space in which he lived.

The first Canadian poet to be aware of his place in this way was Charles
Sangster. Though Sangster has been either ignored or maligned by most recent
critics of Canadian literature, he was, with the sole exception of Charles Mair,
the first poet to be genuinely conscious of the Canadian scene and the Canadian
identity. A poet with a sense of mission, he attempted to record, both for his own
generation and for the future, the wonders of the Canadian landscape. From his
correspondence, the surviving fragments of which have never been adequately
explored, it is apparent that his attention to nature was almost compulsive: to
capture in words the beauty and joy of the natural landscape, and to impress

54

these qualities on his Canadian readers. He said, "the description here is true in both nature and fact",[1] and he remained faithful to this concept in all his poetry.

One characteristic of emerging societies is their tendency to turn to origin-cultures for their aesthetic pleasures. Just as Americans in the first half of the nineteenth century clung to British and French cultures, so the Canadians of the mid-century were unwilling to admit the merits of Canadian writers. Sangster himself comments on the indifference of the reading public of his time to poetry written in Canada.[2] Indeed, it was because he was at first ignored in his own country that Sangster was forced to publish his first volume, *The St. Lawrence and the Saguenay and Other Poems* (1856), at his own expense in Auburn, New York. It might be argued, when one considers the popularity of the later classically educated and oriented poets, Carman and Roberts, that Sangster's limited education militated against his acceptance in the literary circles of his day; however, this explanation alone cannot account for his lack of popularity. Doubtless his dull and unimpressive jobs — proofreading for newspapers, a minor position in the Post Office Department in Ottawa — made him a limited success socially, and in a class-conscious age this may well have lessened his appeal. Though he spent the last years of his life working over his later manuscripts, enough for two solid volumes, they are still — more than eighty years after his death — not published. Except for some praise from Edward Hartley Dewart, who in the 1860's looked for Canadian themes in the writing of his contemporaries, Sangster was largely ignored in his own time; since then even the consideration that is given to his work as one of the few important poets before Confederation has done little to enhance his reputation. Critical comment seems to end in the conclusion that it is a wonder he ever existed.[3]

The key to Sangster's role as a poet is evident in his first volume, *The St. Lawrence and the Saguenay*. At first, the title poem appears to be an epitome of early nineteenth-century verse, stressing well-delivered descriptive passages and solid images, combined with a narrative about a journey down the two rivers, and interspersed with allusions to a love story that never seems to get anywhere but whets the reader's curiosity enough to hold his attention so that he reads on. A closer look at the whole collection of poems reveals a somewhat undistinguished flair for verse-writing, with occasional good passages but not enough consistency among them to reveal an original poet working with an individual voice.

Further consideration, however, suggests that Sangster's individuality may lie in his relationship to what he is doing. He presents himself in the title poem as a "Pale, solitary watcher", for ever re-examining his personal position in relation to what he is examining in the poem. He is the recorder of a scene, the external observer of natural things including landscape and man, drawing back from what he describes, never allowing himself to participate in what he sees, as though he were afraid to involve himself within the context of commitment.

THIS POSITION can be understood as soon as one places Sangster in his historical setting. Because of his weak educational background, his knowledge of poetic mode and poetic tradition tended to be superficial. This is shown by his clichéd approach to image and metaphor. He had learned, indeed, that Keats was "half in love with night"; he was conscious of the rustic direction of Wordsworth and the mystery of Coleridge. He knew the popular modes of the Romantic poets, and he attempted to capture what he thought was their direction and approach. But his knowledge of them seems to have been based on anthologized representations of their poetry rather than on a thorough knowledge of their work through development and change in successive volumes. And because his knowledge of them was general, and because his sensibility was obviously limited in comparison with theirs, Sangster was never able to render the romantic inclination with success and clarity.

As observer-removed-from-the-scene, Sangster puts in all the guide-lines needed for the interpretation of his work. His most prominent metaphor is that of the day, which he divides and extends in all its variants: "dawn", "day", "noon", "evening", "twilight", "night", "midnight". The centrality of his "day" metaphor creates his poetic structure. He relates all the emotions that he feels, the sensations he assimilates, to aspects of the day, using them to integrate a scene as well as to extend and interpret a meaning outside the particular situation he chooses to describe. But as a metaphor, whether used as symbol or as image, the day and its parts have to be cleverly mounted within a poem, or they become too obvious and appear contrived: as when sadness is related to the dark of night; joy to the brightness of noon; new beginnings to the freshness of dawn. But there are nuances and subtleties inherent in the metaphor too, which demand from a poet original insight and supreme control; only rarely did Sangster achieve these.

He was content, it seems, to write poetry as other people had been writing it for some time, or rather as he thought they had been writing it. Though his subject may be the Canadian landscape, his attitude is similar to that of poets writing about England:

Red walls of granite rise on either hand,
Rugged and smooth; a proud young eagle soars
Above the stately evergreens, that stand
Like watchful sentinels on these God-built towers;
And near yon beds of many-colored flowers
Browse two majestic deer, and at their side
A spotted fawn all innocently cowers;
In the rank brushwood it attempts to hide,
While the strong-antlered stag steps forth with lordly pride.

("The Thousand Islands", *The St. Lawrence
and the Saguenay*)

It is description at its most conventional, and deliberately so. Sangster was attempting to give the Canadian scene his own individual interpretation through the romantic sensibility. Perhaps he could do no more, but it is obvious that he felt that what he was writing was what his potential public wanted. He responded to the critics who felt he was a Canadian Wordsworth,[4] and tried to give them what they expected. And he continued in his later poetry to echo Wordsworth, as in "The Meadow-Field":

Do you remember the meadow-field,
Where the red-ripe strawberries lay concealed,
Close to the roots of the scented grass,
That bowed to let the sunbeams pass
To smile on the buttercups clustering over
The drooping buds of honied clover?
Or the golden dandelions, milky-stemmed,
With which the spring fields were begemmed?

It would be some time before an original voice would give expression to the unknown land that was Canada. For the time being, it was left to Sangster, and others like him, to make the beginnings of a tradition, to express a new land-scape in the traditional way.

For Sangster, his poetry was a love affair with Canada. "My idea was to save them [his manuscripts] not to the world, but to this Canada of ours, which . . . has occupied much of my thoughts in the rhyming way for many years."[5] "Rhyming" is indeed the clue to Sangster's attitude towards his task: that it should be poetry that sings, that becomes mellifluous. And his verse does sing, though often turgidly; it becomes too regular, marked by jaded rhythms that at times can cloy even the most insensitive ear. He tries to see English classical allu-sions within the Canadian scene, but for him "No Nymphic trains appear/To charm the pale Ideal Worshipper/Of Beauty." In "The St. Lawrence and the Saguenay" he examines every scene, often with the eye of a photographer, preserving the details of the landscape that all may see them. Yet there remains a desire to people that landscape with classical images, "to fill the breast with fear", and since he cannot find the images he is disappointed. The word "but" recurs often as he searches the landscape in the hope of relating his poetry to the images of Greece of which the Romantic poets were so fond, and it is regretfully that he admits the absence of the references he wants to capture:

> But crystal streams through endless landscapes flow,
> And o'er the clustering Isles the softest breezes blow.

Significantly, the language of this poem changes when the poet leaves the St. Lawrence River and begins to sail up the Saguenay. The description becomes more precise, the rhythms are less stodgy. Sangster is captivated by the strangeness of the scene he views; he becomes fascinated by its particularity, and for a few pages he forgets that he had set out to write a poem whose language would assure his readers that he was a poet writing in an acceptable romantic mode.

The interest in the classical that was always part of Sangster's bent is particularly evident in his second volume, *Hesperus*. But he does not use classical mythology primarily as metaphor; rather he uses the stories of myths to further his quest for "Nature for our guide". He associates the Greek legends with those of Christianity, and retells them within a nineteenth-century context. He goes only far enough to interpret the present; he does not move into heightened metaphor through myth as twentieth-century poets have done. His model for this seems to have been Shelley, and at times he achieves something resembling Shelly's peculiar pompousness:

> With silence, and to the ear
> Attuned to harmony divine
> Begets a strain
> Whose trance-like stillness wakes delicious pain.

It might have been better had Sangster, in his constant rewriting, attempted to apply his personal vision, evidenced by his refusal to see wood nymphs on the Saguenay, to his later work.

Hesperus echoes the devotion of the Romantic poets to the country life and to idyllic rurality.[6] It examines the idealized joys of the pioneers, the Krieghoff-like joys of happy children in the snow, of "bees" and merry dances, at a time when Mrs. Moodie was exposing the flaws of that Canadian legend, of which the

nineteenth-century myth-makers were so fond. Yet the verse which in this volume celebrates Canada's great moments of history echoes the qualities of the earlier poetry, and the notes of patriotism are not excessively chauvinistic. He has "stood upon the Plain/That had trembled when the slain/Hurled their proud, defiant curses at the battle-heated foe", ("The Plains of Abraham"), and he had been moved. "Brock" is replete with statements that show a healthy respect for the Canadian past. Yet even in these poems the excessively regular rhythms create a stilted and pretentious quality that is rarely relieved. But apparently this was a public voice which Canadian readers at that time wanted to hear, and it was also what people outside Canada expected of a country on the threshold of nationhood. Sangster did not look upon his country and his times dispassionately; in those days patriotism was enough, and Sangster displayed it abundantly.

SANGSTER never deviated from the tradition of English literature as he saw it, or from his love for Canada, yet his personal outlook was sombre and lonely. He worked at his manuscripts with a heavy heart, wondering what the public would do with the poetry he gave it. He worried about his work, and often wondered if it were worthwhile.[7] He did not share the contemporary belief in universal improvement, nor did he foresee the coming of an age when the poet in Canada would have a position of respect. He strove to ameliorate the hardships in his life, both mental and physical, without ever expecting that they could be finally removed. But he did have some praise in his lifetime, among others from E. H. Dewart, who in *Selections from Canadian Poets* (Montreal, 1864) talked of "The originality and descriptive power ... the variety of Canadian themes on which he had written with force and elegance." This was true only within limitations, for Sangster's is a poetry that constantly echoes the masters he tried to emulate.

Even in his most original poems, *Sonnets Written in Orillia Woods*, the pace is still one of imitation, the diction is borrowed, though occasionally the subject matter is specifically Canadian. For Sangster uses the unfamiliar setting to develop typically romantic concerns: love for nature, glimpses of God in the cycles of the seasons, faith in man's ability to cope, nostalgia and melancholy at the transience of life. His metaphors are of the woods, of flowers that grow wild, of trees that sway to a musical wind. And over it all is a sadness of spirit, produced not only by his consciousness of being ignored by his contemporary world, but also because

59

his vision of the romantic sensibility included this overpowering quality. His best work from the *Orillia Woods* volume evidences this:

> I've almost grown a portion of this place;
> I seem familiar with each mossy stone;
> Even the nimble chipmunk passes on,
> And looks, but never scolds me. Birds have flown
> And almost touched my hand; and I can trace
> The wild bees to their hives. I've never known
> So sweet a pause from labor.

He was not precise enough to give his poetry the freshness in approach that authenticity of vision would have created.

Often, the fact that early Canadian poetry is imitative is taken for granted, and it is felt that we do not have to say it any more. Yet a recognition of the fact gives the contemporary reader a yardstick for measuring what happened when imitation lost its appeal to our poets. And while one may take Sangster on his own terms, it is equally important to decide what he accomplished as a poet in his time. It was a time when poets elsewhere were experimenting with new forms and concepts: Arnold and Tennyson were decisively discarding the romantic influence, even though it could never be completely eliminated, for most men — and most poets particularly — have a romantic side. But Sangster stood still, looked back, and then looked around him; he knew well the uses of the past, but his vanity in thinking that he would be the first great Canadian poet prevented him from understanding the uses of the future.

Sangster cannot be dismissed out of hand, for his work is at the basis of two of the main trends in Canadian poetry: the role of the spectator as one of the main poetic stances, and the fact that most Canadian poetic metaphor stems from the Romantic movement. Perhaps his vision was blurred, his voice unoriginal. But it was he more than any other poet who transformed from England the romantic influence that was to pervade — and continues to pervade — Canadian poetry. Historically, he is the constant reminder that British influence was maintained in Canada above all in its literature, and that in the case of men like Sangster their devotion to integrating that influence often weakened their own individuality as poets.

Sangster often declared, in his later years as he was reworking his manuscripts, that he was a true servant of Canada, and that his practice showed that this was true. What he served, however, was the past of English poetry. He did not satisfy the taste of his contemporaries, and still less did he serve the true English tradition, which is, after all, based on growth and change. Rather, he expected his readers, like himself, to promote the poetic values that had been handed down to them — or manufactured by literary critics. Unconsciously he used the tradition to distort in his poems the individual flavour of the Canadian landscape, and it is difficult to discern in his work any element of the purely creative poet at work. Sangster had no vision for the future of Canadian poetry except that he was part of its foundation; he had, instead, only a tenacious will to defend the literary past. And though his work is often referred to as the beginning of Canadian poetry, he was in fact the last poet in Canada to be purely English in approach; others would imitate, too, but they would also add their own freshness to create original voices. Sangster's poetry is the end of an era; after him, the beginnings.

(1974)

NOTES

1 Autobiographical fragment, McGill University Library, apparently deposited there by W. D. Lighthall.

2 *Ibid.*

3 Desmond Pacey in *Ten Canadian Poets* (Toronto: Ryerson, 1957) says: "Of the poets who came to maturity in Canada before Confederation it seems to me that Sangster is easily the best, though I am quite willing to admit that the competition was not very intense."

4 The London *National Magazine* said that "there is much of the spirit of Wordsworth in this writer, only the tone is religious instead of being philosophical . . . he may be regarded as the Wordsworth of Canada."

5 Letter to W. D. Lighthall, July 14, 1891, McGill University Library.

6 Desmond Pacey, in *Ten Canadian Poets*, talks of the "fresh image" of "Brightly broke the summer morn/Like a lark from out of the corn," but it appears to be a metaphor contrived for rhyme rather than for originality.

7 Letter to W. D. Lighthall, July 13, 1888, McGill University Library.

POET AND POLITICS:

Charles Mair at Red River

Norman Shrive

THE SIGNIFICANCE OF CHARLES MAIR in the development of Canada and of her literature is today almost unknown. Some Canadian historians, of course, have remembered him — perhaps only too well — as a controversial figure in a controversial event: the Riel uprising of 1869-70. But their accounts, both fair and prejudiced, of the part he played in that historical episode are concerned with only a few months of a life that lasted nearly ninety years, and he has been depicted, therefore, in a very limited context. On the other hand Canadian literary scholars have ignored him altogether or have dismissed him condescendingly, preferring to name Roberts, Carman, Lampman and Scott as their "Confederation Poets", despite the fact that none of these more famous figures was over the age of seven in 1867 or published anything until almost fifteen years after that date. But Charles Mair not only gave Canada what was regarded in 1868 as its first significant collection of verse; he also, unlike Roberts and Carman, retained faith, however dim at times, in his country's future, and, unlike Lampman, lived long enough to see that faith justified. He offers to the Canadian literary historian, in fact, an ideal illustration of the struggle of post-Confederation letters for survival and recognition.

For even when Mair is revealed as a precious fool and a bad poet he provides a singularly striking parallel to the cross-currents of aspiration and frustration, of success and failure, of even tragedy, that marked that struggle. His life gives us a tableau of some of the most significant aspects of Canadian history — of pioneering in the Ottawa Valley, of the Canada First movement in politics, of both Riel rebellions, of the opening up of the West. His writings and the influences behind them reveal the cultural climate in which he lived — more particularly, the way in which nationalism and its judgments intruded into literary matters, not only in the nineteenth century but also in a much later period. Because Mair and his work were so closely associated with the political and cultural development of Canada, there is little wonder that journalist Bernard McEvoy could call him a "marvel of miscellaneousness" who had "the knack of carrying a load of versatility", or that the late Lorne Pierce could describe Mair's life as "a thrilling romance" and his work as part of "the structure of our national life". Or, perhaps, that Louis Riel could find him "a barely civilized" Upper Canadian who found amusement in "uttering follies to the world".

Unfortunately for Mair the published commentaries about his career have been both few in number and limited in value. John Garvin's supposedly authoritative biographical essay in the *Master-Works of Canadian Authors* edition is ludicrous in its bias and pretentiousness, its critical posturing and unscholarly inaccuracies. And the articles on Mair in newspapers and periodicals are of the "popular" type: in them he is invariably depicted as a "great singer of Canadian Literature" or as a "saviour of Canada's nationhood". The suspicions stimulated by such apotheosizing are confirmed of course when one reads those social and political histories that have included Mair in their scope; for in these works he is revealed as a quite different figure. Part of this contrast is often explainable by personal and commercial prejudices (J. J. Hargrave's *Red River*), by religious intolerance (R. E. Lamb's *Thunder in the North*), or by journalistic indulgence to popular taste and by distortion of historical evidence (Joseph Kinsey Howard's *Strange Empire*). But an unattractive Mair is also to be found in works of scholarly excellence such as W. L. Morton's *Alexander Begg's Red River Journal* and G. F. Stanley's *The Birth of Western Canada*; unfortunately once again for Mair, however, the objectives of these latter studies have not warranted more than a rather abstracted interpretation of his role as a literary figure at Red River.

A MORE DETAILED EXAMINATION of Mair that must still remain selective in emphasis would begin, nevertheless, with Red River in 1868-70; for better or for worse, his reputation and subsequent career depended largely upon his actions at that time. How he got on the trail to Fort Garry in the first place is a theme worthy of that writer he himself most esteemed, Sir Walter Scott, but since the melodramatic details have already been tortuously exploited by Garvin[1] it is unnecessary and undesirable to repeat them here. Sufficient it is to note that a trip to Ottawa in May, 1868, to see his first book, *Dreamland and Other Poems*, through the press led Mair to the Canada First Association, then to the attention of the Honourable William Macdougall, the Minister of Public Works and ardent proponent of North-West expansion, and then not to Kingston and Queen's to resume medical studies but to Fort Garry, ostensibly as paymaster of a Government road party. "At once we saw the opportunity", said fellow Canada Firster George T. Denison, "of doing some good work towards helping on the acquisition of the territory." [2] And William A. Foster, another member of the group, promised to arrange with George Brown of the *Globe* that Mair should be the paper's North-West correspondent and therefore the advocate of the western policy that Brown had in common with Macdougall.

The appointment was a last-minute decision by Macdougall, and because the road-party had left days before, Mair's departure was a hasty one. But he began the adventure as best he could. In his pocket he had a letter of introduction from his friend, the Reverend Aeneas Macdonell Dawson of the Cathedral of the City of Ottawa, to the Right Reverend Monsignor Taché, Bishop of St. Boniface, in which Dawson emphasized that "Mr. Mair's great abilities have commended him to the notice of the leading people" of Ottawa, and that, although "Mr. Mair is not precisely of our communion . . . Dr. Pusey himself does not surpass him in respect for Catholics." [3] And when he reached Toronto Mair took advantage of a stop-over, as his expense account reveals — "revolver and ammunition, $15.25" — to prepare himself even further for the eventualities of the West.

The letters that Mair wrote to his brothers in Perth, Ontario — letters immediately given to the Perth *Courier* and subsequently copied by the Toronto *Globe* and other papers — provide a detailed record of his trip to Fort Garry as well as considerable critical comment on the land and peoples he encountered on the way. The letters in fact are so full of information and are so enthusiastic about the greatness of the new land that with certain exceptions they were almost certainly intended not for private reading but for newspaper publication as a form of "immigration literature".

From Toronto he travelled, as did all who wished to get to Red River in less than a month, by rail to Chicago, and thence by a combination of water, rail and road to Fort Abercrombie, North Dakota, where he hoped to overtake superintendent John Snow and his party. The trip under the best of conditions could be only an arduous one, but Mair, either because of youthful enthusiasm or because of his patriotic obligation, reveals in his reports little if any sense of hardship. Petty annoyances are not mentioned or are treated humorously, and the more obvious deprivations concomitant with travel through a primitive West are either understated or are exploited as intrinsic to the romance of the great new land. The letters in fact continually emphasize the ease and comfort that the new settler would experience once he had left his Ontario town or farm. In the *Globe* of December 27 Mair reported that after three days on the train to Chicago and LaCrosse, he journeyed by "immense steamer" up the Mississippi to St. Paul — "a splendid two days' sail" made constantly enjoyable by "magnificent and striking" scenery. A further 170 miles by rail brought him to St. Cloud "in time to attend Judge Donnelly's political meeting"; and "four splendid horses, changed every fifteen miles" pulled his stage-coach to Sauk Centre, seventy miles farther west. There, "after great difficulty" (which he does not detail) and "valuable fact! only on account of being a Mason", he obtained a driver to take him to Abercrombie, "where I found Mr. Snow, the Surveyor, waiting for me".

Mair and Snow then travelled together the 250 miles to Fort Garry, this time by a horse and buggy bought by the latter at St. Paul and with "every luxury, even *condensed milk*, an admirable thing". The record of this part of the journey (Perth *Courier*, January 14, 1869) reads like a idyllic travelogue:

> No description of mine can convey to you an idea of the vastness and solitary grandeur of these prairies. Sometimes for a whole day you will drive through a perfect ocean of luxurious grasses now yellow and decaying, and perhaps the next day your tracks will be through an immense expanse of inky soil where the prairie fires have consumed the herbage. The prairies are a dead level, and the traveller drifts along in a sort of a dream between earth and sky over roads as solid and even as marble.

Mair and Snow reached the edge of the Red River settlement one evening in late October just in time to hear "the convent bells of St. Boniface sounding sweetly over the water " (*Globe*, December 27, 1868) and within a few minutes had registered at "Dutch George" Emerling's hotel.

But Mair's stay at Emerling's was brief, for he lost little time in finding his Queen's College friend, John Schultz; and for the few days prior to his leaving with Snow to set up road headquarters at Oak Point, thirty miles to the east, he lived with Schultz at the latter's combined medical dispensary and trading store. There is no extant correspondence between Mair and Schultz prior to 1869, and it is therefore difficult to determine whether or not Mair had more than superficial knowledge about Schultz's standing in the Red River settlement. This point is of some importance because historians have emphasized the "error" committed by Mair and other "Canadians" in intimately associating themselves with Schultz. To Mair especially, however, such association was not an "error". If he was aware before he arrived at Red River that Schultz was extremely unpopular among the great majority of the settlement, it must be concluded that he would have discounted such an attitude as being unreasonable and short-sighted, for Schultz represented to Mair an *avant-coureur* and agent in Red River not only of his own theories on North-West expansion, but also of those of the Minister of Public Works and of the Canadian Government itself.

Dr. John Christian Schultz had had a stormy career at Red River since his arrival there in 1861. Perhaps he had never really intended to practise medicine, for within a year he had established a lucrative fur trade and a thriving general store. In 1865 he had acquired control of the settlement's only newspaper, *The Nor' Wester*, and had continued with ever-increasing frankness the policy on which that paper had been founded — the necessity for ending Hudson's Bay rule and for opening the country to settlement. Because of this and other factors, by 1868 he had emerged as the most notorious figure in the settlement. In 1864 he had been instrumental in forming a Masonic Lodge; in 1867 he had married a Miss Anne Farquharson just in time to prevent her conversion to Roman Catholicism; and in early 1868, after refusal to pay a debt in favour of his half-brother and partner, Henry McKenney, he had to be taken to jail by force. In this affair, even his release was dramatic. No sooner had he been carried off by carriole than his bride of a few months "forthwith caused all the doors and windows to be barred and secured with nails and spikes, so as to guard the shop against a fresh entry on the part of the Sheriff". Then,

> towards one o'clock on the Saturday morning about fifteen persons, among whom was Mrs. Schultz, forcibly entered the prison where Schultz was confined, overpowered the constables on duty, and, breaking open the door leading to his cell, liberated him. This done, the party adjourned along with him to his house, where report says "they made a night of it."[4]

The special *Nor' Wester* of the following day not only presented Schultz's side of the story but also took the occasion to point up the complete incapacity of the Hudson's Bay Company as both a judicial and executive authority.

Schultz is one of the ambiguous personalities of Red River history. He obviously had many qualities of the natural leader: he was strikingly handsome, of great physical strength, aggressive, ambitious, decisive and intelligent. He was also known as a man of kindness and reserve, even of scholarship; articles he wrote on

Red River botany had been recognized by the Royal Botanical Society of Canada and those on primitive western fortifications and on the Eskimo later led to his election to the Royal Society of Canada. Certainly among his devoted "Canadian party" associates he was an almost archetypal figure of the national patriot and champion against tyranny. Professor W. L. Morton fairly conceded: "He sincerely sought to develop the North-West; he saw its possibilities with the vision of the statesman as well as the eye of the speculator."[5] Schultz's enemies and many other historians, however, saw not the visionary statesman but only the arrogant speculator. The *métis* and the Roman Catholic clergy disliked his Masonic Protestantism and feared his bold expansionist policies; the Hudson's Bay Company resented his abusive vilification of its authority; and those traders and colonists of the settlement who opposed the transfer of the Territory to Canada found it easy to distrust him as a selfish, unscrupulous adventurer.

Mair's immediate association with Schultz at Red River was not in itself a matter of resentment to the anti-"Canadian" group. He himself records the warmth of welcome extended to him by representatives of both the main factions: "We had a very pleasant stay at Fort Garry and received all sorts of entertainment," he reported (*Globe*, December 27, 1868); "they live like princes here"— even to the extent of "nuts of all kinds, coffee, port and sherry, brandy punch and cigars, concluding with whist until four o'clock a.m". And at the home of Alexander Begg, an anti-"Canadian" free trader, he was offered "hospitalities to my heart's content" (*Globe*, January 4, 1869).

But such initial relationships were soon put to test. Mair and Snow made their headquarters in a log and mud hut at Oak Point and prepared to build their road; by Christmas the former's intimacy with Schultz and his support of the "Canadian party" had become obvious enough to cause resentment where previously there had been friendly acceptance. Begg, no longer the hospitable host, wrote that both the road officials "severed the confidence . . . by their joining hands with this ultra and dangerous party".[6] The activities of the road-party itself were also a matter of concern, particularly to the *métis*. Actually, the Canadian Government had as yet no right to construct a road over what was still the territory of the Hudson's Bay Company, although some justification for the project did exist in the oral permission Snow had received from Governor Mactavish. And to those *métis* and settlers who were suffering famine following a grasshopper plague of the previous summer, the announced intention of the road-party to provide money and provisions in return for work was more than welcome. But the first trees were hardly felled when news of trouble was reported back to Fort

Garry. The relief programme had proved a disappointment: fewer men than expected were hired, and these few (about forty) claimed their wages were low. In addition was the more serious charge, according to J. J. Hargrave, "that Messrs. Snow and Mair were purchasing from the Indians portions of land to which the actual occupants laid a pre-emption claim". The actual occupants were *métis* and such was their indignation that "Mr. Mair was brought to Fort Garry under compulsion of an excited crowd of French half-breeds who required he should forthwith quit the country, as he was, in their opinion a man likely to create mischief."[7] Governor Mactavish intervened, however, and "after some altercation" Mair was permitted to return to work. Snow was not quite so fortunate. For having sold liquor to the same Indians he was fined ten pounds in Petty Court and later accused by Riel of trying "to seize the best lands of the *métis* . . . at Oak Point".[8]

Because of the welter of conflicting evidence and bias it is difficult to determine the truth of these charges. Hargrave, nephew and secretary of Governor Mactavish and no supporter of Mair, admits that the episode that he himself reports was the result of a misunderstanding about payment for work on the road. The Mair Papers include "private vouchers" from Mair to Alexander Begg for considerable quantities of brandy and gin, but such transactions between a trader and the paymaster of a road-party would hardly be unusual. Snow's sale of liquor was proved; but surely it is irresponsible to state blandly, as Joseph Kinsey Howard does, that "Snow started dickering with the Indians for property . . . and one of his favorite mediums of exchange was whiskey."[9] Professor Morton suggests instead that there may have been "some *treating* of Indians to induce them to tolerate the claim-staking".[10] In any case these irritations might have been forgotten or pardoned if they had not been aggravated by Mair himself, not only by his association with Schultz, but also by what Begg described as his "preaching a doctrine sufficient of itself to cause distrust in the minds of the Red River people".[11]

THIS "DOCTRINE" was contained in the supposedly private letters Mair's brothers gave to the newspapers and in those Mair himself later sent when he was appointed special correspondent. The young poet (*Dreamland* appeared in the bookshops while Mair was en route to Red River) either did not realize that his commentary would cause "distrust", or was indifferent to such a consequence. His correspondence indicates that he saw himself as a professional writer from the East with a responsibility both to his own newly-acquired reputation as a man of letters and to his special appointment as a Governmental agent. And certainly his reports in the newspapers contain some of the most vivid descriptive prose ever written in Canada. It is effortlessly fluent, revealing the same sensitivity to sights and sounds that mark the better lines of *Dreamland* (Mair's notebooks give ample evidence of his propensity to jot down whatever interested him at a particular time). The letters are lengthy — in some cases over 2,500 words — but they are consistently stimulating. A description of the prairie may be followed by historical or even geological comment. That of a "genuine out west political meeting" includes the humorous "tall tales" related by the speakers and the earthy, sarcastic observations of their listeners. And pictures of the river steamers, the mule-trains, the Red River carts, of the Indians, the half-breeds, the white settlers are all made more vivid by interpolated accounts of incidents and events that may befall the frontier traveller or immigrant. It is when Mair's depictions seem exaggerated, a little too lush, even though always maintaining a tone of sincerity, that the reader is reminded that the letters were written not for their own sake nor, as Hargrave innocently — or ironically — suggested, "to vary the monotony of existence in the backwoods",[12] but to convince Canadians of the desirability of settlement in the North-West and of the great possibilities of Canada's future. "So far as I have yet seen", Mair informed his readers (*Globe*, January 4, 1869),

> the country is *great* — inexhaustible — inconceivably rich. Farming here is a pleasure — there is no toil in it, and all who do farm are comfortable, and some wealthy. What do you think of a farmer within a bowshot of here, being worth seven or eight thousand pounds sterling, and selling to the Hudson's Bay Company last week £5,000 stg. worth of cattle: a man who came from Lower Canada nineteen years ago, not worth sixpence?

Beyond Red River is the prairie (*Globe*, May 28, 1869):

> There the awful solitude opens upon the sight and swells into an ocean, and the eye wanders over the "silent space" of the West. The man must be corrupt as death who, unaccustomed, can look unmoved upon this august material presence, this calm unutterable vastness. Man is a grasshopper here — a mere insect, making way between the enormous discs of heaven and earth.

Portage la Prairie, is not just a thriving settlement; it is really a *portal*, through which will flow "the unspeakable blessings of free government and civilization".

It is there that the Canadian "for the first time clearly recognizes the significance and inevitable grandeur of his country's future". Far behind him "are his glorious old native Province[s],[13] the unsullied freedom of the North, the generous and untiring breed of men"; before him "stretches through immeasurable distance the larger and lovelier Canada — the path of empire and the garden of the world".

The letters seemed to justify the high hopes of Macdougall and Mair's Canada First friends when they had urged him to open "the sealed book" of Rupert's Land. The Toronto *Globe* of June 11, 1869, remarked that "the greatest interest has been manifested in every section of Ontario in the letters . . . from Mr. Charles Mair," and emphasized with some specificity Mair's call for settlers. "We hope to see", it said, "a new Upper Canada in the North-West Territory — a new Upper Canada in its well-regulated society and government — in its education, morality and religion." Denison wrote Mair (March 10, 1869) of his pleasure in reading "such good accounts . . . of the great North-West", and added characteristically that "together we Men of the North . . . will be able to teach the Yankees that we will be as our ancestors always have been, the dominant race." But such bold confidence might have been somewhat qualified if Denison had known that his friend's ardently nationalistic journalism had a few weeks before caused him to undergo a most humiliating experience.

The *Globe*s containing the first two or three of Mair's letters began arriving in the settlement some time in January, 1869. To a people already tense over recent events and the implications of the approaching transfer the letters were little short of sensational. Their glowing accounts of the possibilities of the West were in themselves enough, as Begg states, to cause "distrust" among the settlers and natives; but certain passages of a more personal nature infuriated them. The *métis*, said Mair (*Globe*, December 14, 1868), "are a harmless obsequious set of men and will, I believe, be very useful here when the country gets filled up". But they are "a strange class", he continued (*Globe*, December 27, 1868); "they will do anything but farm, will drive ox-trains four hundred miles — go out on the buffalo hunt — fish — do anything but farm." The *métis*, indeed, said Mair — and this annoyed many settlers receiving or awaiting assistance as a result of the famine — "are the only people here who are starving"; of the rest, "not one of them requires relief other than seed wheat which they are quite able to pay for." But to add to this impression of a lazy, self-indulgent *métis* and to that of himself as a rather superior being viewing the lower orders with disdain was one especially offensive passage in the *Globe* of January 4, 1869:

70

After putting up at the Dutchman's hotel . . . I went over and stayed at Dr. Schultz's after a few days. The change was comfortable, I assure you, from the racket of a motley crowd of half-breeds, playing billiards and drinking, to the quiet and solid comfort of a home. I was invited to a dinner-party at Beffs [sic], where were the Governor's brother-in-law, a wealthy merchant here, Isabister [sic] and other Nor' Westers. Altogether, I received hospitalities to my heart's content, and I left the place thoroughly pleased with most that I had met. There are jealousies and heart-burnings, however. Many wealthy people are married to half-breed women, who, having no coat of arms but a "totem" to look back to, make up for the deficiency by biting at the backs of their "white" sisters. The white sisters fall back upon their whiteness, whilst the husbands meet each other with desperate courtesies and hospitalities, with a view to filthy lucre in the background.

MAIR SURELY NEVER INTENDED that such lines would be made public and had hoped his brothers would use greater discretion in giving them to the papers. He later defended them as reflecting "the usual freedom and flippancy of a private letter to a friend", and himself as a victim of "an unpardonable indiscretion" that "allowed the letter to be published *verbatim*". He sincerely regretted the letter's appearing in print, for he "had received much kindness in Red River, and certainly bore no feelings of dislike or ill-will to anyone. But political and monopolist antagonisms ran high, and . . . this letter . . . , amongst sensible people, at any other time would have only provoked a smile" (Saskatchewan *Herald*, March 15, 1880).

The good folk of Red River, however, were not amused. Hargrave records that one of the first to react was "Dutch George" Emerling, who "threatened that should the author of these philippics ever enter the house he had maligned, he should be expelled". Much more severe was the anger of the Red River ladies:

One lady pulled the poet's nose, while another used her fingers rudely about his ears. A third confining herself to words, said his letters would be productive of serious mischief by circulating doubts about the reality of the destitution, of which they gave an account highly calculated to mislead and to paralyse the efforts being made to raise money abroad for the relief of the suffering poor.[14]

The scene of the settlement post office, as recorded by Abbé Georges Dugas, the Roman Catholic director of St. Boniface College, was even more violent:

Mair, having committed the indelicacy of writing, in the Ontario papers, some words offensive to the women of Winnipeg, underwent the humiliation of being horse-whipped in the town post-office, by the wife of one of the most notable citizens, Mrs. Bannatyne. She asked the clerk of the store in which the post-office was located to let her know when Mair came at his regular time on Saturday at four o'clock in the afternoon, when the store was full of people. Daniel Mulligan, the clerk, seeing Mair coming, ran to tell Mrs. Bannatyne. She quickly threw a shawl on her head and arrived like a bomb at the post-office; she held a large whip in her hand. Without hesitating, she seized him by the nose, and administered five or six strokes of the whip to his body: "There," she told him, "you see how the women of Red River treat those who insult them."

The scene lasted only half a minute. But it seemed long to Mair who hastened to leave, daring neither to speak nor retaliate. That evening the episode was known throughout the district.[15]

The unfortunate affair made Mair the object of all the resentment that the majority of the populace felt for the "Canadian" party. A "French gentleman" wrote to his friend Hargrave: "The indignation against Mr. Mair is going on furiously."[16] According to another witness it was so great "that he was ordered to leave the territory", but through the intervention of Governor Mactavish he was allowed to return and remain "after apologizing to the leading half-breeds and promising that he would write no more letters of such a nature".[17] This latter report probably inspired Joseph Kinsey Howard's glibly inaccurate comment that Mair "apologized abjectly, abandoned journalism, and thereafter confined himself to epic verse".[18]

Mair's enemies made certain that their impressions of his early conduct at Red River would never be forgotten. Hargrave, Begg and Dugas were not only antagonistic participants or spectators in the events of this time and afterwards; they were also, to varying degrees of proficiency, journalists, and some of their works have become basic documents. Begg in particular carried on a form of literary harassment, and among his many writings is what is considered the first historical novel of the North-West, *Dot-It-Down*,[19] a smugly naive and rather clumsy satire in which Mair plays a notorious role and for which — by his propensity for note-taking — he even provides the title. As Begg describes "Dot", he is a bumptious and cocksure young man constantly trying to impress the modest, hospitable Red River settlers with his social and literary prowess. He is also depicted as a would-be gallant, too free with both wine and ladies. As a result Dot's friends are soon only "Cool" (Schultz) and "Sharp" (Snow); but after several brushes with the law and the righteous folk of Red River — one is over claim-staking — these three are reduced to utter disgrace and leave the settlement. "Ah! Canada, how your champions suffered for your sake! Ah! Canada, how you have also suffered by their deeds." Sharp becomes the proprietor of "a third-rate boarding house" in St. Paul; Cool disappears to some other community where "assuredly there was trouble in store for them", and Dot,

> the unfortunate correspondent, found to his cost that he had got into bad company, and felt that he was consequently a loser by the connection. His land speculations were frustrated by the action of the settlers in the matter. His expenses while in Red River had been enormous, through his extravagance, and he found that he possessed few friends on account of his untruthful letters to Canada. He, therefore, decided to follow in the footsteps of Cool; and it is to be hoped when he reached Canada he tried to make some reparation for the evil he did while in Red River.[20]

How much of *Dot-It-Down* can be accepted as a realistic depiction of personalities and events at Red River is difficult to determine. Begg certainly deviates from fact when he disposes of his villains: Mair, Schultz and Snow were to play even more dramatic roles in the near future. His characters and situations, although they may have historical basis, are mainly caricatures — Begg did not have the skill to make them any other. Unfortunately for Mair, however, his friends in the East have helped to confirm the impression that Begg created. Fellow Canada Firster, R. G. Haliburton, reviewing *Dreamland* (Halifax *Daily Reporter*, July 13, 1869) refers to him "as brimful of fun and frolic as a schoolboy . . . as if cricket or croquet, boating and flirting, were more likely to be engrossing his thoughts, than the quiet mysteries of nature." The correspondence of Foster and of Henry J. Morgan (the other founding member of the Canada First group) contains more than one reference to the frivolity of a rather dubious quality that enlivened their evenings when Mair was with them in Ottawa. "Speaking of girls", wrote Morgan (April 4, 1869), "reminds me that information has reached here of a little mishap on your part with a little feminine Nor'Wester. Haliburton and I had a good laugh over it, but the elderly gentlemen frown dreadfully, and say all sorts of things against you." These eastern friends treated Mair's adventures with the good humour and tolerance that common interests and distance could allow, and they sympathized with Mair in his self-imposed banishment. As Denison said (March 29, 1868): "I do not doubt that you are lonely enough out there, and you ought to have some friends — white folks — with you. It is not right you should be entirely alone among those wretched, half-starved half-breeds."

73

Fʀᴏᴍ ᴍᴀɪʀ ʜɪᴍsᴇʟf there is little even to be guessed concerning the charges against him. The liquor vouchers in the Mair Papers are doubtful evidence; other documents are similarly ambiguous. Three days after John Garrioch of Portage la Prairie had reported that there was "a perfect misunderstanding" between Mair and the Indians over what land "they would allow immigrants to occupy" (June 18, 1869), Mair wrote to Macdougall that he had applied "a modest pressure" upon the Indians by "pointing out their insignificant numbers compared with the incoming multitude and the obvious necessity, hence, of acting friendly and honestly".[21] In the same letter, however, he decries the methods used by certain landseekers and advises Macdougall that one of the greatest problems will be "to devise a method of distributing Indian annuities in such a manner that they shall be of real service to the recipients and not find their way into the pocket of the rum-seller as soon as paid". The only indication of Mair's personal acquisition of land is a quit claim deed between himself and one Charles Demerais, with Schultz as witness, by which he bought a thousand square chains of property at Portage for eighty pounds sterling — a quite reasonable price.

The memory, certainly, of his humiliation at the post office was to haunt Mair for many years. Ten years after the event an official of the Hudson's Bay Company recalled it during a newspaper-letter controversy with him. Of the Reverend Georges Dugas, when his *Histoire Veridique* appeared in 1905, Mair wrote to Denison: "[He] impales your humble friend as the *Advocatus Diaboli*."[22] And in a letter of 1911 from a relative in New Zealand, a significant comment — "I saw . . . a Judge Mair had been horsewhipped at Prince Rupert, I think; surely he is not one of our Mairs" — is underlined, undoubtedly by Mair, in red pencil.[27]

Whatever his feelings may have been on those occasions, during the first months of 1869 Mair must have felt beleaguered by friend and foe alike. For despite the good-natured levity of his Canada First cohorts, there was another friend whose whole future depended upon the manner in which the transfer of the territory was effected and who had to view Mair's conduct from a perspective different from that of Denison and company. This was the Honourable William Macdougall, who on June 13, 1869, wrote to his paymaster-*cum*-correspondent:

> I regret to have heard some rumours, which upon enquiry I found too true, that prevent me from doing all I had intended in your case. I need not be more precise, but you will at once admit — your own good sense will tell you — that full confidence cannot be placed in one who sometimes forgets himself, and what

74

is due to those who become answerable for his conduct. I hope for the best. Your future is in your hands. You have talents and genius of a high order — don't follow bad examples, or the end will be like theirs. I write you as a friend who is willing and may be able to do you service, but not if you become your own enemy.

There was also another correspondent, but one who obviously did not write "as a friend", and who expressed his opinion publicly in the pages of the Montreal *Nouveau Monde* of February 25, 1869:

Red River, February 1, 1869.

Mr. Editor:

Please be so good as to give me a little space in the columns of your journal, in order that I too may write of Red River.

I cannot resist that desire since I have read the enormities which a journal of Upper Canada, the *Globe*, has just uttered, in publishing a letter of a certain Mr. Mair, who arrived in Red River last fall. This gentleman, an English Canadian, is, it is said, gifted in making verses; if such is the fact I should advise him strongly to cultivate his talent, for in that way his writings would make up in rhyme for what they lack in reason.

Scarcely a month after his arrival in this country, Mr. Mair desired to describe it and its inhabitants. He succeeded rather like the navigator who, passing by a league from the coast, wrote in his log: "The people of this country seemed to us to be well disposed . . . ."

I know some men who have more than two weeks' experience and who say the opposite to this gentleman. He says finally: *the city of Portage la Prairie is destined to become one of the most important in the country: however, I shall not speak to you of it until I have seen it.*

And why not? You speak of a great many other things that you have not had time to see or know; that would be worth as much as the remainder of your letter; as much as the scarcely courteous terms, I will even say barely civilized, which you use in speaking of the ladies of the country, who certainly by all reports are equal to the ladies of your country.

Be it said in passing, Mr. Mair, if we had only you as specimen of civilized men, we should not have a very high idea of them. If I wished to amuse myself by wielding the pen as you do for the sole pleasure of uttering follies to the world, I should have some amusing things to say on your account . . . .

L. R.

The editor of *Le Nouveau Monde* noted that the letter had been written "by a half-breed . . . rightly indignant of the stupidities which a certain Mr. Mair" had published. If "L.R." was "almost certainly"[24] Louis Riel, he would later have an opportunity to show his indignation in a much more forceful and personal manner.

But that is part of another story, one that is more familiar to Canadians because of its tragi-comic elements of bravado and bloodshed, because of its central importance in their history. Not so well known is how a minor versifier from a small village in the Ottawa Valley provided significant material for its opening paragraphs. For Charles Mair, less than a year after he had journeyed to Ottawa with his manuscript of *Dreamland*, a work intended to sound a key-note of a new, unified nation, had by his pen, ironically, helped to create a situation of potential danger to Confederation itself. This Upper Canadian had brought to the West the attitudes and prejudices that had been formed over a period of thirty years and then sharpened by his alliance with a particularly aggressive group of other Upper Canadians; one of them, Macdougall, was even a "Father of Confederation". In Ontario such pro-British, Protestant attitudes and prejudices could flourish with little or no opposition. In the melting pot of the new West they were almost bound to provoke conflict.

(1963)

NOTES

[1] John Garvin, *Master-Works of Canadian Literature*, vol. XIV (Toronto: Radisson Society, 1926).

[2] G. T. Denison, *The Struggle for Imperial Unity* (Toronto: Macmillan, 1909), pp. 13-14.

[3] Queen's University Library, Mair Papers, October 6, 1868. All subsequent references to Mair's correspondence and papers, unless otherwise indicated, are from this source.

[4] J. J. Hargrave, *Red River* (Montreal: John Lovell, 1871), p. 426.

[5] W. L. Morton, *Alexander Begg's Red River Journal* (Toronto: The Champlain Society, 1956), p. 22.

[6] A. Begg, *The Creation of Manitoba* (Toronto: Hovey, 1871), pp. 20-21.

[7] Hargrave, *Red River*, p. 458.

[8] Morton, *Begg's Journal*, Document XXVII, "Memoir of Louis Riel," p. 528.

[9] J. K. Howard, *Strange Empire* (Toronto: Swan, 1965), p. 87.

[10] Morton, *Begg's Journal*, p. 528, n.5.

[11] Begg, *The Creation of Manitoba*, p. 41.

[12] Hargrave, *Red River*, p. 451.

[13] Thus Mair corrected his own copy of the *Globe*; but it is highly likely that his letter read simply "Province", as the newspaper had it.

[14] Begg, *Red River*, p. 456.

[15] G. Dugas, *Histoire veridique des faits qui ont préparé le mouvement des Métis à la Rivière Rouge en 1869* (Montreal: Librairie Beauchemin, 1905), p. 27. The quotation is translated from the French of Dugas.

[16] *Ibid.*, p. 455.

[17] Thomas Spence, deposition, "Report of the Select Committee on the Causes of the Difficulties in the North-West Territory in 1869-70," Canada, Parliament, House of Commons, *Journals*, 3d Parl., 1st Sess., 1874, app. 6., p. 133.

[18] Howard, *Strange Empire*, p. 86.

[19] A. Begg, *Dot-it-Down: A Story of Life in the North-West* (Toronto: Hunter, Rose, 1871).

[20] *Ibid.*, pp. 354-56.

[21] Public Archives of Canada, Public Works Files, ser. 98, subj. 429, June 21, 1869.

[22] *Ibid.*, Denison Papers, 5148, June 2, 1905.

[23] Ethel Harrington to Mair, December 20, 1911. Mair did become a Justice of the Peace in Prince Albert.

[24] Morton, *Begg's Journal*, p. 399, n. 2. The translation of the letter and the original appear on pp. 399-402 and pp. 567-69, respectively.

ISABELLA VALANCY CRAWFORD

The Canoe

John B. Ower

E VEN THE CASUAL READER of the best poetry of Isabella Valancy Crawford can hardly fail to be impressed by its boldness, vigour and originality. In passage after passage, he will meet with an extraordinary energetic imagination which, while obviously neither uneducated nor insensitive to literary influence, has succeeded in creating an art that is as distinctively individual and "Canadian" as anything in our literature. The aim of the present limited study is not so much to praise these obvious virtues of Crawford's best work as it is to suggest, by means of a relatively detailed study of her lyric "The Canoe", that in her finest pieces we have a poetry which is not only vital and distinctive, but also rich in symbolic significance and sophisticated and subtle in technique. James Reaney, in his brilliant pioneering essay on Crawford's poetry[1] has of course outlined a symbolic myth and a "grammar of images" which seem to form the backbone of her work. However, although Reaney has certainly told us a great deal about her art as a whole, I feel that Crawford is a poet of sufficient substance to warrant a closer scrutiny of some individual pieces. It is also only through a relatively close analysis of individual poems that it is really possible to show the virtuosity of Crawford's technique.

A convenient starting point for an analysis of "The Canoe" is the fact that the poem constitutes, both in the viewpoint of its narrator, the canoe, and in her account of her "masters twain", a study in the psychology of the primitive mind. Particularly notable is Crawford's remarkable awareness of the animating and myth-making proclivities of primitive man. That is, as is evident in some of the most striking similes and metaphors in "The Canoe", the poet is familiar with the tendency of the primitive to see everything in terms of life, and of human life in particular:

> Thin, golden nerves of sly light curl'd
> Round the dun camp, and rose faint zones,
> Half way round each grim bole knit,
> Like a shy child that would bedeck
> With its soft clasp a Brave's red neck;
>
> Sinuous, red as copper snakes,
> Sharp-headed serpents, made of light,
> Glided and hid themselves in night.

Another significant aspect of Crawford's treatment of the primitive mentality is her romantic sense of its primal and direct character. In "The Canoe", as in D. C. Scott's "At Gull Lake: August 1810", the poet evidently finds in the behaviour of the "savage" Indian a sort of psychological apocalypse of the basic forces of human nature. This is particularly evident in Crawford's lyric in the love-song of the two braves, with its frank expression of impulses and emotions which at first appear scarcely less elemental than those of the hounds who dream of "the dead stag stout and lusty":

> My masters twain sang songs that wove
> (As they burnish'd hunting blade and rifle)
> A golden thread with a cobweb trifle —
> Loud of the chase, and low of love.
>
> "O Love, art thou a silver fish?
> Shy of the line and shy of gaffing,
> Which we do follow, fierce, yet laughing,
> Casting at thee the light-winged wish.

Even if "The Canoe" were simply a poetic study in the psychology of un-civilized man, it would still do considerable credit to Crawford's powers of insight and imagination. However, as Reaney has shown, Crawford is not merely a clever poetical dilettante, but an artist with a vision of sufficient dimensions to come to grips with the great questions of human existence. It is therefore reasonable to assume that her remarkable re-creation of the primitive mind in "The Canoe" is not simply an anthropological study, but possesses a wider frame of human reference. One obvious possibility follows from the supposition that Crawford sees in the primitive the direct expression of man's primal psychic impulses. This is that she is using the mentality of the Indian in essentially the same way as Wordsworth employs that of the peasant: to exemplify or explore in the workings of a simple and uninhibited mind certain basic principles of man's psychic activity which are normally buried, suppressed or modified in the case of the civilized person. In terms of modern psychology, Crawford might be dealing in "The Canoe" with those forces which in the European normally belong to the realm of the subconscious, but which nonetheless exert a pervasive influence upon his life. It would then of course be possible that the external world as it is seen through the myth-making and animating focus of the primitive mind becomes a symbolic projection of the psychological realities with which the poet is dealing.

An analysis of "The Canoe" along the lines just proposed may begin with the love-song of the two braves. This lyric occupies a central position in Crawford's poem, and we may divine that it is intended to stand out as a kind of climax or core, to which the preceding and following lines function essentially as a prologue and epilogue. It is accordingly significant for our line of argument that the song is concerned with a paradox involving one of the fundamental impulses of man's psychic life. The paradox, which under normal circumstances would exist only in the sub-conscious of civilized man, is that human love in its sexual aspect is also violence, and is destructive as well as creative, death-dealing as well as life-giving:

> O Love, art thou a silver fish?
> Shy of the line and shy of gaffing,
> Which we do follow, fierce, yet laughing,
> Casting at thee the light-wing'd wish,
>
> . . . .
>
> O Love! art thou a silver deer,
> Swift thy starr'd feet as wing of swallow,
> While we with rushing arrows follow;
> And at last shall we draw near,
> And over thy velvet neck cast thongs —
> Woven of roses, of stars, of songs?

The darker aspect of sexuality is expressed in the song of the braves in terms of the pursuits of fishing and hunting. These images of force and slaughter are of course offset in the song by what Reaney would term the "golden daffodil" images of laughter, song, lily, rose, gold, silver and gems.[2] However, the manner in which the song is introduced ironically undercuts the positive implications of these images:

> My masters twain sang songs that wove
> (As they burnish'd hunting blade and rifle)
> A golden thread with a cobweb trifle —
> Loud of the chase, and low of love.

Similarly, the predominance of "golden daffodil" symbols in the second stanza of the lyric is implicitly offset by the imagery of violence and death in the line immediately following. In the primitive or sub-conscious context of "The Canoe", the creative and life-giving aspects of sexuality are thus paradoxically accompanied, and even overshadowed, by a dark lust for destruction and death. In terms of the symbolic scheme outlined by Reaney, "The Canoe" is thus a "black daffodil" poem, in which the chase of love is still essentially the dark line of the rush to annihilation. It is only near the conclusion of Crawford's poem that we receive symbolic hints that this black line is becoming the "black circle" in which evil is ordered and redeemed.[3]

The dark vision of sexuality in the love-song of the braves is reinforced by the imagery in the passages which precede and follow it. Thus, the almost domestic tenderness of the "erotic" treatment of the canoe with which Crawford's poems open is ironically undercut by the grim references to the hunting and fishing activities of the braves, which involve numerous images of shooting, stabbing, binding and hanging. We should particularly notice in the lines preceding the love-song the description of a deer, which has been shot, bound and hung from boughs:

> My masters twain the Slaughter'd deer
> Hung on fork'd boughs — with thongs of leather.
> Bound were his stiff, slim feet together —
> His eyes like dead stars cold and drear . . . .

The psychological paradox just outlined, with its emphasis on the dark aspects of human sexuality, is also reflected in the animating and myth-making images of "The Canoe", of which there are several striking examples in the lines preceding the love-song of the braves.[4] It will be noted that the relevant similes and metaphors are all images of light. The source of this light is in each case the campfire of the two braves, whose designation as a "camp-soul" indicates that it serves as a symbol of the source and centre of primitive consciousness in the psychic activity of the "savage" mind. In the images under consideration, either the light of this "camp-soul" or what is revealed by it carries sinister implications of malignity. Thus, the extended simile concerning the "faint zones" of light cast by the campfire on the trunks of pine trees (ll. 12-20) expresses the frightened paralysis of human innocence and love in the face of the dark powers of cruelty and violence that reside in man. A similar sense is conveyed by the image in which the firelight becomes a human figure who lays an "anxious" hand on the foam-flecked shoulder of a hanging deer, and peers into his dead eyes. In this strange metaphor, we evidently have a recognition of the consequences of a lust for violence and slaughter in which there is a child-like mixture of fascination and fear. The two images just mentioned thus depict an essentially naive conscious-ness suddenly becoming aware of the innate capacities for evil in the human soul. However, in neither of them is the firelight itself seen as something sinister, as it is when it becomes "Thin, golden nerves of sly light", or "Sharp-headed" snakes slithering into the darkness. In both of these latter images there is a suggestion, not of the naiveté which we find elsewhere in "The Canoe", but of the subtlety of the serpent who tempted Eve.

Seen with regard to the traditional value of light as a symbol of goodness, love and life, the above images with their sinister implications apparently involve an ironic reflection of the psychological paradox which Crawford is treating else-where in "The Canoe". In connection with "primitive" sexuality, and perhaps the whole of man's fundamental psychic life, creativity is overshadowed by des-tructiveness, and love by bloodlust and violence. On a symbolic level, the light of the "camp-soul" which represents the psychic life of the primitive is thus really akin to darkness. This paradox of a light which embodies blackness is suggested symbolically by the redness of the firelight in three of the above images. This colour has of course appropriate associations with blood and burning, together with its connotations of violence, lust and death. This "demonic crimson" is in turn probably intended to be contrasted with the silver fish and the silver deer of love which we find in the song of the two braves.

The symbolic pattern which runs through the myth-making and animating imagery of the "prologue" to the love-song is of course carried on into the "epi-logue" in the radical simile in which "slaughter'd" fish, reddened by the light of the campfire, are compared with scimitars stained with the blood of "new-dead" wars. However, in the final myth-making image of "The Canoe", there is a reversal of the symbolic values of the images just discussed:

> The darkness built its wigwam walls
> Close round the camp, . . .

This metaphor is of course an image of darkness rather than of light, but the darkness in this case is evidently that of the "black circle", in which the line of evil and destruction has become the whirl from which the golden daffodil will ultimately re-emerge. This positive connotation is implicit in the reference to the weaving of a wigwam wall, which is not only an image of an upward gyration,[5] but also one of creation rather than of destruction. Thus, in symbolic opposition to a light which is really darkness, we have in the last myth-making image in "The Canoe", a darkness from which light and order are beginning to be born, just as they are in the first stages of the Creation in Genesis. The nascence of light from blackness, and of cosmos from chaos, is likewise suggested in the last two lines of the poem by the white shapes, albeit still "thin-woven and uncertain", which press at the "curtain" of shadows. In psychological terms, we presumably see in the closing images of "The Canoe" a representation of the first stages of a transformation of the dark side of man's nature into sweetness and light.

"The Canoe" thus evidently constitutes a symbolic exploration of the human psyche. However, there is another of Crawford's poems which indicates that "The Canoe" has a further dimension of symbolic significance. This is the "Epilogue" to "Gisli, the Chieftain", in which the poet evidently conceives of the universe as a whole in terms of the same inextricable union of good and evil, creation and destruction, darkness and light, which we see in the primitive mind in "The Canoe".[6] This suggests that for Crawford the psychological paradox explored in "The Canoe" is really a microcosmic reflection of a metaphysical situation, and that she therefore sees a definite analogy between the constitution of man's psyche and that of the cosmos which he inhabits. This correspondence would follow as a consequence from the origin of both man and nature in the same great cosmic flower.

Whatever its basis, such an "analogical" vision would have important implications with regard to the symbolic value of Crawford's poetry. The perception of a radical correspondence between the internal and external worlds would make it possible for her to write a "double-barrelled" poetry, in which metaphysical and psychological questions were treated in one and the same set of symbolic images. The action of a poem like "The Canoe" could in this case take place within the human mind, and yet at the same time extend to embrace the whole of the cosmos. Crawford's poetry would thus involve a double apocalypse, in which the depths of man's mind and those of the universe surrounding him were simultaneously revealed.

These presumptions about the nature of Crawford's poetry are supported in the case of "The Canoe" by the way in which certain of the images in the poem override the logical distinction between man and the world which he inhabits.

Thus, we have the similes and metaphors in which external phenomena are represented in anthropomorphic terms, together with those of the song of the braves in which human love becomes a fish and a deer, and a wish is represented as "light-wing'd". Such imagery of course implies that for Crawford man's psyche and the external world are in some manner analogous, and therefore imaginatively interchangeable. The same implication is also conveyed, although less directly, by the images in "The Canoe" which confound the extensions of man's personality in the world of art with the "untouched" realm of nature. The poet's representation of fire-lit fishes as swords and scimitars, and the play of shadows around the camp as the weaving of wigwam walls, have already been noted. Such representation of the outside world in human terms, and vice versa, points towards a poetry in which a close correspondence is seen between man's inner life and the external universe, and which could therefore deal simultaneously with both. Thus, the outlook of the primitive in "The Canoe" may very well involve not only a psychological projection, but also a metaphysical vision. It would then represent an insight into an external world which displays the same paradoxical union of good and evil, death and life, light and darkness which we have in the depths of man's mind.

If "The Canoe" really does function symbolically on two levels, what would be the significance of its dual revelation in terms of the frame of reference provided by Crawford's overall vision of man and the universe? How could the double apocalypse of the poem fit into the Biblical pattern of Creation, Fall, Redemption and Apocalypse which Reaney sees as the backbone of Crawford's poetic system?[7] To put a further question which is closely related to the first two, what message could "The Canoe" be meant to convey to the civilized European who is the poet's intended audience? On the psychological level, we have already indicated that the primitive outlook of "The Canoe" is intended to illustrate a sinister paradox in the fundamentals of human psychology, which would in turn be of basic importance for civilized man, even if in his case it were suppressed or buried below the level of his normal consciousness. In terms of the Biblical schema which Reaney sees as providing the "bigger subjects" of poetry, this inseparable union of creativity and destructiveness, good and evil, in man's basic mental activities may be seen as the psychological aspect of his fallen state, with its frightening ramifications of his life. For Crawford, this fallen condition is presumably shared by the savage and the civilized man alike. In the case of the European at least, its negative side may be repressed or sublimated through the censorship of morality, but this control is at best imperfect, and for Crawford it will never bring humanity back to heaven. The good and evil, creation and destruction, which are so intimately linked in the depth of the human psyche are in fact complementary aspects of the "golden daffodil" unity which is man's spiritual goal, and both are necessary for its attainment. What is needed is not for man to attempt to suppress the evil side of his fallen nature, but rather to organize and transform it by means of his powers of creativity and love. In order for him to do so, it is necessary for him to plunge into its darkness, as Dante descends into the Inferno on his way to God.[8] Only by so doing will man's nature finally be redeemed, and return to its unfallen unity. The Indian braves of "The Canoe" may be seen as pointing out this dark journey which must be taken by all men, including the European, in order to achieve redemption. The emphasis in "The Canoe" falls upon the negative aspect of this process although, as we have seen, there is a symbolic suggestion at the end of the poem of the ordering and transmuting of the evil in man.

The significance of "The Canoe" on a metaphysical level can be best approached by a consideration of the wilderness landscape of the poem as it is seen by the primitive mind. In all probability, the forest whose trees become grim warriors in the light of the "camp-soul" represents for Crawford what Blake terms "Eututhon Benython": the dark wood into which the Garden of Eden has degenerated as a consequence of the Fall.[9] Nature, instead of being subordinate to man as it was in the prelapsarian world, is now an independent enormity which surrounds humanity and threatens to overwhelm it. Like the evil within his soul, this menacing Leviathan must be redeemed through a process of organization and re-creation. As Reaney points out in connection with "Malcolm's Katie", Crawford sees the task of the European in the New World as being the redemption of the dark wood by converting it into a garden once again.[10] However, in order to "save" the wilderness, he must first plunge into it like the Indian braves of "The Canoe", and temporarily experience the terrors of its darkness. This preliminary step in the process of redeeming nature is of course analogous to the psychological plunge into his own fallen soul which is an essential part of man's return to the golden daffodil. In fact, Crawford undoubtedly sees the two processes as being inseparably related in actual practise. The settling of a country like Canada would involve for her a simultaneous redemption of both the outer and inner worlds. In "The Canoe", Crawford emphasizes the essential element of evil and terror which is involved in this re-creative process, with only suggestions towards the end of the poem of the rebirth of light and order from darkness and chaos.

85

In the course of this analysis, it has been indicated that the poet's "myth" and imagery have in "The Canoe" both a psychological and a metaphysical reference, exploring simultaneously the spiritual secrets of man's mind and those of the universe. This symbolic richness is accompanied in "The Canoe" by a subtle sense of paradox and a skilful use of irony which make the poem seem surprisingly modern, and which might not be expected from an artist as thoroughly romantic as is Crawford. These merits of "The Canoe" should serve to indicate that at her best the poet deserves neither the apologetic tone which Reaney sometimes adopts towards her,[11] nor yet damnation with faint praises.

(1967)

NOTES

[1] See James Reaney, "Isabella Valancy Crawford," in *Our Living Tradition*, ed. Robert L. McDougall (Toronto: University of Toronto Press, 1957).

[2] *Ibid.*, pp. 276-79.

[3] *Ibid.*, pp. 276-77.

[4] "The Canoe", ll. 12-20, 24-26 and 31-38.

[5] Reaney, "Isabella Valancy Crawford," pp. 277-78.

[6] *Ibid.*, pp. 279-80.

[7] *Ibid.*, p. 275.

[8] *Ibid.*, pp. 279-80.

[9] Northrop Frye, *Fearful Symmetry* (Princeton: Princeton University Press, 1947), p. 380.

[10] Reaney, "Isabella Valancy Crawford," pp. 286-87.

[11] *Ibid.*, pp. 270-71.

A CHOICE OF WORLDS

God, Man and Nature in
Charles G. D. Roberts

W. J. Keith

THE MAJOR VICTORIAN POETS left a bewildering literary legacy to their successors. Tennyson had posed one of the great questions of the century: "Are God and Nature then at strife?" The intellectual exertion required to answer this question in the negative — and so to protect the Victorian world-picture — was in itself an index to the seriousness of the challenge. Browning, through the mouth of Pippa, had offered the popular, comforting assertion that "God's in his heaven —/All's right with the world!", but his own optimism was more qualified, complex and hardly-won; the "will-to-believe" again involved conspicuous effort. Matthew Arnold, registering a sense of irreparable loss that has touched a more sympathetic chord in the ethos of our own century, pictured himself "wandering between two worlds, one dead,/The other powerless to be born". The Wordsworthian dawning had given way in less than a century, to a comfortless "darkling plain".

For Charles G. D. Roberts, encountering these divergent but sobering views in the Maritimes of the 1870's, the situation must have seemed both challenging and uncertain. Intellectually at least, it was an age of tradition and authority, and the cultural ties with Britain remained strong; at the same time, however, the Canadian perspective proved inevitably different. A young country looking to the future rather than to the past was unlikely to view the present in such bleak terms as Arnold's, and the untamed, uncultivated areas of Nova Scotia and New Brunswick contained wilder, more disturbing aspects of "Nature" than were to be found in the Lake District of Wordsworth ("romantic yet manageable" Grasmere, as E. M. Forster was later to call it), in Tennyson's Lincolnshire or Arnold's Oxford countryside.

Besides, Roberts' personal circumstances were a complicating factor. He would have been conscious not, like Arnold, of two lost worlds but of the conflicting interests of worlds readily available. The son of a clergyman, he was brought up in a religious atmosphere which, without being piously oppressive, must none the less have emphasized the distinction between the secular and the divine. At school in Fredericton, the classical education inculcated by George R. Parkin introduced him to Hellenism as a counter, again in Arnold's terms, to the Hebraism of church and rectory, while his exploration of wilderness and ancient wood implied a further opposition between the civilization and sophistication of the drawing-room and the primitive, even primeval conditions of the non-human world. Moreover, the fledgling writer was beginning to explore the possibilities of the related but none the less separate imaginative worlds of prose and poetry.

God, man and nature. The words, together with the concepts they represent, seem distinct enough, but what of the relations between them? From time immemorial, poets have considered these relations; the following extracts mark some of the climaxes within the English tradition:

> ... And justify the ways of God to man.

> ... who takes no private road,
> But looks through Nature up to Nature's God.

> On Man, on Nature, and on Human Life,
> Musing in solitude....

> ... And one far-off divine event,
> To which the whole creation moves.

It may appear tactless to quote such inimitable examples here, but the young Roberts was nothing if not ambitious, and he was well aware of the established masterpieces against which his own writings would inevitably be judged. I have discussed Roberts' poetry from an evaluative viewpoint elsewhere;[1] here I am concerned not primarily (or, at least, not initially) with the quality of his work but rather with his attitude towards and treatment of these major themes. Is a consistent presentation of man's place in nature and his relation to an unseen God discernible within Roberts' poetry? Can the "nature" exhibited in the poems be reconciled with the natural world which forms the background to his stories of the wilderness?

I shall attempt in the following pages to bring together some of the evidence upon which any informed answers to these questions must be based. The importance of collecting such evidence has now been increased by the conflicting opinions on these matters that have arisen from the notable revival of interest in Roberts' work over the past few years. Robin Mathews has argued, for example, that "all Roberts' work is a piece," that "all makes a philosophic whole" — a view which, as he admits, conflicts with earlier assessments (including my own).[2] It would be pleasant to be able to agree with him; unfortunately, however, his method of approach involves the construction of a simplified but attractively coherent philosophical position that is then "proved" by means of highly selective reference. Any passages that conflict with this position are either ignored or belittled. There follow numerous generalized assertions which vigorously uphold the original principle without in any way demonstrating its validity (a tactic which, as we shall see later, Roberts was fond of employing himself). Thus we are informed that " 'nature's never ceasing war of opposites' is in continuum with divine 'control,' divine wisdom and silence" and that "the wilderness is drawn into mysterious [*sic*] relation with divinity"; Roberts' philosophical and mystical poems can then be described as "deeply suggestive, precise statements, poetic and beautiful".

The resultant picture represents Roberts as Mathews would like him to have been. It is an admittedly tidy portrait, but does not, I think, take all the facts into account. Naturally the evidence to be offered here will be equally selective, but my motive in assembling it is not to prove a thesis but to illustrate the varieties of intellectual attitude that Roberts took up and used in the course of a long and multifaceted career. If it is possible to fit all the pieces into a consistent pattern (with no pieces left over) I shall welcome the achievement, but — to anticipate the results of my inquiry — I have been unable to perform the feat myself. In my view, Roberts not only continually shifts his position, but often blurs his meaning by the use of a richly metaphorical but conceptually misleading language. The present essay makes no claim to provide a neat, straightforward assessment of Roberts' beliefs; rather, it tries to offer a faithful account of the bewildering profusion of ideas that can be found side by side within his writings.

R OBERTS' EARLY VERSE contains a number of poems devoted, very much in the Victorian tradition, to classical subjects. Of these "Orion", "Actæon" and (a little later) "Marsyas" are the best known.[3] At first sight they read like set exercises within the limits of established convention, and in many respects that is what they are; but they command an added interest in reproducing a traditional poetic world in which the relationships I am here concerned with could be explored in preparation for the later depiction of Canadian landscape and wilderness in *Songs of the Common Day* and elsewhere, and the dream-worlds posited in his "Poems Philosophical and Mystical". The classical setting is one in which boundaries between the divine, the human and the animal were less clear-cut. Gods and goddesses (Pan, Apollo, Eos, Artemis) walked the earth in human form; centaurs and goat-footed satyrs testified to a physical relation between man and animal, and Actæon, we remember, was even transformed into a stag. Moreover, although the myths were apparently set and unalterable, Roberts had in fact more freedom to manipulate them than we might at first expect. Not only could he select for extended treatment the stories most suited to his purpose, but, as we shall see when discussing "Orion", he could adapt and modify them and invest them with his own particular interpretation.

The relation between god, man and nature is especially well illustrated by "Orion". Indeed, the story of a man who is the son of a god and the beloved of a goddess and whose main occupation is hunting in the wilderness can legitimately be interpreted as an oblique but deliberate exploration of my chosen theme. In this poetic world, links between man and nature are particularly close. Nature can be seen in human terms:

> The sunset with its red and purple skirts
> Hung softly o'er the bay, whose rippled breast
> Flushed crimson.

And by the same principle man can be described in terms of nature — the royal priest's hair is

> made aware
> Of coming winter by some autumn snows.

This is a kind of reference that for the most part Roberts abandons in his later verse (in the first quotation, "banners" is substituted for "skirts" in later editions), but it is reasonable to assume that his intention here is to accentuate the closeness of man to the world of nature.

But the most conspicuous point to be noted in "Orion" is that Roberts makes a definite distinction, in terms of the response shown to human beings, between wild creatures and the natural world itself. Wild creatures are unquestionably enemies. Orion's task has been to rid Chios of lions, leopards, bears, lynxes and wolves. The opening scene includes the ritual slaying of "a tawny wolf,/Blood-stained", and when Roberts wants to convey the wickedness of Œnopion, he uses imagery which in context suggests not the Garden of Eden but the jungle — the king's words are "crooked, serpent-smooth". On the other hand, perhaps because of his divine ancestry, the natural world is presented as actively co-operating with Orion:

> The strong earth stayed me, and the unbowed hills,
> The wide air, and the ever joyous sun,
> And free sea leaping up beneath the sun, —
> All were to me for kindly ministrants.

When Orion is blinded by Œnopion, he is assured by the Nereids that the whole of nature — comprising the sea, the night, the air, the wind, the sun, the waters, the rocks, the hills, the earth — mourns for him. All natural phenomena, indeed, are under the aegis of separate gods who duly reward man's reverence, and although there is an allusion to "the indomitable fates" that cannot be bent, the gods none the less have the power to restore Orion's sight.

It is, however, the ending of the poem that proves most revealing for our purposes. Roberts chooses to cut the myth short with the union of Orion and Eos the dawn-goddess, and their journey to Delos is smoothed by the intervention of the gods. The last we see of them is their fading, like Keats' nightingale, into the forest dim:

> And so they reached
> Delos, and went together hand in hand
> Up from the water and their company,
> And the green wood received them out of sight.

But in Greek myth the story generally ends with Orion's death at the hands of Artemis, sister of Apollo, either because the love affair with Eos is displeasing to the gods, or because Apollo, afraid that Orion will fall in love with Artemis, tricks her into killing him. Roberts' conclusion belongs more to the realm of dream and fairy-tale. Nature becomes the protective sanctuary in which man can live god-like in security and in peace.

It is true, of course, that in other mythological poems the relation between man and the gods is less happy, though it is equally evident. In "Actæon", for example, the goddess Artemis uses the hounds to punish the man who has unwittingly invaded her privacy, and in "Marsyas", though the poem ostensibly limits itself to a moment before the climax of the original myth, Apollo's cruel revenge is implicit within it. Both Actæon and Marsyas, however, are found lacking in the all-important "reverence". The same is true in Roberts' best-known Indian myth-poem, "The Departing of Clote Scarp [Gluskâp]", where the god-figure leaves the world because

> All the works
> And words and ways of men and beasts became
> Evil.

But the escape into the protective "green wood" at the close of "Orion" is of particular importance because it looks forward to a dominant motif in his later poems about the wild. The openly escapist quality of much of this poetry is immediately apparent. Indeed, Roberts sees it as a distinguishing characteristic of such verse. When editing an anthology of *Poems of Wild Life* in 1888, he took pains to bring together what he defines in his introduction as "that characteristically modern verse which is kindled where the outposts of an elaborate and highly self-conscious civilisation come in contact with crude humanity and primitive nature". And he continues:

> The element of self-consciousness, I think, is an essential one to this species of verse, which delights us largely as affording a measure of escape from the artificial to the natural. Such escape is not to be achieved unless the gulf between be bridged for us. This the poet effects by depicting wild life and untrammelled action in the light of a continual consciousness of the difference between such existence and our own.[4]

This is of special interest because it claims, I believe, a very different significance for wilderness-literature from that which Roberts later establishes in his wilderness stories, where a basic aim seems to be the demonstration that life in the wild is less distant from the image of civilization than we care to think. It is worth noting, however, that Roberts' own "poems of wild life" rarely concern themselves with heroic or violent action. In them the wilderness usually offers a more conventional escape — a refuge, a town dweller's haven. The opening of "On the Creek" is representative:

> Dear Heart, the noisy strife
> And bitter carpings cease.
> Here is the lap of life,
> Here are the lips of peace.
>
> Afar from stir of streets,
> The city's dust and din,
> What healing silence meets
> And greets us gliding in!

"Birch and Paddle" is rather more subtle, but derives from the same response. Dedicated to Bliss Carman, the poem opens with an evocation of wilderness in which images of rest and peace are varied with other involving action and movement. On the one side we have "shy streams" and "the quiet lake", on the other "wildcat rapids" and "leaping waves". But about two-thirds of the way through the poem the rapids are left behind. They represent a barrier to be overcome; the excitement they offer is not an end in itself. The ultimate goal, we discover, is not wildness but escapist calm:

> And then, with souls grown clear
> In that sweet atmosphere,
>
> With influences serene
> Our blood and brain washed clean,
>
> We've idled down the breast
> Of broadening tides at rest,
>
> And marked the winds, the birds,
> The bees, the far-off herds,
>
> Into a drowsy tune
> Transmute the afternoon.

Roberts seems torn, as it were, between Wordsworth and the tropics, and by the end of the poem the vigorous reality of the wilderness is succeeded by a poetic dream-world:

> We need no balm but this, —
>
> A little space for dreams
> On care-unsullied streams, —
>
> 'Mid task and toil, a space
> To dream on Nature's face!

In her examination of the language of Canadian poets, Sandra Djwa has conclusively demonstrated that "dream" was a favourite word for Roberts.[5] It is worth adding, however, that dreams (and the same applies to related words like "peace", "calm" and "rest", etc.) are frequently associated with a rural setting and a life spent close to "Nature".

This emphasis on "dream" is also prominent in the series of sonnets from *Songs of the Common Day* that contains many of Roberts' best and best-known poems. Although the sequence is generally (and properly) praised for its minute and delicate description of the farming countryside of Nova Scotia and New Brunswick, the tendency to inlay a dream-landscape upon the reality is persistent and has not been sufficiently recognized. The meditative and passive observer of "Frogs" is typical:

> My view dreams over the rosy wastes, descrying
> The reed-tops fret the solitary sky.

Just as the speaker in "The Tantramar Revisited" looks down upon his home region from the perspective of the hills, so in these sonnets the landscape is seen lovingly but from a distance — an intellectual distance from which idealization is possible and the "wastes" can therefore be seen as "rosy".

Moreover, the observer extends the capacity to dream from himself to his subjects. A careful examination of these poems reveals the interesting but unexpected fact that, at least as often as not, the dreamers are not human beings but animals — and sometimes, indeed, natural objects. Both "In an Old Barn" and "Midwinter Thaw" end with descriptions of winter cattle dreaming of summer. The whole sestet of the former is relevant:

> Far down, the cattle in their shadowed stalls,
> Nose-deep in clover fodder's meadowy scent,
> Forget the snows that whelm their pasture streams,
> The frost that bites the world beyond their walls.
> Warm housed, they dream of summer, well content
> In day-long contemplation of their dreams.

In "Burnt Lands", the blackened trunks of dead trees feel "phantom leafage" rustling faintly "through their parched dreams", and the idea is repeated in the later poetry — in "The Logs", for example, where logs floating down the rivers are imagined dreaming of their previous life in the forests ("perchance they dream", Roberts writes, with an inappropriate echo of Hamlet). Even in "The Iceberg", where for the most part he offers an admirably bald account of its progress from the berg's viewpoint, we encounter the lines:

> Slowly now
> I drifted, dreaming.

Once again there are some interesting comparisons to be made between these human attributes shared by the other animals and objects of the natural world on the one hand, and the situation in the animal stories on the other; but before proceeding to this, I want to consider some of Roberts' more ambitious, inspirational poems in which he attempts to express his sense of the ordered but mysterious workings of the universe. Many of these, which vary radically in poetic quality, were collected into the section "Poems Philosophical and Mystical" when Roberts issued his *Selected Poems* in 1936. Here, the relations between God, man and nature constitute the prime subject.

Roberts' God, whose function (as opposed to His attributes) generally resembles a process rather than a person, is rarely to be identified directly with the God of Christianity. It is noteworthy, for instance, that although God is frequently mentioned in the verse, there are hardly any references to Jesus Christ — "When Mary the Mother Kissed the Child" is one of the few poems to employ an explicitly Christian reference. More often, the divine figure exists outside the boundaries of specific religions; in "Beyond the Tops of Time" (or "The Tower Beyond the Tops of Time", as it was called in the 1936 edition) the architecture of Heaven is deliberately eclectic, consciously constructed by Roberts to combine elements from Christianity ("Cities of sard and chrysoprase"), Norse mythology ("Valhallas of celestial frays") and Buddhism ("lotus-pools of endless peace"). A distinction has to be made, however, between the philosophical attitudes behind the poetry and the language in which the poetry is expressed. While God is seldom asserted to resemble human form — a rare example may be found in "Ascription" ("... him Thou madest most like Thee") — anthropomorphism is continually implied by Roberts' imagery. In poem after poem we encounter references to the face of God ("In the Wide Awe", "Beyond the Tops of Time", "Child of the Infinite", "Origins", "Earth's Complines"), the hands of God ("Kinship"), the knees of God ("Recessional"), the dreams of God ("The Unsleeping"), God's finger ("The Marvellous Work"), God's smile ("The Silver Thaw"). As a consequence, the reader gains a distinct impression of a personal deity even when the intellectual foundation of the poem seems to be positing an abstract principle.

If required to generalize about Roberts' presentation of this metaphysical process that he calls God (and I submit that only a dominant impression can be communicated, since Roberts does not write all his poems from a consistent philosophical viewpoint), one is forced to conclude that it is separate from, but paradoxically in control of, the natural universe. He (or It) exists "beyond the bournes of space" ("Origins"), "in deep beyond deep" ("A Song of Growth"). The impression conveyed by these poems is of infinite distance and sublime ascent into a vast and unimaginable new dimension. The paradox is well caught in "The Falling Leaves". God controls the natural process that determines autumn, but

95

is at the same time so remote that "leaves and ages are as one to Him." This is the "God of order and unchanging purpose" celebrated in an early poem.[6]

The controlling principle finds its most direct expression in the opening lines of "Ascription":

> O Thou who hast beneath Thy hand
> The dark foundations of the land, —
> The motion of whose ordered thought
> An instant universe hath wrought.

"Control" is, indeed, a recurring word in these poems — in "Immanence", for example, and in "O Solitary of the Austere Sky" where it is specifically characterized as "benign". When translating "New Year's Eve" from Louis Honoré Fréchette, Roberts was conveying congenial sentiments in asserting that God alone "conceives and orders the mystery."

As in traditional western thinking, Roberts sees man as poised precariously but perhaps miraculously between God and nature. Man has "God for kin and clay for fellow" ("Kinship"), and the relation is summed up clearly enough in "Wayfarer of Earth":

> And good is earth, —
> But earth not all thy good,
> O thou with seed of suns
> And star-fire in thy blood!

As an "atom of the Eternal Soul" ("O Solitary") man is greater than he seems. As "child of the infinite", although physically vulnerable he is spiritually invincible and even (shocking as it may sound to the orthodox) coequal with deity.

For Roberts, indeed, man is capable of identifying, blending, merging with both God and nature. "Child of the Infinite" is a good example of the former ("I was of the fiery impulse/Urging the Divine Desire"), "Origins" of the latter —

> We feel the sap go free
> When spring comes to the tree;
> And in our blood is stirred
> What warms the brooding bird.

Similar statements concerning the unity of human and animal life are scattered throughout his poetry; moreover, the connection is often made with natural objects — when, for example, the flow of blood in his veins is likened to the restless movement of the tides (*Ave*, "The Vagrant of Time"). Occasionally, Roberts' thought is animistic in the stricter sense of positing the existence of souls within the natural creation. Thus in "Earth's Complines" he writes:

> I felt the soul of the trees —
> Of the white, eternal seas —
>   Of the flickering bats and night-moths
> And my own soul kin to these.

Most often, however, the connection is a vaguer intimation of the unity of all life.

In attempting to draw a general philosophical position from these poems, we are inevitably faced with a difficulty. Only the most rigid literary critic would insist that a poet must write all his poems consistently from the viewpoint of a single system. Indeed, a number of poets — Thomas Hardy is a well-known example — deliberately explore their subjects by emphasizing differing viewpoints and assuming different hypotheses from poem to poem. It is not difficult to detect apparent contradictions in Roberts' poems, or to find examples, even within the category of "Poems Philosophical and Mystical", that take their origins from incompatible metaphysical assumptions. But can we accurately describe such poetry as exploratory or experimental?

The problem here is that Roberts employs a rhetorical tone in these poems so confidently assertive that we cannot but conclude that he is expressing his firmest convictions. "In the Wide Awe and Wisdom of the Night" provides a useful instance. The sestet reads as follows:

> I compassed time, outstripped the starry speed,
>   And in my still soul apprehended space,
> Till, weighing laws which these but blindly heed,
>   At last I came before Him face to face, —
> And knew the Universe of no such span
> As the august infinitude of Man.

The sentiment is bold and bracing, yet it is not easy to reconcile with other equally assertive statements concerning man's position in the scheme of things. Here man is presented as so superior to the rest of the universe that no comparison is possible. But "The Native" begins, "Rocks, I am one with you," and the fir tree is a "kinsman" whose sap runs in his veins. The tone is similarly assured, but we can hardly accept both as equally and simultaneously "true"; the result is to raise doubts concerning the validity of Roberts' claim to visionary inspiration.

"O Earth Sufficing All Our Needs" leads to even greater difficulties. Its very title presents a challenge to earlier poems, and Roberts' conclusion is in striking contrast to many of the assertions already discussed:

> I have sought God beyond His farthest star —
> But here I find Him, in your quickening dust.

The heavens in which Roberts' aspiring soul could once move with remarkable ease are now designated "alien". The poem seems to refute and cancel many of the earlier poems that proclaimed a different faith ("How obstinate in my blindness I have been," the poet confesses) — yet it exists side by side with them in the 1936 *Selected Poems*. I find it difficult to escape the conclusion that, despite the persuasive rhetoric, Roberts' philosophical beliefs were as restless, wayward and uncertain as his biographical wanderings.

M Y MAJOR CONCERN here is with Roberts as poet, but it would be improper to conclude this discussion without raising the question: to what extent is the presentation of God, man and nature in his poetry reconcilable with his treatment of the same subjects in his animal stories and other "stories of the wild"? The answer, I think, must be that there are considerable differences, and that these are evident not merely in Roberts' attitudes but in the manner in which they are communicated.

First and most obviously, God has virtually disappeared from the scene. Indeed, the only significant references occur in the story titles "Do Seek their Meat from God" and "The Young Ravens that Call upon Him", both of which appeared in Roberts' earliest collection of short stories, *Earth's Enigmas* (1896). In both cases the quotations are from the Psalms (104:21, 147:9, respectively) and it is difficult to believe that Roberts is not attempting an ironic effect. The meat that the panthers seek "from God" is a human child who is only saved (from the human viewpoint) by happy chance, and the young eagles (for such they are in the second story) are fed with the body of a new-born lamb whose own call presumably went unheeded. In the first story, the irony is extended further when Roberts, in describing the panthers, refers to "that for which nature had so exquisitely designed them";[7] the phrase, we realize with a decided shock, is a periphrasis for killing. But Roberts seems unskilled in these effects — and possibly even uncomfortable about their implications; in his subsequent stories, the extraphysical dimension is almost wholly expunged, and the emphasis falls squarely upon man and nature.

But the two stories already named are as effective as any of his fiction in challenging some of the over-generalized statements expressed in the poetry. In both, the marauders (panthers and eagles) are desperately hungry, and it is only too clear that the earth is *not* "sufficing at all [their] needs." In the wilderness, such comforting statements fail to stand the test of reality. Remembering the fate of the panther-cubs and the lamb, we may find it more difficult to respond sympathetically to "Ascription", where God is addressed as one

> Who hear'st no less the feeble note
> Of one small bird's awakening throat,
> Than that unnamed, tremendous chord
> Arcturus sounds before his Lord.[8]

The wilderness stories "place" such assertions as (at best) simplistic. It is, I hope, unnecessary to insist that my critique here is literary, not theological. I am not implying that Roberts is "right" in the stories and "wrong" in the poetry; I am merely observing that the various metaphysical assumptions are not always reconcilable with each other, and that the vulnerability of his more pious, high-sounding sentiments is often revealed by the hard-headed realism of his less ambitious writings.

As might be expected, man's position in the wilderness varies according to his temperament, attitudes and deeds. Only the townsmen-adventurers in *Around the Camp Fire* see the natural world as an escape: "We fled from the city and starched collars, seeking freedom and the cool of the wilderness."[9] Those who live in closer contact with the wild know better.[10] It is clear, moreover, that man must win by his own exertions the respect that Orion was able to claim by right. The following passage from "Eyes of the Wilderness" expresses an extreme form of the relation:

> From every direction, above, below, around him, anxious eyes, timorous eyes, curious or scornful or malevolent eyes — but none that were indifferent; for this blundering, heavy wayfarer with the flaming red kerchief at his neck was Man, the eternal and irresistible enemy. Moreover, he was so obviously a stranger, an alien, to the wilds.[11]

Here the animals obviously reject any idea of man as "kin". But some individuals, including "the Boy" who appears in a series of impressive stories scattered through Roberts' volumes and the hunters and trappers whose adventures are brought together in *The Backwoodsmen*, have penetrated the wilderness and become a part of it. They have learned the all-important lesson that, to survive in the wild, they must develop their animal heritage of strength, courage, keen observation and (above all) cunning.

The complex interrelationships of man and animal in the wilderness are well illustrated by one of Roberts' best stories, "The Vagrants of the Barren". Pete Noel's cabin has burnt down, leaving him without food or snowshoes in bitterly cold weather at least fifty miles from the nearest human habitation. That he had snatched up blankets, coat, rifle and cartridge-belt while making his escape is attributed to "his [animal] instincts" which "were even quicker than his [human] wits".[12] Peter realizes that what we inadequately term "nature" has become "the savage and implacable sternness of the wild":

> There was no blinking the imminence of his peril. Hitherto he had always managed to work, more or less, *with* nature, and so had come to regard the elemental forces as friendly. Now they had turned upon him altogether and without warning. His anger rose as he realized that he was at bay.

The last phrase, normally used of animals, is depressingly apt; at the same time, the passage continues: "The indomitable man-spirit awoke with the anger." In order to survive, Pete must employ his animal and human traits to the fullest.

His success involves both returning to the primitive animal responses and rising above human greed. Employing all his powers of woodcraft, he manages to kill a caribou bull, and gains nourishment by drinking its blood ("he was an elemental creature, battling with the elements for his life"). Then, tempted to kill another stranded bull in the interests of future profit, he desists — partly because "a sympathy passed between the man and the beast", partly because he realizes shrewdly that the living warmth of the animal is more valuable to him as he rides out the blizzard than possible payment for the dead carcass. Nature, then, both threatens and sustains; man, combining his animal and spiritual qualities, has the means to endure. "The Vagrants of the Barren" is more than an exciting adventure story; it includes, I suggest, a profound commentary on our human inheritance that is not merely asserted but imaginatively realized in artistic form.

Criticism of Roberts' wilderness stories has generally centred upon the vexed question of his allegedly endowing his animals with excessively human traits. The controversy is real enough, but I hope to have shown by the preceding discussion that it is in fact only part of a much broader subject. Basically, indeed, the point at issue is at least as much a matter of literary technique as of scientific principle. Roberts is here employing yet another artistic device to illustrate his recurring theme: the numerous possible connections between the human and animal worlds.[13] We have encountered a number of comparable effects in Roberts' work — the metaphorical identification in "Orion"; the mythological interrelations in all the early classical poems; the dreams that link the human, animal, vegetable and even mineral worlds in much of the poetry from *Songs of the Common Day* onwards; the assertions concerning the unity of all life in "Poems Philosophical and Mystical"; the reverse process of human beings drawing upon primitive animal instincts in the stories of the backwoodsmen. Without in any way detracting from the authority of Roberts' testimony as a student of the wild, it is important to insist that he is above all an imaginative writer and must be judged accordingly.

It seems indisputable that the philosophical assumptions upon which he based his works fluctuated considerably — that the "Fate" or "Doom" so prominent in the wilderness stories is very different from the controlling and habitually personalized God of the poems, that the whole ethos of the prose can never be fully harmonized with that of the verse. From a strictly literary point of view, there is no particular reason why this should trouble us (though it may well lower our assessment of his importance within the history of ideas); but we cannot help being conscious that this verdict would almost certainly have disturbed Roberts himself. He was sufficiently a child of the great Victorians to imitate their impressively solid achievement by attempting to hammer his thoughts into a unity. Hence the assertive rhetoric and *ex cathedra* tone of the philosophical poems in remarkable contrast to the unostentatious directness of the prose. Our own age, however, has learnt to be wary of the grandiloquent gesture, and we should therefore be in a position to appreciate what I believe to be his characteristic strength: his ability to evoke, whether in verse or prose, the rich multiplicity of experience in the wild. His choice of worlds, then, was a fortunate circumstance that he put to good effect — not by explaining but by exploiting for imaginative purposes the varied and complex interrelationships between the divine, the animal and the human.

(1974)

NOTES

1 See *Charles G. D. Roberts* (Toronto: Copp Clark, 1969), ch. 2; and my introduction to *Selected Poetry and Critical Prose of Charles G. D. Roberts* (Toronto: University of Toronto Press, 1974).

2 Robin Mathews, "Charles G. D. Roberts and the Destruction of Canadian Imagination," *Journal of Canadian Fiction*, 1 (Winter 1972), 55. I should perhaps

state that in my opinion the argument concerning Roberts' philosophical consistency is the only part of this unwisely intemperate article that merits an answer.

³ The most accessible editions of Roberts' poetry are his *Selected Poems* (Toronto: Ryerson, 1936) and my own selection (see note 1 above). The majority of poems mentioned in this essay can be found in either edition. The exceptions are as follows: for "Earth's Complines", "Immanence", "Kinship", "Origins", "Recessional", "A Song of Growth", "The Unsleeping", "Wayfarer of Earth", "When Mary the Mother Kissed the Child", see *Selected Poems*; for "The Departing of Clote Scarp [Gluskâp]", "New Year's Eve" and "Orion", see *Selected Poetry and Critical Prose.*

⁴ Introduction to *Poems of Wild Life*, reprinted in *Selected Poetry and Critical Prose*, p. 265.

⁵ See Sandra Djwa, "Canadian Poetry and the Computer," *Canadian Literature*, 46 (Autumn 1970), 43-54.

⁶ "The Marvellous Work," in *In Divers Tones* (Boston: Lothrop, 1887), p. 62.

⁷ *Earth's Enigmas* [1896] (Boston: Page, 1903), p. 23.

⁸ It is difficult to reconcile this quotation with Mathews' statement that "the God of his poetry is not one who watches and cares for each sparrow" (53). In context, surely, "hear'st" carries within it the implication of positive response.

⁹ *Around the Camp Fire* (New York: Crowell, 1896), p. 1.

¹⁰ It is interesting to note, however, that the backwoodsmen in the poem often differ from those in the stories. The squatter in the poem of that name is a dreamer:

> His chores all done,
> He seats himself on the door-sill,
> And slowly fills his pipe, and smokes, and dreams.

He is closer to the introspective observer of the sonnets than to the backwoodsmen of the prose. Contrast Old Dave the lumberman in *The Heart of the Ancient Wood* who, in a comparable situation, "slept the deep undreaming sleep of the wholesomely tired" (Toronto: McClelland and Stewart, 1974), p. 23.

¹¹ *Eyes of the Wilderness* (London: Dent, 1933), p. 248.

¹² *The Backwoodsmen* (New York: Macmillan, 1901), p. 1.

¹³ For a more detailed discussion of the relation between man and animal in the "stories of the wild," see my *Charles G. D. Roberts*, ch. 4.

LAMPMAN
AND RELIGION

Barrie Davies

THE RELIGIOUS BELIEFS and religious position of Lampman, as Desmond Pacey points out in *Ten Canadian Poets*, have been almost entirely ignored or taken for granted by previous critics with the exception of Pacey himself and Roy Daniells. In the *Literary History of Canada* Daniells writes that Lampman's "connection with the Christian tradition is of the most exiguous and awkward kind".[1] Desmond Pacey is concerned "to document the case for believing that he (Lampman) had severe religious doubts".[2] The present essay is an attempt to enlarge upon the insights and intuitions of these two critics.

Lampman — like Emerson, Thoreau, and many of the English Romantics — was not irreligious but did experience a growing revulsion against orthodox religion. It is convenient to deal with Lampman's religious experience in three stages; his rejection of institutional religion, his perplexity and doubt, and the nature of his religious beliefs. At the same time, it is important not to forget that such an order is artificial in that it fails to reflect the fluctuations between rejection, belief, doubt, and affirmation.

In context, it is useful to remember Lampman's background. For the first twenty-one years of his life Lampman lived in a staunchly Anglican environment. Is it not significant, therefore, that there is no evidence which shows that Lampman considered following in his father's footsteps? At the same time, the fact that Lampman did not enter the ministry is representative in the sense that it can be duplicated in the experience of many literary men in the nineteenth century throughout Canada, America, and England. Charles G. D. Roberts was born in the rectory at Douglas, and D. C. Scott in a Methodist parsonage in Ottawa. W. W. Campbell, born in the Anglican Mission at Berlin, eventually entered the ministry but like Emerson publicly renounced it. The nineteenth century was a time when many sensitive men and women found it difficult to accept an orthodox religion increasingly undermined by the findings of science, anthropology, and the Higher Criticism. Having established that Lampman's distrust of institutional religion was broadly representative and not unique, it is necessary now to detail his disagreement. Such details also imply, because of negative emphasis, the religious ideas which he affirmed.

In his essay on Shelley, "The Revolt of Islam",[3] written whilst he was still at Trinity College, Lampman is shocked by what he calls the "atheistic opinions and daring blasphemy"[4] of Shelley's poem. But the essay does not reflect a straightforward, orthodox reaction. Lampman clearly admires Shelley and we have an example here of something which was to become characteristic of Lampman's writing, the transference of religious terms to nature. Shelley is a "pure worshipper of nature" and "one of her peculiar priests".[5] The essay seems to me to foreshadow Lampman's own quest, which is best described by the words he uses to portray Shelley's search for "some natural code of faith which to his mind conformed more closely to the workings of his only instructress, nature's self ".[6]

Like Emerson and Thoreau, and the Deists and Unitarians before them, Lampman rejected many aspects and beliefs of institutional Christianity. His own time he described as "a philosophic age when people are beginning to realize with a sort of poetic clearness their true relations with nature and life."[7] Elsewhere, whilst protesting against contemporary translations of the Bible, he has a further comment upon the changing temper: "The men of the sixteenth century knew how to translate the Bible, because they believed it in a sense which is not intelligible even to the devout people of our day, and because they were saturated with its spirit."[8] Both these comments imply that for the sensitive, thoughtful and informed man, subscription to orthodox beliefs with the passionate intensity of earlier eras was no longer possible.

At the same time, Lampman realized that the majority of people clung to a moribund Church and regarded with suspicion any attempts to establish a personal belief which provided an intensity and meaning lacking in institutional religion.

Lampman hated anything which followed blind custom both in religion and in other aspects of life. Throughout his work, Lampman clearly and without histrionics established his own point of view which was always in reaction to the deadening quality of the experience of the mass of mankind. W. W. Campbell, his flamboyant contemporary, during the first three weeks of the column in the *Globe*, in which he and Lampman collaborated, used the findings of anthropology to show that much of the Old Testament and the Story of the Crucifixion were mythic and condemned as "poor and tottering" a religion "bolstered up by ignorance".[9] Emerson had done much the same thing fifty years earlier as a prelude to a statement of his own belief, but clearly the religious attitudes in Canada were still rigid, for Campbell's article brought a shocked rebuke in the Monday editorial, which expressed "strongest disapproval" and condemned and repudiated "most emphatically his religious ideas".[10]

W. W. Campbell had begun his *Globe* column with some reflections on the growing class distinctions, the increasing disparity between the rich and the poor in Canada, and had castigated the churches for their indifference to the "destitution, degradation and misery both within the shadow of the same church spire, or within the sound of the same Sabbath bell". He ended: "Religionists may cry out about the hopelessness of mere humanity as a religion, but it would be better did they put a little more hope into the anguish of the world by putting more of the humanities into their religion."[11]

There have been many who have felt that institutional religion has often been conservative and reactionary. Thoreau, for example, believed the Church to be a very timid organization and a tool of materialism. A criticism of this kind of collusion is implicit in Lampman's "The Story of an Affinity" which emphasizes the richness of the church, the "grandeur", the "silken ceremonies", and the "velvet stalls". The pastor preaches on love and the brotherhood of man, but to a congregation composed of the "rich and the proud", who remain indifferent. The Church thus continues to announce the radical doctrines of Christ but has made them largely ceremonial. It is no wonder that Lampman in the *Globe* column for May 1892, like Emerson in "The Divinity School Address", calls for "genuine and effective" sermons to be delivered only by the most gifted preachers moving from parish to parish.

In the same column for September 1892 where he is attacking excessive wealth, there occurs the clause, "if it be true that there is a life beyond the grave". An orthodox Christian would not have expressed qualifications or doubt. Lampman seems not to have shared the belief in an afterlife, or rather he was concerned with the possibilities of the present life and this is where he wished to place his emphasis. In the column for November 1892 he incidentally dissociates himself from the popular belief in the afterlife. The tone of the language, which has a touch of Thoreauvian mockery, disapproves of the devaluation of the present life for something illusory: "Whether we accept with the mass of mankind the belief in a happy immortality of the soul, or whether we refuse to busy our thoughts with that great after-blank into which we cannot see how we shall penetrate with profit, in neither case will the sound-hearted man and the true lover of humanity and life look upon death as in anywise a hideous and desperate thing."

Lampman did not endorse the doctrine of Original Sin. As early as his essay, "The Revolt of Islam", he approves Shelley's "magnificent dream", when men freed from the corrupting social institutions are able "to follow the instincts of natural goodness and virtue which should gradually lead them to perfection, to pure, glorious, unselfish happiness, without the further aid of laws and systems of morals".[12] Lampman continuously played down the other world of orthodox religion in order to assert the infinite possibilities of the present life and the innate capacities of human beings. Man needs neither Divine Grace, the Church, priests, nor theology and dogma. With Emerson, Lampman regarded the belief in a "system of post-mortem rewards and punishments", to use his words from the *Globe* column for April 1893, as false and degrading.

His poem, "Virtue", is an explicit rejection of external control and fear. Men cannot be bribed or frightened into virtuous behaviour. The only authority for the virtuous life comes from the "inward light", which produces "the God-like habit". Only when he thought of the Hon. John Staggart did Lampman regret "that the old theological fable of hell fire is not true".[13] In the poem the reaction to orthodox religion is openly contemptuous. Religion is a "grudged control", producing not virtue, but something peevish, crabbed and rancid, a "sour product". Religion has become petrified and reactionary, a "custom" maintained by the "sharp-eyed", and relying heavily on the enforcement of crude conceptions of a "painted paradise" or a "pictured hell". By contrast the reader familiar with Lampman's work realizes how personal and characteristic at times are the religious insights found here. By this I mean the emphasis on clarity, light, flowing movement, and self-fulfilment, whilst the line "Bathed in the noon-tide of an inward light" is more informative of one aspect of that most typical of his poems, "Heat", than many pages of critical commentary.

An untitled poem, left in his manuscript book for 1889 to 1892, is significant in showing how radically Lampman's religious ideas had changed in the ten years since he had left Trinity College:

> How dealt the world, Oh Christ, with thee,
> Who shrank not from the common rod,
> Whose secret was humility?
> They mocked and scourged; then hailed thee god.
>
> And built out of thine earnest speech,
> Who gifts had for the simplest needs,

> Whose meaning was in all men's reach,
> The strangest of phantastic creeds.[14]

Like the New England Transcendentalists, Lampman no longer believed in the supernatural origin of Christ. He considered, as Emerson did, that Christ was a great ethical and moral teacher but nevertheless a man whose meaning could be understood and attained by all men. The moral precepts of Christ had been corrupted and perverted by orthodox religion and made into an elaborate mystery.

Lampman's impatience with sectarian theology may be partly explained from two points of view. He had been influenced by the findings of anthropology and archeology and was very much aware of the rise and fall of religions. In the poem, "In October", the sound of the falling leaves resembles the "failing murmur of some conquered creed". Later it will emerge that Lampman did not believe that the truth was confined to any particular religion but that many religions testified to truth.

Because of his view of Christ, Lampman maintained that there were central and constant truths in original Christianity. The variety of dogma had confused and distorted their simplicity and beauty. Such attitudes motivate "To An Ultra Protestant". The poem is an explicit rejection of institutional religion, and, with it, all the impediments which Emerson and Thoreau saw as "crutches", propping up a frigid and lifeless creed.

A letter from Lampman to E. W. Thomson, dated November 2, 1897, is an important document in this context. It provides a summary of Lampman's quarrel with orthodoxy and further details of the nature of his rejection. For these reasons, I quote the letter in full and restore a meaningful passage which is missing from it as quoted by A. S. Bourinot in his edition of Lampman's letters:

> Yesterday was a holiday and the day before was Sunday and I went to Church, a thing I do about three times a year. It always depresses me to go to Church. In those prayers and terrible hymns of our service we are in the presence of all the suffering in the world since the beginning of time. We have entered the temple of sorrow and are prostrate at the feet of the very God of Affliction.
> "Lead kindly light
> Amid the encircling gloom"
> Newman hit it exactly. It is the secret of the success of Christianity. As long as there is sorrow on earth, the pathetic figure of Christ will [next three words mutilated] days when men were children, they were worshippers of light and joy. Apollo, and Aphrodite and Dionysias were enough for them, but the world is

grown old now. It has gone through so much. It is sad and moody and full of despair and it cleaves to Christ its natural refuge. I must say, however, that Sunday is a day that drives me almost to madness. The prim black and stiff collars, the artificial dress of the women, the slow trouping to the church, the silence, the dreariness, the occasional knots of sallow and unhealthy zealots whom one may meet at street corners whining over some awful point in theology, — all that gradually presses me down till by Sunday night I am in despair and would fain issue forth with paint and brush and colour the town crimson.[15]

L AMPMAN CONTINUED to go to church infrequently until the end of his life, but it is clear that orthodox religion was not only unsatisfying but also profoundly distasteful to him. The original insights of Christ are no longer in evidence. Orthodox Christianity is prim and restrictive, a dreary ceremonial maintained largely by people who are themselves sick and whose interest is chiefly aroused by sterile casuistry. Most important, there is expressed here a conflict between Paganism and Christianity. Lampman valued the experience of the Greeks because he felt that in their vision of the world the emphasis was placed upon an easy correspondence between the world of man, gods, and nature. What Lampman sought was a belief which would give man a sense of "light and joy" and in which there was room for the spontaneity, total absorption, and imaginative play of childhood. In other words, he could not be content with a religion which appeared to encourage men to remain in a crippled state, dependent upon "the very God of Affliction", or with a ceremony which was an expression of gloom and despair.

Thus eventually, for Lampman, Christianity became synonymous with human distress, and was unacceptable because it failed to give men a greater sense of their own potential. Further evidence for this statement is provided by "Storm Voices". This poem is not, as many other poems of Lampman are not, simple description. The besieged house is the contemporary individual, and his condition is critical. Inside the house, the poet is aware of the tremendous forces for dissolution, and the darkness and rain blot out any kind of perception from a window already "narrow". Only if the poem is read in this way do such phrases as the "surging horror" in the night become meaningful. The storm stands for all of the contemporary conditions which Lampman felt diminished man. The poem is especially relevant because the storm is explicitly identified with a religious crisis. The fury of the storm is the "thunder" of organs and the "burst" of hymns, and the darkness is the "gloom" of a cathedral. Once more orthodox Christianity is experienced as a religion of desperation and despair, contributing to the sadness and vexation of men who have lost the capacity for wonder and the ability to respond to the infinite which is at the centre of religious feeling.

It is understandable, therefore, that in "The Land of Pallas", expressive both of Lampman's ideals and criticisms of contemporary society, the "robes" and "sacred books" of "many a vanished creed" are kept only as a reminder and a warning. In this land worship is "priestless", but of course Pallas is a religious state. Religion here, freed from its institutional aspects, has taken on a new intensity. The men and women of the land do in fact appear to be divine, and the worlds of man, nature, and the spirit are in continuous intercourse and harmony. Nevertheless it is men and women that Lampman is describing. He is indeed setting forth the ideal, but the ideal for Lampman is synonymous with the potential and the attainable. The religious faith and beliefs of the people are clearly not orthodox or traditional. Later I shall attempt to set forth the characteristics of Lampman's beliefs which are close to those found in the land of Pallas. For the moment it is enough to point out the close connection here between religion and nature, the sense of the immanence of spirit in the world, and the divinity of the human. Such characteristics are hardly compatible with orthodox Christianity.

The question of Lampman's religious doubts, using the word religious here to describe not only Christianity but other beliefs as well, may be dealt with briefly. Lampman's feeling that the Church had become moribund and oppressive can be found in many writers and intellectuals of the nineteenth century and is part of the general cultural dislocation of the century. As long as Lampman was deprived of a tradition, and until he was able to replace it with beliefs forged out of personal knowledge, there were bound to be evidences of despondency and nihilism. At the same time, his personal convictions, always elusive and hard won, sometimes failed him and brought further moments of deprivation. However, when observed in the context of his work as a whole, uncertainty and disbelief are not dominant. Moreover, these feelings must not be confused with the anguish often evinced in his work, which was the result of Lampman's awareness that the mass of mankind were ignorant of, or indifferent to, knowledge and powers which the poet believed could transform the quality of man and his existence. Desmond Pacey has pointed to some of these moments of doubt in "Despondency" and "Winter Evening". The poem "To Chaucer" is very important here as it charts the historical decline in orthodox faith from the Middle

109

Ages, down to the "doubt" and "restless care" of the contemporary situation.

In the introduction to his book, *The Disappearance of God*, J. Hillis Miller portrays the nineteenth century as a time when poets came to feel that either the lines of communication between man and God had been dislocated or God had fled from the world. One consequence of this feeling is the evocation of a Golden Age when God dwelt on earth and a close affinity existed between the divine and the human. Miller goes on to write that the Romantic poets,

> still believe in God, and they find his absence intolerable. At all costs they must attempt to re-establish communication. They too begin in destitution, abandoned by God. All the traditional means of mediation have broken down, and romanticism therefore defines the artist as the creator or discoverer of hitherto unapprehended symbols, symbols which establish a new relation, across the gap between man and God. The artist is the man who goes out into the empty spaces between man and God attempting to create in that vacancy a new fabric of connections between man and the divine power . . . . The central assumption of romanticism is the idea that the isolated individual, through poetry, can accomplish the "unheard of work", that is create through his own efforts a marvellous harmony of words which will integrate man, nature, and God.[16]

"To Chaucer", and several other poems by Lampman, belong to the category which Miller is describing. The Middle Ages are seen as a Golden Age and are significantly described in seasonal and youthful imagery. By contrast the present is felt to be a fallen world, a Paradise lost, or a Heaven which must be laboriously sought. But the present is not totally unredeemed, and this fact accounts for the paradoxes which become apparent in the poetry about to be examined and for the sense of struggle alternating between joy and hope which accompanies the attempt at "a new fabric of connections between man and the divine power".

Underlying many of Lampman's poems on the seasons is the theme of death and resurrection. By this I mean that the seasonal movement arouses in the poet a religious emotion similar to what the Christian has towards the death and resurrection of Christ. Furthermore the poet is so closely identified with the seasonal pattern that he too undergoes a death and rebirth which is felt to be physical, emotional, and spiritual. This theme viewed from a slightly different angle may also be interpreted in terms of separation and reunion. It is the theme of the Prodigal Son, of the child who has lost its mother, of the sense of being cut off from the natural sources of grace as in "The Ancient Mariner".

The tone of "In October" is defined by religious imagery — the "tall slim priests of storm" and the leaves which utter "low soft masses" for the death of the year. For the poet, too, it is a time of penance, and his heart goes out to "the ashen lands".

In "Ballads of Summer's Sleep", the alternation of the seasons becomes a religious struggle in which victory will be obtained only when "the slayer be slain". This image is very close to that of Christ's victory over death. It is also similar to the battle of the priest-kings at the beginning of Frazer's *The Golden Bough*, a battle which Frazer later identifies with vegetation rituals of death and revival. The same emphasis is there in "Winter Hues Recalled" where February is "the month of the great struggle twixt Sun and Frost". In "The Coming of Winter", the seasons are personified throughout. Summer is a god dying in the shadow of the mighty "slayer" winter whilst the earth prays and mourns in black. The earth is now a widow who will be forced into marriage with winter.

Several other poems, such as "Autumn Waste", "The Ruin of the Year", and "The March of Winter", marked by the same theme and similar structure and imagery, serve to underline that such a preoccupation is not merely fortuitous. Moreover, the two Greek myths most pertinent here, Adonis — Persephone and Demeter — Persephone, are explicitly referred to in Lampman's poem "Chione", which is another poem of death and descent into the underworld.

In "Sirius", Lampman provides variation by drawing on Egyptian mythology, but the concern is the same as in the poems already mentioned. Isis or Hathor was the wife of the fertility god, Osiris, also identified with the sun. The great star of Isis was Sirius, which betokened the rising of the Nile and the resurrection of Osiris. In Lampman's poem the waning of the "old night" and the rising of the star cause the poet to cry aloud to Hathor for he is "smitten by her star".

Clearly for Lampman, Spring, Autumn and Winter are the equivalent emotionally of Easter, Lent and the Passion, and it is interesting to read in Frazer something which Lampman may have intuited or thought out:

> When we reflect how often the church has skilfully contrived to plant the seeds of the faith on the old stock of Paganism, we may surmise that the Easter celebration of the dead and risen Christ was grafted upon a similar celebration of the dead and risen Adonis[17]

It is worth speculating, too, that when Lampman expressed his disgust with orthodox religion in the letter to Thomson which I quoted earlier, and opposed the pale figure which institutional religion had made of Christ with Apollo, Aphrodite, and Dionysus, he might have been setting up his own Trinity. The choice is significant, for Apollo is associated with the sun and light and his return was celebrated by festivals in the spring. Likewise Aphrodite is associated with the fertility of the spring and Dionysus is a vegetation god who underwent the pattern of death and rebirth.

In the general context, the poet tends to dramatize himself in two significant and interrelated ways. He is both a dead god awaiting the moment of rebirth and a man divided from the divine source within himself and the world of nature. The possibility of re-entry into a divine harmony still exists, but the occasions are limited in the contemporary situation as opposed to a past when union between man, nature, and god was continuous and characteristic. Christianity, especially in its institutionalized form, is for the poet one of the factors which has contributed to this fragmentation.

In "Favourites of Pan", the god flees before the "new strains" of "hostile hymns" and "conquering faiths". The synthesis caught in "A Vision of Twilight":

> When the spirit flowed unbroken
> Through the flesh, and the sublime
> Made the eyes of men far seeing,

is no more. However, "the infinite dream" may be attainable "for them that heed". In the "Return of the Year", characterized as the title suggests by imagery of conflict and rebirth:

> This life's old mood and cult of care
> Falls smitten by an older truth
> And the gray world wins back to her
> The rapture of her vanished youth.

At such times, the poet knows, "The Gods are vanished but not dead." Hence, like the loons, in the poem of the same title, the poet will search for the exiled Glooscap, or in "The Lake in the Forest" will experience in the wilderness the spirit of Manitou.

Contemporary man has been left only with the fragments of the medieval symbols of faith and correspondence with the Divine. Lampman puts it thus in "Voices of Earth":

> We have not heard the music of the spheres,
> The song of star to star . . . .

But in this poem there is not that sense of poignancy and horror as, for example, in Arnold's "Dover Beach", because earth does have voices, signs and symbols, which awaken in man organic knowledge, "bedded" in his heart.

In Lampman's poetry, nature is nearly always called "Mother" or "Great

Mother", terms synonymous with Rhea or Cybele, the "Mother of the Gods" of the Ancients. In "Freedom" the poet leaves the city and is re-united in the arms of his mother. Cast out of Paradise or Heaven the poet's heart in "Among the Timothy", which was a "heaven", is dead like the white leaves that hang through winter. But the poet lies in the earth as if buried, and his spirit passes into "the pale green ever-swaying grass" to return re-invigorated. In "The Meadow", as the earth burgeoned with April so the poet's spirit "sprang to life anew". Finally, in "Storm", the dead poet buried in his grave, "his narrow girth of need and sense", experiences divinity in moments of "demonic birth".

THE DISCUSSION of Lampman's dissatisfaction with orthodox religion has led logically to the world of nature which gave the poet an outlet for, and an image of, his religious sentiments.

"Life and Nature" provides a transition from the rejection of orthodoxy to Lampman's later religious position as it emerges through rather than in nature. To put it simply at the outset, nature is felt to be an intermediary, a means whereby the religious experience is expressed and realized. The title is misleading because it compresses too drastically the ideas behind the poem. Essentially the poem contrasts life or nature with orthodox religion, which the imagery indicates to be synonymous with death. Once again the poem is an example of Lampman's ability to find correlatives for a state of mind, for a spiritual struggle. The poet enters the city which is still and deserted and is overcome by the desolation which the inhabitants offer as worship to their God. Tormented by a lack of purpose and direction, driven to the point of distraction and madness he finds his attempts to assert life perverted into their opposite. He leaves, goes into the depths of nature where he lies down and undergoes a metamorphosis, a dying into life achieved by the loss of self in the procreative sound and movement.

Lampman, then, found "a natural code of faith". The several influences which moulded the correspondence between matter, mind, and the Divinity appear to be diverse, but all contributed to the essentially eclectic religious position arrived at by transcendentalism; they include Plato and Greek philosophy, Shelley, Emerson, Coleridge, Eastern mysticism, Amiel, Arnold, and W. W. Campbell.

The parts of "A Story of an Affinity", which tell of Richard's quest for knowledge are a likely guide to Lampman's own reading. Richard meditates on "Plato's vast and Golden dream": Lampman's writing shows that he had absorbed Plato's belief in another world beyond the material, a world of immutable essences, Forms or Ideas, especially beauty, truth, and harmony. Later Richard learns from Coleridge the "heavenly likeness of the things of earth". Coleridge, of course, is central to any discussion of transcendentalism. He had absorbed the ideas of the German idealists, especially those of Kant, and was a major formative influence upon Emerson. What is most relevant here is Coleridge's preoccupation with spiritual unity and the belief that the Platonic Ideas, manifested in the material world, may be perceived by the imagination, which is essentially the faculty that reconciles opposites in a new harmony.

The poem "Earth — The Stoic" reveals other classical influences apart from Plato which help to build up our picture of Lampman's cosmology. In the poem, Lampman speaks of the "fiery birth" of the universe and the "sheer will" which earth communicates to the heart of man. The original meaning of spirit was the conception of the Stoics of a fire-like principle, animating and energizing the Cosmos. The earth is the Stoic and is imbued with the spiritual principle, especially as it manifests itself in the force of heat. With all the images of light and heat in Lampman's poetry, and one central poem entitled "Heat", there is surely little need to emphasize how important the Stoic conception of the universe is to our understanding of Lampman's poetry.

Carl F. Klinck, tracing the spiritual difficulties of W. W. Campbell, Lampman's friend and, as we have seen, his collaborator in the *Globe* column in 1892 and 1893, writes: "Until the end of his life, he [Campbell] was Canada's chief popularizer of what he called idealism, and what the historian will call transcendentalism."[18] It is at least probable that Campbell was able to provide Lampman with opportunities for discussion of the ideas and major documents of transcendentalism, especially those of Emerson, with whose work Campbell was very familiar.

Indeed Emerson was probably the most congenial and important influence upon Lampman in the particular area under discussion. There are striking similarities between both men's work, and I propose to allow Lampman's religious position to emerge in conjunction with references to the ideas and writings of Emerson. Lampman considered Emerson to be a nature poet "in the fullest sense". His "sympathy with nature" is a "sympathy of force" which draws him to nature because "in the energies of his own soul he is aware of a kinship to the forces of nature, and feels with an elemental joy as if it were a part of himself, the eternal movement of nature."[19] In his essay on Keats, Lampman stated that the concern of poetry was with "essences" which accorded with "That divine and universal harmony". He also writes in the same essay:

> Whatever creation of the human imagination is genuinely beautiful is produced by an impulse derived from, and allied to the power of the Divine Creator himself, and it has the right to exist. There is an energy in the spirit of the true poet which realizes what he creates . . . . [20]

An unpublished essay, "The Modern School of Poetry in England", also asserts that "all true art must rest upon a sense of wonder — a sense of the invisible that is around everything."[21]

In these various statements, it seems to me, are to be found the aesthetic and moral sentiments usually associated with the transcendental vision of experience, and since the beautiful is "allied to the power of the Divine Creator", the experience is essentially religious. Nature in "Earth — the Stoic" is conceived of as being imbued with an animating principle known interchangeably as force, energy, or spirit. Emerson is a true nature poet because he is aware within himself of an energy akin to that of nature which partakes of universal movement. The central essence is harmony, and this is universal and divine. The imagination, or the poetic faculty, is concerned with the perception of invisible harmony and so "realizes", that is, creates, a reality which is both divine impulse and a divine achievement. Thus nature, art, the imagination of the poet, and the divine mind are one. The religious experience is synonymous with a sense of unity between the individual, nature, and what Emerson called the Oversoul, or is a correspondence between the spirit or energy in nature, the spirit or energy in man, and Divine Spirit or Energy. These last two terms are both Lampman's and Emerson's favourite expressions for their God. Man at such mystical moments is divine, and Deity, Spirit, Force, or Energy is both immanent within man and nature and transcendant or beyond the creation. Thus to describe Lampman as a pantheist is not exact. The more accurate term would be pantheist for God is more than the spiritual presence permeating the universe. Furthermore, the idea of a Christian dualism has no place in Lampman's belief, since he envisages no division between spirit and matter. Here we are close to the insights which make up Lampman's religious position.

Man, then, looking at nature with his imagination, would see analogies between mind and matter and understand them as diverse manifestations of the universal harmony which is the divine unity. For Lampman "true art" rested upon a "sense of wonder" because of the "invisible that is around everything".

Likewise for Emerson the visible creation was "the terminus or circumference of the invisible" and the "invariable mark of wisdom is to see the miraculous in the common". It is clear why Emerson felt that the task of the teacher was "to acquaint man with himself" and why with Lampman he was saddened by contemporary man, "a god in ruins", "the dwarf of himself".

There exists a close similarity between Lampman's and Emerson's attitude towards science and its effect upon the religious view of experience. Broadly speaking one of the effects of scientific findings in the nineteenth century was to make orthodox religious beliefs less tenable, but science could apparently provide sanctions for orthodox beliefs because, as Douglas Bush writes, "much of what crumbled under the pressure of science was rather the adventitious accretions of religion, such as the scientific validity of Genesis, than religion itself."[22] If we consult "The Story of An Affinity", we see that Lampman meant by science primarily astronomy, geology, and biology, those branches which most directly challenged orthodox religious beliefs. The protagonist of the poem, Richard,

> explored the round
> Of glittering space, the heavenly chart, and saw
> The giant order of immense worlds,
> The wheeling planets and our galaxy;
> And far beyond them in the outer void
> Cluster succeeding cluster of strange suns
> Through spaces awful and immeasurable,
> Dark systems and mysterious energies
> And nebulous creations without end —
> The people of the hollow round of heaven
> In trackless myriads dwelling beyond search
> Or count of man — beneath his feet this earth
> A dust mote spinning round a little star
> Not known, nor named in the immensity.
> He probed the secrets of the rocks, and learned
> The texture of our planet's outer rind,
> And the strange tale of her tremendous youth.
> He touched the endless lore of living things,
> Of plant, of beast, of bird, and not alone
> In the mere greed of knowledge, but as one
> Whom beauty kindled with a poet's fire.

The last three lines are particularly important, for though Lampman and Emerson did not object to science itself, they were opposed to the scientific fact uninformed by the poetic imagination as an end in itself.

For Lampman and Emerson, scientific discovery was a welcome ally in changing moribund beliefs, but only as a prelude to newer and essentially religious convictions about the meaning of life. This is one of the themes of a lecture, "Historic Notes of Life and Letters in New England", given by Emerson in 1880.

The essay is close in idea and phrasing to Lampman's essay in his *Globe* column for April 1893.[23] He begins with a pessimistic view of human nature, human history, and the worst tendencies of his own age, but "in a time when these things are becoming most apparent" he offers a new hope, "a new conception of the higher life". This new conception he identifies as "the child of science" but is careful to emphasize that it is "reinforced by the poetry inherent in the facts of the universe and all existence". Viewed in this way the conception "is not a materialistic one, although at first it may seem so." Instead it is "poetic and intrinsically religious". Men armed with "the new knowledge" can achieve "a breadth and majesty of vision" and this "new spiritual force" will enable men to live "in the very presence of eternity".

Emerson's religious beliefs were influenced by his reading of oriental religions and mysticism. There is evidence that Lampman, too, had read and thought about Eastern philosophy and religion. A knowledge of this aspect of Lampman's reading is useful because it affected all levels of his work, from his thought to the structure and imagery of his poetry. The preponderance of the image of the circle, for example, in his work, as in Emerson's, may well have derived from an acquaintance with Hinduism. In a manuscript book of poems and notes, for 1894 to 1899, there is the following jotting:

Mir-han-oya — final complete self-consciousness
Manvantara — the great process of expansion and contraction — the day of Brahma
Pralaya — the period of concentration, the night of Brahma[24]

These rather cryptic notes are in fact a condensation of many aspects of Hindu religious beliefs and cosmology. Hinduism postulates a universe immense in size and duration, passing through a continuous process of decline and development. The fundamental cosmic cycle is the day of Brahma which is equal to 4,320,000,000 years and known as a kalpa. The god sleeps for a further kalpa known as the night of Brahma and then repetition takes place. Brahma is in the infinite, the unchangeable, the eternal, absolute pure Being on which all that exists depends and from which it derives its reality. The world is an immense series of repetitive cycles and is thought of as being periodically absorbed into, and emanating from, the Divine Being. Brahma is the inmost essence of all things animate and inanimate, and the ultimate is the impersonal world spirit with which the soul of the individual is mystically identical. The true self is universal consciousness and exists both in itself and for itself or, as Lampman writes, in "the very presence of Eternity". Other attributes of the Divine Being as it appears in Lampman's poetry, such as divine light and energy emanating to the individual soul and the immanence of God in man and the universe, clearly derive from Lampman's acquaintance with Eastern religions.

Perhaps by now Lampman's religious position and beliefs are clearer, and this essay may be concluded by an examination of how these ideas operated in, and shaped, a number of poems apart from those already scrutinized.

The impulse behind these poems is religious in the sense that Lampman sought to re-create, as he said, the knowledge that "with the fullest intensity of sympathy we are of one birth with everything about us"[25] and to make known the "heavenly likeness of the things of earth". The poems fall into two categories, the alternate sides of the same theme. Man is a god in ruins because in his increasingly mechanized and urbanized society he has lost contact with the vital forces of the natural world. These forces are varied manifestations of the central essence of nature, the spiritual unity of the One, the World Spirit. To recover himself man must die to the material world and resurrect the god within, his true identity. The religious experience occurs when the real self experiences itself simultaneously through nature in the presence of the World Soul. Then all opposites are reconciled, and the feeling is characterized by a sense of clarity and harmony which accompanies the unbroken flow of spirit.

In "Freedom" men have lost their relationship with nature. Though their souls originally "were sprung from the earth" they are now here "degenerate children". "A Prayer" uses the recurring image of modern man physically handicapped and spiritually maimed, "weak", "halt", and "blind". The poet, in a way which recalls the work of D. H. Lawrence, asks nature to recover the men, "Born of thy strength", from the partial, mechanical existence of industrialized society and restore them to integrated, organic wholeness by endowing them with some of her energy and creativity. "Sight" is a series of detailed contrasts. The irony of life is that beauty, harmony, and infinite possibilities surround men, but, shut in by walls and the perpetual winter of the spirit, men cannot attune their inmost selves to the wonders outside and thus remain unconscious to both.

"An Athenian Reverie" is another poem in which man is depicted as a being unaware and unfulfilled. Man ought to be in a state of metamorphosis. Instead he is unable to free himself from the chrysalis. This theme is developed in the image of the tree. Man sits beneath it, half-asleep, enjoying its shade, but is unable to go beyond the simply sensual and immediately apparent to the majestic formal harmony of the source. By contrast, the poet, alert and receptive, struggles with "watchful dreams" to add a little to the "wrought sculpture" and "never-finished frieze" of life. The exact choice of image to convey the fullest meaning is impressive here. The frieze is the middle portion of an entablature linked by the architrave to the column below and by the cornice to the roof above. Life is a magnificent structure, like a Greek temple, and the poet occupies a mediating position between earth and heaven.

"Peccavi Domine" was written as "an act of self-relief".[26] It is an important poem because it displays many characteristics of Lampman's belief, and its paradoxes, abrupt oppositions, and contrasts are akin to the technique, as well as the theme, of Emerson's "Brahma". Emerson's poem is about the absolute unity underlying Maya, or the Hindu principle of illusion and variety.

Lampman's poem is a study in dejection, a lament in which the poet chastises himself for ignoring his deep perceptions of the unity of the universe and the intuitions of his real self and its relationship with the World Spirit. God has many names and many attributes, "Power", "Poet-Heart", "Maker", "Riddle", and "Energy". The World Spirit is like a sphere composed of interpentrating circles and is present throughout the universe:

> Within whose glowing rings are bound,
> Out of whose sleepless heart had birth
> The cloudy blue, the starry round,
> And this small miracle of earth.

Because the Divine Being "livest in everything", and since "all things are thy script and chart", the task of the poet is to remain alert and interpret the manifold signs of the world. Thus he is constantly moving from the border of illusion to the centre of reality. The Divine Being — "protean", "ever-old" and "ever-new" — is also the central reality of the poetic self. But here the poet feels that he has betrayed the promptings of the "God within" and consequently is separated and alienated from the emblems of spirit in the natural world. Instead of being led beyond the forms of nature to an awesome awareness of unity, as in "Heat", for example, the poet here experiences no expansion of self but rather a spiritual rebuttal which leads to the sorry spectacle of his "broken soul". His torment is made more unendurable by the evidences of spirit with which the earth shines and glows, evidences which no longer beckon to him but mock and enhance his self-division.

Elsewhere Lampman turns from self-division and the spectacle of fallen man to affirm the correspondence between universal spirit, the spirit of nature, and the soul of man. On these occasions, man is rejuvenated, resurrected from his sensual grave, aware of the infinite in the finite, and of the poetic soul, the imagination, intensely sympathetic to the emblematic quality of nature, and becomes the "expositor of the divine mind".[27]

A characteristic quality of Lampman's poems at such times is that the landscape seems to glow as if lit from within. The natural world, in other words, becomes luminous and transparent as spirit shines through. This experience, accompanied by its characteristic terminology, is a leading motif of Emerson's essay "Nature" because the main concern is to show "how the universe becomes transparent, and the light of higher laws than its own shines through it".[28] Lampman, of course, was not writing an essay, but that the experience I have attempted to define, and which Emerson's essay describes in part at least is there, can be demonstrated in several poems. The poem, significantly titled, "Cloud-break", concretely realizes the experience:

> The islands are kindled with gold
> And russet and emerald dye;
> And the interval waters outrolled
> Are more blue than the sky.
> From my feet to the heart of the hills
> The spirits of May intervene,
> And a vapour of azure distills
> Like a breath on the opaline green.

There is a sudden intensification of colour and the landscape "distills" its essence, becoming "opaline" or translucent with spirit. The experience is momentary and then,

> The chill and the shadow decline
> On the eyes of rejuvenate men
> That were wide and divine.

In "The Bird and the Hour", diverse visual and auditory experiences coalesce to manifest the underlying spiritual essence. At sunset the valley and sky dissolve in molten gold. The song of the hermit bird, the "golden music", is part of the unifying aspects of the landscape and prolongs the vision which appears to emerge:

> from the closing door
> Of another world.

The frogs in the poem of the same name, are the expositors chosen by nature of "her spirit's inmost dream". "Distance" expresses simply the transcendental vision which is looking beyond the surface of natural phenomena:

> Till this earth is lost in heaven
> And thou feel'st the whole.

In "Peace", "Nature" and "Eternity" are interchangeable since the earth is a "daedal spectacle", an "open radiance", and a "script sublime". The fulfilled man is he whose reality is found "only in the flawless mind". Finally, the source of "The Largest Life" is the recognition of universal spirit, the knowledge that salvation is self-salvation. This salvation enlarges, so to speak, in a universe which is felt to be dynamic, the area of spirit. The "Great Light" becomes "clearer for our light", and the "great soul the stronger for our soul".

Both Emerson and Lampman entitled one of their poems "Xenophanes", and a passage from Emerson's essay "Nature" makes clear why both were fascinated by the ideas and experience of this early Greek philosopher and rhapsodist. Emerson writes:

> Herein is especially apprehended the unity of nature, — the unity in variety which meets us everywhere. All the endless variety of things make an identical impression. Xenophanes complained in his old age, that, look where he would, all things hastened back to unity. He was weary of seeing the same entity in the tedious variety of forms.[29]

Xenophanes asserted a divinity who is true existence as opposed to appearance, the One and the All, undivided and eternal and underlying the universe. Lampman portrays Xenophanes as a wanderer and a searcher after truth, weary in extreme old age of the world of appearance and longing for the reality which he has seen. It is the same "hunger" of Xenophanes which occupies the poetic imagination.

The esemplastic nature (to use a work coined by Coleridge to explain the synthesizing power of the poetic imagination) of universal spirit is the theme of "The Passing of the Spirit". Characteristically the theme is worked out through images of nature and music. The wind is one aspect of the World Spirit, an invisible cause with clearly visible effects. It is also called "the world-old rhapsodist" or, in other words, a professional reciter of Homeric poems, an expositor of the elemental and universal. The movement of the wind of universal spirit finds its response in a world which is intensely sympathetic and attuned to the universal cause. Tree after tree begins to sway and sing, blending into a chorus composed of strophe and antistrophe, an "infinite note" which is both initiated by, and a paean to, the universal presence of spirit. Likewise the finite life of individual man, "at sacred intervals", is transformed and completed in the presence of spirit. It is at such moments that "we dream ourselves immortal and are still". Without perplexity or doubt we are awesomely aware of universal harmony which is completed by the soul of man. This, for the poet, is the essential religious experience.

Much has already been said about "Heat", but by way of a conclusion it ought to be added that this is a fine transcendental poem. The landscape liquefies and dissolves and all contraries are unified in the presence of the manifestation of spiritual force. This explains why the poet believes that he has been brought to the experience by "some blessed power". The god within the poet is resurrected and lives in the eternal presence of the divine as it shines through nature. God, who through the centuries became more and more remote, has returned to earth in his original guise, man, and the poet need no longer envy the men of old, for he has vindicated their myth, and re-entered "The glittering world" of that "Immortal", "divine" and "Gay-smiling multitude".

(1973)

NOTES

[1] R. Daniells, *Literary History of Canada*, ed. Carl F. Klinck (Toronto: University of Toronto Press, 1965), p. 394.

[2] D. Pacey, *Ten Canadian Poets* (Toronto: Ryerson, 1957), p. 127.

[3] Archibald Lampman, "The Revolt of Islam," *Rouge et Noir*, I, no. 4 (December 1880).

[4] *Ibid.*, p. 6.

[5] *Ibid.*, p. 5.

[6] *Ibid.*, p. 6.

[7] Archibald Lampman, "At the Mermaid Inn," the Toronto *Globe*, Saturday, November 26, 1892.

[8] *Ibid.*, Saturday, August 20, 1892.

[9] *Ibid.*, Saturday, February 27, 1892.

[10] *Ibid.*, Monday, February 29, 1892.

[11] *Ibid.*, Saturday, February 6, 1892.

[12] Archibald Lampman, "The Revolt of Islam," *Rouge et Noir*, I, no. 4 (December 1880).

[13] Letters from Lampman to E. W. Thomson, MS Group 29940, Vol. I, February 10, 1883, Public Archives of Canada.

[14] MS book, 1889-1892, Trinity College Library, Toronto.

[15] Letters from Lampman to E. W. Thomson, MS Group 29940, Vol. I, Public Archives of Canada.

[16] J. Hillis Miller, *The Disappearance of God* (Cambridge, Mass.: Harvard University Press, 1963), pp. 13-14.

[17] J. G. Frazer, *The Golden Bough* (London: Macmillan & Co., 1957), p. 455.

[18] Carl F. Klinck, *Wilfred Campbell: A Study in Late Provincial Victorianism* (Toronto: Ryerson, 1942), pp. 56-57.

[19] Archibald Lampman, "At the Mermaid Inn," the Toronto *Globe*, Saturday, April 22, 1893.

[20] Archibald Lampman, "The Character and Poetry of Keats," pref. note by E. K. Brown, UTQ 15 (July 1946), 357.

[21] Archibald Lampman, "The Modern School of Poetry in England," MS 29940, Vol. I, Public Archives of Canada.

[22] Douglas Bush, *Science and English Poetry* (New York: Oxford University Press, 1950), p. 136.

[23] Archibald Lampman, "At the Mermaid Inn," the Toronto *Globe*, Saturday, April 8, 1893.

[24] Archibald Lampman, MS Group 29940, Vols. 3 and 4, Public Archives of Canada.

[25] Archibald Lampman, "At the Mermaid Inn," the Toronto *Globe*, Saturday, July 2, 1892.

[26] Letters from Lampman to E. W. Thomson, MS Group 29940, March 5, 1894, Public Archives of Canada.

[27] Ralph Waldo Emerson, "Nature," *Selections from Ralph Waldo Emerson*, ed. Stephen Whicher, Riverside Editions (Boston: Houghton Mifflin Co., 1960), p. 50.

[28] *Ibid.*, p. 35.

[29] *Ibid.*, p. 40.

LAMPMAN'S
FLEETING VISION

Sandra Djwa

READING THE POETRY of Archibald Lampman, we are reminded again of the Victorian capacity for dualism: he appears to accept both the Socialist vision of human progress and the Calvinist sense of man's inescapable evil; a professed non-believer, he explores the ways of Stoic and hedonist without ever losing his own devotion to a reinstated Pale Galilean; a pacifist of sorts, he shrinks from violence yet writes several fascinated explorations of the psychology of brutality. In Arnoldian frame, Lampman regularly suggests the need to "moderate desire" despite which some of his best poems are celebrations of anarchic passion. An idle dreamer, a self-proclaimed troubled soul, a Utopian, a feminist, and a critic of society . . . . The list of epithets gleaned from the poetry are often self-contradictory; yet, most often, Lampman's varied poetic stances are related to his exploration of an abyss which he perceives gaping between the benevolent nature which he would like to affirm and the often unpleasant "reality" of everyday life.

This rift between the real and the ideal world is bridged, although not always successfully, through the metaphor of the "dream". Lampman's first poems are superficially descriptions of the peace, beauty and truth received by the poet as he "dreams" in nature, but the reader is always made aware of the unpleasant "real" which the idyllic vision attempts to subjugate; the "dissonant roar of the city" intrudes into the "easeful dreams" of even such idylls as the early poem "April". The Victorian parable of the high dream struggled into fruition ("The Story of an Affinity") and the Utopian vision ("The Land of Pallas") are all undercut in Lampman's canon by assaults of human viciousness and cruelty ("The Three Pilgrims") or by the perversions of human reason expressed in the nightmare vision of the coming machine world ("The City of the End of

Things"). In fact, a characteristic development of many of Lampman's later poems is that of the dream dissolving into the nightmare as in his sonnet, "Winter Evening":

> Tonight the very horses springing by
> Toss gold from whitened nostrils. In a dream
> The streets that narrow to the westward gleam
> Like rows of golden palaces; and high
> From all the crowded chimneys tower and die
> A thousand aureoles. Down in the west
> The brimming plains beneath the sunset rest,
> One burning sea of gold. Soon, soon shall fly
> The glorious vision, and the hours shall feel
> A mightier master; soon from height to height,
> With silence and the sharp unpitying stars,
> Stern creeping frosts, and winds that touch like steel,
> Out of the depth beyond the eastern bars,
> Glittering and still shall come the awful night.

In his earlier work, Lampman appears to accept the truth of the visionary experience: dreaming in nature, he can proclaim "dreams are real and life is only sweet." But the primary difficulty with continuing in the dreaming state, as even an Endymion must discover, is that the poet is not always able to keep "reality" at bay. Eventually, he does find it necessary to ask himself whether the visionary experience is indeed a true insight into higher truth or simply the embroidery of a cheating fancy. The question is stated quite explicitly in Keats' "Ode to a Nightingale": "Was it a vision or a waking dream/ Fled is that music: do I wake or sleep?" Lampman's aspiring "Vision of Twilight" concludes with a similar questioning of reality: "Comes my question back again — / Which is real? the fleeting vision?/ Or the fleeting world of men?" Is the true reality the product of our imagination, "the fleeting vision", or is it "the fleeting world of men"? Lampman's use of the same adverb to describe both states (and the fact that both are perceived through a poem which is itself a "vision") points up his transitory sense of both states and may be taken to support the view that he often sees the "visionary" and the so-called "real" world from the essentially passive state of the observer in the dream.

Curiously, Lampman began to write poetry not as a direct response to the dream visions of the major Romantics (Keats' *Hyperion*, 1819, or its Victorian descendent, Hengist Horne's *Orion*, 1843), but rather under the influence of a derivative Canadian work in the late Victorian stream, the *Orion* (1880) of

125

Charles G. D. Roberts. Orion, a latter day Endymion, is "a dreamer of noble dreams"[1] and Lampman, when first reading Roberts' *Orion*, was plunged into a state of "the wildest excitement": "A little after sunrise I got up and went out into the college grounds... but everything was transfigured for me beyond description, bathed in the old-world radiance of beauty." Lampman was particularly delighted that "those divine verses... with their Tennyson-like richness" had been written "by a Canadian ... one of ourselves".[2]

Lampman's first books, *Among the Millet* (1888) and *Lyrics of Earth* (1895), are clearly a response to Roberts' *Orion* and *Songs of the Common Day* (1893). But although Lampman adopts much of Roberts' romantic dream mythology, (the "sleep" of time and winter, the "dream" as a description of human life, and the Pan myth as it relates to nature's "dream" and poetic experience) his stance in nature is somewhat different from that of Roberts. From a comparison of Lampman's early sonnet, "In November", with Roberts' sonnet, "The Winter Fields", we can see that Lampman's "dream" is not only transcendental metaphor but also poetic process. The octave of each sonnet describes the wintry landscape, but in the sestet Roberts then deserts the fields for a dream-wish projection of the future; Lampman, in opposition, brings the reader back to the still figure of the poet:

> I alone
> Am neither sad, nor shelterless, nor gray,
> Wrapped round with thought, content to watch and dream.

This conclusion reinforces our awareness that the poem itself has come about because the poet, as observer, has stood and "dreamed". In that sense, his conclusion is a low modulated affirmation of the impartial "truth" of the experience just described.

As John Sutherland and Roy Daniells both have noted, it is the figure of the poet as apparent idler and dreamer which appears throughout Lampman's poems, especially in such poems as "Among the Timothy" or "At the Ferry" where the narrator states, "I look far out and dream of life."[3] In this "dream" or "reverie" he gives himself up to the "beauty" of sense impressions from nature. These impressions are analogous with high truth because Lampman prefers, as did the early Keats, the easy equation of beauty and truth. Furthermore, the truth of nature is a truth spontaneously given:

> ... I will set no more mine overtaskèd brain
>   To barren search and toil that beareth nought,
> Forever following with sore-footed pain

> The crossing pathways of unbournèd thought;
> But let it go, as one that hath no skill,
>   To take what shape it will,
> An ant slow-burrowing in the earthy gloom,
> A spider bathing in the dew at morn,
> Or a brown bee in wayward fancy borne
>   From hidden bloom to bloom.

Similarly, the poems "Ambition" and "The Choice" declare that for "poet" and "dreamer" it is all sufficient to "Sit me in the windy grass and grow/ As wise as age, as joyous as a child."

The romantic inheritance from which Lampman derives this wise passiveness is almost surely Wordsworth's "Expostulation and Reply". Wordsworth's conclusion, "Think you . . . That nothing of itself will come,/ But we must still be seeking?" would seem to underlie Lampman's assertion that he will "let it go . . . / To take what shape it will." No longer will he attempt to impose his willed structure on the world outside and so shape the poetic happening (as do, for example, Heavysege, Crawford, and Roberts) but he will rather sit passively and so allow the powers of nature to impress themselves upon poet and his art as do the minutiae of "ant", "spider" and "bee" from "Among the Timothy".

This formulation would seem to be a fairly accurate description of Lampman's nature poetry; if in Roberts' work there is most often an active straining for apotheosis, Lampman's poems, such as his sonnet, "Solitude", are most often a series of associations tied together by natural sequence and by the fact that they are the related perceptions of the recording poet:

> How still it is here in the woods. The trees
>   Stand motionless, as if they did not dare
>   To stir, lest it should break the spell. The air
> Hangs quiet as spaces in a marble frieze.
> Even this little brook, that runs as ease,
>   Whispering and gurgling in its knotted bed,
>   Seems but to deepen, with its curling thread
> Of sound, the shadowy sun-pierced silences.
> Sometimes a hawk screams or a woodpecker
>   Startles the stillness from its fixed mood
> With his loud careless tap. Sometimes I hear
>   The dreamy white-throat from some far off tree
> Pipe slowly on the listening solitude
>   His five pure notes succeeding pensively.

But the point should be made that this is not only passive sense impression. Lampman's characteristic stance is one in which, Meredith-like, he insists upon cultivating the faculties of seeing and hearing: "Let us clear our eyes, and break/ Through the cloudy chrysalis." No longer "blind", man is enabled to see "The threads that bind us to the All,/ God or the Immensity" ("Winter-Store"). In the sonnet "Knowledge", Lampman describes the life which he would like to live as one "of leisure and broad hours,/ To think and dream" while "An Athenian Reverie" states explicitly that the function of these "broad hours" is to inquire into the deeper meaning beyond the surface phenomena of life. This whole association of "dream" and "knowledge" is given an Arnoldian context in the earlier poem "Outlook" where it is asserted that the true life is "Not to be conquered by these headlong days" but to allow the mind to brood "on life's deep meaning": "What man, what life, what love, what beauty is,/ This is to live, and win the final praise."

Despite the easy conventionality of these lines, Lampman's work does suggest a genuine preoccupation with the nature of the buried life, the hidden stream, the authentic self which Arnold in "Resignation" describes as lying unregarded beneath life's phenomena, a hidden self which must be tapped if man is to find peace and a moral guide for his existence. The protagonists of Lampman's major narrative poems — the dreamer of "An Athenian Reverie", Perpetua, David and Abigail as well as Richard and Elizabeth of "The Story of an Affinity" — all ask variations on the general question "What is this life?" More often than not, their moral struggles with themselves lead to an affirmation based on the fleeting "vision", a glimpse of that higher reality which they understand to underlie surface phenomena.

THE INSISTENCE that the poet should put himself in touch with nature's underlying truth seems to have been a part of Lampman's early thought. F. W. Watt (writing in *The University of Toronto Quarterly* in 1956) describes Lampman's early fable "Hans Fingerhut's Frog Lesson" which was first published in the periodical *Man* (1885). Clearly an allegory of the artist in society, it describes a young poet failing to receive popular recognition who then reviles man and nature. For this *hubris*, he is metamorphosed into a frog until he learns to interpret nature's cosmic plan, described by Watt as "cosmic optimism based on a stoical acceptance of one's lot and faith in Nature's maternal purposes".[4] Initiated through suffering, Hans Fingerhut undergoes a moral transformation: "From that day the great songs that he made were nothing like his former ones. There was never anything bitter or complaining in them. They were all sweet and beautiful and wise."[5] This easy parable of the poet's reconciliation with himself and with society might be compared with Lampman's own pronouncements on the nature of unhappiness:

> All our troubles in reality proceed from nothing but vanity if we track them to their source. We form an ideal of ourselves and claim what seems to be due to that ideal. The ideal of myself is entitled to love and approbation from my fellow creatures: but the love and approbation does not appear, and I fret and abuse the constitution of things. To the ideal of myself money and power and practical success are no doubt due, but they do not come, and again I abuse the constitution of things. (1896)[6]

Lampman's early complaints that his poetry was not properly appreciated, his continued penury, his unhappiness with the tedium of the Ottawa Post Office, grief over the death of a young child, suggestions of an unrequited love, and, above all, his fatal illness and early death are all legendary and have contributed to the view of Lampman as a Canadian John Keats. Despite the evidence of D. C. Scott's letter to Ralph Gustafson (17th July, 1945) which argues "the cast of Lampman's nature was not towards melancholy,"[7] much discussion of Lampman has interpreted the poetry to infer that Lampman did consider himself heir to "The woe and sickness of an age of fear made known". The truth of Lampman's situation may have been somewhat less onerous; writing for the *Globe* in 1892, he proclaims: "No man is more serious than the poet; yet no man is more given to expressing under different circumstances the most opposite statements."

Implied in Scott's letter to Gustafson and in his Introduction to *Lyrics of Earth: Sonnets and Ballads*, 1925, is the suggestion that some of the "ills" which plague Lampman's poetic world may have been an imaginative recreation of Socialist thought rather than Lampman's actual experiences in Ottawa, *circa* 1890. Certainly, we do notice there are very few poems referring to Ottawa life which are grounded in the realistic mode. Even when presented in a poem specifically titled "Ottawa", the city is not recognizable as any place having a Canadian habitation and a name but is instead the city of misty romantic towers or the city of industrial greed and social oppression. It is also true that other than for the sensitive nature poetry of the first two books, Lampman's later work does become a repository for the Victorian stock concerns of religious bigotry ("To an Ultra Protestant"), social injustice ("Epitaph on a Rich Man"), evolutionary progress ("The Clearer Self"), the machine age and utopias ("A Vision of Twilight").

However stereotyped the invocation, there is a note of genuine melancholia running throughout Lampman's poetry. The early sonnet "Despondency" bleakly views the future: "Slow figures in some live remorseless frieze/ The approaching days escapeless and unconquered". He concludes that life itself is "Vain and phantasmal as a sick man's dream". A poem such as "Sapphics" which urges man to follow the stoical fortitude of nature also presents a personal application: "Me too changes, bitter and full of evil,/ Dream after dream have plundered and left me naked,/ Grey with sorrow." "Loneliness", like Margaret Avison's "The Mirrored Man", starkly reveals an inner self:

> So it is with us all, we have our friends
> Who keep the outer chambers, and guard well
> Our common path;
> For far within us lies an iron cell
> Soundless and secret, where we laugh or moan
> Beyond all succour, terribly alone.

Other than for a large cluster of images which makes reference to the "dream" or "vision" in relation to the "beauty" of nature, Lampman's poetic vocabulary is often concerned with the negative emotions of "pain", "misery", "fear", "loneliness", "loss" and "emptiness". The particular association of the "dream" with "grief" and "death" which begins to dominate about 1894 particularly in relation to poems such as "Chione" and "Vivia Perpetua", suggests Lampman's grief at the death of his infant son. Similarly, the long narratives, "David and Abigail" and "The Story of an Affinity", parables of impossible love brought to fruition, may be given a new rationale if they are viewed in the light of the autobiographical "A Portrait in Six Sonnets" and Lampman's stifled affection for Katherine Waddell.[8] It is perhaps because of this growing burden of unhappiness, coupled with the beginning of his own fatal illness, that Lampman writes in 1895:

I am getting well weary of things. I was so far gone in hypochrondria on Saturday last that I had not the spirit to go to my office at all. I went straggling up the Gatineau Road, and spent the whole day and most of the next under the blue sky and the eager sun; and then I began to perceive that there were actually trees and grass and beautifully loitering clouds in the tender fields of heaven; I got to see at last that it was really June; and that perhaps I was alive after all.[9]

For the early Lampman, as for his alter-ego Hans Fingerhut, the cure for melancholy was to return to nature. And, as in the early poetry of Keats ("I Stood Tip-Toe Upon a Little Hill" or "Sleep and Poetry") the realm of "Flora and old Pan: sleep in the grass" is invariably associated with the poet's "dream". In addition, Lampman endows nature with the instinctive apprehension of eternal truths. Throughout Lampman's verse, there runs a conscious-unconscious antithesis in which the creatures of nature are associated with the instinctive knowledge or "dream" which underlies creation, while man is made miserable by his own nagging consciousness. Consequently, in poems such as "An Old Lesson From the Fields" and "Comfort of the Fields", the lesson given to man is the injunction to experience the true "power" and "beauty" of life by putting away conscious knowledge. At one with the other creatures of the field, he can drain "the comfort of wide fields unto tired eyes".

This emphasis on a wide passiveness would seem to be related to the idea that the poet, standing a little apart from both nature and himself, is not only in a position to be impressed upon by the moving "frieze" of nature, but is also enabled to see into the fixed plan or "dream", which he hypothesizes as underlying the active surface motion of nature and the universe. In Lampman's work, as in the early verse of Roberts, the frogs have a special function as emissaries of the poet's "dream". In the poem "The Frogs", they are specifically associated with a lack of conscious thought: "Breathers of Wisdom won without a quest,/ Quaint uncouth dreamers". For Lampman, the frogs become a way of communicating with the eternal first principle:

> Often to me who heard you in your day,
>   With close wrapt ears, it could not choose but seem
> That earth, our mother, searching in what way,
>   Men's hearts might know her spirit's inmost dream;
>   Ever at rest beneath life's change and stir,
>   Made you her soul, and bade you pipe for her.

As he listens, "The stillness of enchanted reveries/ Bound brain and spirit and half-closed eyes,/ In some divine sweet wonder-dream astray," so that the "outer roar" of mankind grows "strange and murmurous, faint and far away":

> Morning and noon and midnight exquisitely,
>   Wrapt with your voices, this alone we knew,
> Cities might change and fall, and men might die,
>   Secure were we, content to dream with you,
>   That change and pain are shadows faint and fleet,
>   And dreams are real, and life is only sweet.

In effect, the peace and comfort of the eternal dream, unconsciously experienced by the frogs, is passed on to the poet who lays himself open to this experience. In another poem "Favourites of Pan", Lampman adapts Roberts' earlier poem "The Pipes of Pan" to suggest that the poetic voice of Pan (the "dream") is carried by the frogs.

In the first two books, the "dream" is the direct result of sense impressions from nature; in the long narrative poems, "The Story of an Affinity" and "David and Abigail", re-worked during the early 1890's, the "dream" carries the implications of religious or social "vision". In the first of these (title given as "My Story of an Affinity" by Bourinot[10]) we find in Margaret, a woman of sensitivity and independence, an embodiment of the topical feminism of Lampman's essay for the *Globe*:

> Give [women] perfect independence, place them upon an exactly even footing with men in all the activities and responsibilities of life and a result for good will be attained which is almost beyond the power of the imagination to picture
>
> (1892-93)[11]

Both Margaret and Abigail are women of charm and dignity whose actions have overtones of the philosopher-queen of "The Land of Pallas". Lampman's stress on the "Beauty" and "Peace" of this utopian land and the detail in which "the wise fair women" are described as bringing out baskets of food to their men in the fields, all suggest William Morris' *News from Nowhere* (1890), as does this conventional passage of Socialist economics:

> And all the earth was common, and no base contriving
> Of money of coined gold was needed there or known,
> But all men wrought together without greed or striving,
> And all the store of all to each man was his own.

The insertion into this utopia of a "ruin" describing "The woe and sickness of an age of fear made known" is equally suggestive of the museum of machines and the attack on codified religion from Samuel Butler's *Erewhon* (1872):

> And lo, in that gray storehouse, fallen to dust and rotten,
> Lay piled the traps and engines of forgotten greed,
> The tomes of codes and canons, long disused, forgotten,
> The robes and sacred books of many a vanished creed.

Most interesting is the concept of Pallas, "the all-wise mother" which seems to blend the earth goddess of the first nature poetry with "the wise fair woman", a development, perhaps, of the Pre-Raphaelite Burne-Jones' ideal by way of Morris' Ellen and Katherine Waddell. The noble women of Lampman's major narratives are all characteristically "grey-eyed", conforming in stature and in dignity to that ideal figure of "A Portrait in Six Sonnets":

> Grey-eyed, for grey is wisdom — yet with eyes,
> Mobile and deep, and quick for thought or flame
> A voice of many notes that breaks and changes
> And fits each meaning with its vital chord,
> A speech, true to the heart, that lightly ranges
> From jocund laughter to the serious word,
> And over all a bearing proud and free,
> A noble grace, a conscious dignity.

In "David and Abigail", the spiritual vision is associated with its feminine exemplar in the manner of Keats' *Hyperion;* Abigail's "high dreams" are related to the desire to emulate "those great women praised of old," a Miriam or Deborah whose courage and wisdom supported the tribe. To the lovestruck David who is plunged into "dreams" at the first sight of Abigail, she is, as the maidservant Miriam astutely remarks, "the vision of the wise fair woman". Similarly, in the long narrative poem, "The Story of an Affinity", the "vision" of Margaret is the catalyst which "burst[s] the bolted prison of [Richard's] soul" and transforms an aimlessly violent existence into the nobler "dream" of a formal education and the development of the self which will enable him to claim Margaret's love. Margaret's own dreams are for a life of which William Morris might have approved: "full of noble aims,/ A dream of onward and heroic toil/ Of growth in mind, enlargement for herself/ And generous labour for the common good." For Richard, the "dream" of Margaret proves a passport to the authentic self which guides him through ten years in the city and undergirds the shared "dream" of their future together.

This insistence on the "dream" or "vision" as the mainspring of human experience is sometimes likely to strike the modern reader as a somewhat naive wish-fulfilment device: Nabal, Abigail's gross, wine-bibbing husband is indirectly but conveniently dispatched from a love triangle by the after effects of a great, black "dream". Yet, even while amused at the facility of this structure, we are somewhat sobered by Lampman's earnest attempts to re-define the primary experience of his poetry, the "dream", in terms of a moral guide for man's behaviour in society. Like faith, the dream has the great advantage of being undeniable as it is at once its own genesis and justification.

Among the Millet and *Lyrics of Earth* demonstrate that the dream enabled

Lampman to write some of his most striking poems; the charm of the unusual narrative "In November" is the evocation of the tranced state in the mind of the observer-poet. Loitering in the November woods, he finds himself motionless amidst a group of mullein plants, and feels as if he has become "One of their sombre company/ A body without wish or will". A sudden ray of thin light, (associated with the glimpse "of some former dream") induces a moment of "golden reverie" to man and plant. The attraction of this poem lies in the nicely understated kinship between man and nature and also in the narrator's shock of emotional discovery, a discovery which we as readers share:

> And I, too, standing idly there,
> With muffled hands in the chill air,
> Felt the warm glow about my feet,
> And shuddering betwixt cold and heat,
> Drew my thoughts closer, like a cloak,
> While something in my blood awoke,
> A nameless and unnatural cheer,
> A pleasure secret and austere.

In this poem, as in the earlier poems, "Among the Timothy" and "At the Ferry", the dream is linked with Lampman's passive apprehension of nature and as such it does not interfere with his observations. In fact, it adds an effective (because unexplained) suggestion of the supra-natural. But serious problems do arise in later poems when Lampman attempts to invoke the dream in connection with vague abstractions and unrealized experience; the dream then becames a substitute for reality rather than an agent for perceiving it.

A rationale for the early "dream" experience together with some of Lampman's most characteristic uses of the word itself is to be found in the long narrative poem "An Athenian Reverie". A Greek watching "before the quiet thalamos" falls into a "reverie" compounded of the memories and associations of his past and present life. He views the land itself as if it were "breathing heavily in dreams" and speculates on the "dim dreams" of the wedding guests. Moving to a larger generalization, he concludes that love itself is "one all pampering dream" but this he rejects with the alternative of Tennyson's "Ulysses": "to me is ever present/ The outer world with its untravelled paths,/ The wanderer's dream." In this same Tennysonian vein, he describes as "greedy and blind" the multitude of people for whom life is a "dull dream" to which they never awaken. In contrast is the rich life of the man "who sees":

> to whom each hour

> Brings some fresh wonder to be brooded on,
> Adds some new group or studied history
> To that wrought sculpture, that our watchful dreams
> Cast up upon the broad expense of time,
> As in a never-finished frieze.

The process described here is actually the process of the poem itself, the dream or reverie which moves over the surface of the dreamer's life casting up memories and associations upon the mind. The Keatsian romantic rationale for the experience, reminiscent of *Endymion*, is also quite explicit:

> Happy is he
> Who, as a watcher, stands apart from life,
> From all life and his own, and thus from all
> Each thought, each deed, and each hour's brief event,
> Draws the full beauty, sucks its meaning dry
> For him this life shall be a tranquil joy.
> He shall be quiet and free. To him shall come
> No gnawing hunger for the coarser touch,
> No made ambition with its fateful grasp;
> Sorrow itself shall sway him like a dream.

The dream which is also the poetic process becomes at once a means of apprehending life and an antidote to it; detached from the surface flux of life man acquires both the god-like vision and the god-like immunity to pain.

The importance of this whole cluster of associations in Lampman's poetry is perhaps the imaginative conversion which he is enabled to make; in effect, he is able to reverse the categories of "dreams" and "reality". Because the "true life" of existence is available only to the detached observer in the dreaming state, reality itself can be dismissed as a harmless dream; the inspired dreamer will find "sorrow itself shall sway him like a dream". The great advantage of this structure is that the dream, coupled with the stoic stance, becomes a way of circumventing the pain of everyday reality.

THE PROBLEM inherent in this way of looking at the world is that it is not always possible to maintain the dream and so keep reality at bay. This difficulty is particularly apparent in poems such as the revised "Winter-Store" from *Lyrics of Earth* (1895). In the earliest poems, the high "dream" is sufficient to hold unpleasant reality in check; the "dissonant roar" of the city intrudes into the poetic dream but it does not take over. But, in the second version of the poem "Winter-Store", there is a schism between the two thirds of the poem which deals with the poet's "dream" in nature and his tranquil winter recollections, and the last third of the poem which is a sudden intrusion of the Socialist vision of the unhappy city. Lampman is no longer able to rest in a Meredith-like beneficent nature, at "one with earth and one with man". Instead the poem develops into a sudden and forceful "vision sad and high/ Of the laboring world down there":

> . . . through the night,
> Comes a passion and a cry,
> With a blind sorrow and a might,
> I know not whence, I know not why,
> A something I cannot control
> A nameless hunger of the soul.

If the voices of the frogs can bring assurance of nature's cosmic plan, the "dream" which underlies the flux of existence, there are other voices which remind Lampman of the fear and sorrow which are also a part of human life. The voice which comes out of the depth, "the crying in the night" of Lampman's much anthologized "Midnight" would seem to be part of a larger sequence of poems dealing with the fearful aspects of existence. In this sense, the comforting noon-tide "dream" has its complement in the midnight sleeplessness which will not allow "dream", ("New Year's Eve") or, as in Roberts' work, in the nightmare which grows out of the dream itself.

In the poem "Winter", strange voices rave among the pines, "Sometimes in wails, and then/ In whistled laughter, till affrighted men/ Draw close". The protagonist, Winter, becomes a fearful artist prototype:

> . . . Far away the Winter dreams alone.
>   Rustling among his snow-drifts, and resigns,
> Cold fondling ears to hear the cedars moan
>   In dusky-skirted lines
> Strange answers of an ancient runic call;
>   Or somewhere watches with his antique eyes,
>   Gray-chill with frosty-lidded reveries,
>   The silvery moonshine fall
> In misty wedges through his girth of pines.

The voice of Winter's "ancient runic call" becomes associated with cruelty and death: "The shining majesty of him that smites/ And slays you with a smile". In "Storm", the "blind thought" which impels the wind's cry is associated with repression. "All earth's moving things inherit/ The same chained might and madness of the spirit":

> You in your cave of snows, we in our narrow girth
>   Of need and sense, for ever chafe and pine;
> Only in moods of some demonic birth
>   Our souls take fire, our flashing wings uptwine;
> Even like you, mad Wind, above our broken prison,
> With streaming hair and maddened eyes uprisen,
>   We dream ourselves divine.

In "Midnight", the landscape is again desolate and associated with cold and snow; the narrator, alone and sleepless at midnight, hears some unidentified "wild thing" crying out of the dark. Because of his implied spiritual isolation, we tend to speculate that the voice which the poet hears is a projection of his own grief. Yet, significantly, Lampman does not admit the personal reference which indicates a consciousness of interaction between man and his surroundings as does say, Coleridge, in "Frost at Midnight", but prefers to assign the voice of fear to some undefinable part of the external world.

This poem seems to indicate some of the disadvantages of a theory of poetry which postulates that the mind must wander freely the better to apprehend nature's infinite dream. When weary and despairing, the poet's mind might well find quite opposite principles in nature to that of Hans Fingerhut's "cosmic optimism" yet even intimations of demonic forces must be equally accepted as truth because the mind has given up his own autonomy. We can speculate that as Lampman became more depressed — the burden of death, ill-health, a stifled affection and apparent public indifference to his work detailed in the letters to Edward Thomson; — the press of this reality becomes too strong for the protective dream structure and its opposite, the nightmare, takes over. Such a development is implicit in the metaphor and, we might infer, in Lampman's own personality. This tendency is prefigured even in the first book where the poetic voices of frog and cicada are replaced by the fearful cry of "Midnight".

In Lampman's work we see mirrored the dilemma of the later Victorian romantics; he accepted a romantic mythology — the Wordsworthian belief that it is possible to be "laid asleep in body" and so "see into the life of things" — at the very moment when changing social structures, the Darwinistic imperative, and above all, the loss of a settled faith, made it impossible to assert man's spiritual transcendence in nature. For most of his poetic career, Lampman seems to have willed himself into a denial of these facts: "Pan is gone — ah yet, the infinite dream/ Still lives for them that heed" until that time came when he was no longer psychologically able to participate in the comfort of nature's dream. It is then that there is a great press of new realities — assertions of man's continued cruelty to man, bitter indictments of social injustice, and horrible visions of religious persecution.

Perhaps, as Lampman's own "high dreams" for the future are shaken, he turns to the example of the protagonist of Tennyson's *Maud* and engages himself in the pursuit of the social good. The aspiring "dream" of social progress begins to replace nature's "dream", and this new direction in Lampman's thought is pointedly indicated by the title of his last book, *Alcyone* (1899). The name of this star is meant to suggest man's "wider vision", and this perspective, a Socialist evolutionary vision of cosmic design, is perhaps meant to be contrasted with the narrow and destructive insularity of the man of no vision, the "Idiot" (Greek, *idios*) from the poem "The City of the End of Things". This poem, a nightmare vision of the logical end of man's selfishness and greed, is a descriptive *tour de force* of the death-bringing city of machines.

At this time, Lampman was a member of an Ottawa group which met regularly to discuss Socialism and Science. Animations of Socialist thought, particularly the attack on wealth and social injustice ("To a Millionaire", "Avarice") and Socialist utopias ("A Vision of Twilight", "The Land of Pallas") now begin to fill the vacuum left by the "dream" in nature. Lampman has sometimes been described as a Fabian but his insistence on the social function of "Beauty" and "Art" would seem to suggest that he had been influenced by the aesthetic of William Morris. Certainly, the conclusion of "A Vision of Twilight" is particularly suggestive of the social "dream — vision" structure of Morris' conclusion to *News From Nowhere*. Yet, despite the framework of cosmic optimism provided for *Alcyone*, Lampman's Socialist heavens do not carry with them the beneficent assurance of nature's "infinite dream"; the poet-wanderer returns from his vision of the ideal city, as the first version of "The Land of Pallas" makes explicit, no longer able to find his way back to the social vision, and unable to make the inhabitants of the real city listen to his dream of a better world. In poems such as "The Land of Pallas" and "A Vision of Twilight", Lampman raises the same questions which had hovered on the fringes of his earlier verse — an inquiry into the meaning of life, especially the problem of evil. Such a rationale is provided by the inhabitants of vision city, "They declare the ends of being/ And the sacred need of pain"; but unfortunately, the narrator can no longer accept this truth and unquestioningly agree that "dreams are real, and life is only sweet." Instead, "A Vision of Twilight" concludes with an admission of a loss of faith: "But in veiling indecision/ Comes my question back again — / Which is real? the fleeting vision?/ Or the fleeting world of men?"

Yet, if we are to accept the pattern of rebellion and reconciliation implicit in Hans Fingerhut's experience, or to note the continually remade "dreams" of an Abigail or a Margaret which reassert themselves in lowlier forms in the face of adversity (Lampman was rewriting "David and Abigail" at the time of his "spiritual revolution") and to note that he was actively attempting to move out of the restrictions of his old nature poetry, we might conclude that Lampman was developing beyond the youthful Keatsian realm of "Flora, and old Pan" into a concern with "a nobler life . . . the agonies, the strife of human hearts". Lampman's later poetry, in particular, "A Portrait in Six Sonnets" dated by Scott 1895-99, is a direct inquiry into human personality in a manner that far exceeds the lovesick "dreams" of "The Growth of Love". This sequence also implies that the higher vision is now to be associated with Katherine Waddell: "Touched by her,/ A World of finer vision I have found."

Further, his stoic observation of 1895, "It is necessary for every man when he reaches maturity of understanding to take himself carefully to pieces and ascertain with pitiless scientific accuracy just what he is, then he must adjust his life accordingly," is a far cry from that boyish romanticism which had earlier led him to identify with Keats, and suggests that Lampman was undertaking that mental stock-taking which leads to a new vision of the self and of the world. In particular, his interest in Socialism would appear to be an attempt to move out of the restrictions of nature poetry into what he saw as the real world of men. Writing for the *Globe* in 1893, he argues that "the greatest poets . . . have been men of affairs before they were poets, . . . those men who have been poets only have belonged, however illustrious, to the second class." In April 1894, writing of an early poem derivative of Keats, he asserts, "I am only just now getting quite clear of the spell of that marvellous person."[11] In this context, we may see Morris' Socialist "vision" as Lampman's vehicle of escape. Such a movement from the romantic "dream" to a new sense of social reality would be consistent with the experience of Lampman's good friend and fellow poet, Duncan Campbell Scott. Like Lampman, Scott began to write under the influence of Keats and Charles G. D. Roberts but soon began to move away from the infantile reaches of dream (*The Magic House*, 1893) when he encountered the realities of Indian life (*New World Lyrics and Ballads*, 1905).

The poem which Lampman was working on four months before his death in 1899, "At the Long Sault: May, 1660", does reconcile man, nature and the social vision. It also suggests a new view of nature which is neither the entirely beneficent nature of the dream nor the entirely fearful nature of the nightmare: instead both beauty and fear co-exist within nature and are reconciled. If the poem begins in the old ideal mode, "The innocent flowers in the limitless woods are springing," Lampman for the first time admits that even a beneficent nature might have its serpent, the soaring "grey hawk" of the first stanza. Again for the first time, he does not try to escape this evil by assigning responsibility for it to the intrusion of the "toiling city", his own antithesis to a comforting nature. As a result, "At the Long Sault" becomes a moving acceptance of all "the savage heart of the wild" as Daulac's men, one by one, fall before the Iroquois:

> Each for a moment faces them all and stands
> In his little desperate ring; like a tired bull moose
> Whom scores of sleepless wolves, a ravening pack,
> Have chased all night, all day
> Through the snow-laden woods, like famine let loose;
> And he turns at last in his track
> Against a wall of rock and stands at bay;
> Round him with terrible sinews and teeth of steel
> They charge and recharge; but with many a furious plunge and
>   wheel
> Hither and thither over the trampled snow,
> He tosses them bleeding and torn;
> Till, driven, and ever to and fro
> Harried, wounded, and weary grown,
> His mighty strength gives way
> And all together they fasten upon him and drag him down.

The dream, no longer a passive gratification of the senses, is now the high ideal of heroic action for the good of society, the "sleepless dream" which impels Daulac and his men "To beat back the gathering horror/ Deal death while they may/ And then die." The town, safe and unknowing, does not "dream" that "ruin was near/ And the heroes who met it and stemmed it are dead." In the last stanza, reconciliation is achieved as violence modulates into pastoral: the metre of the poem changes to the lyric elegiac as the flowers of French chivalry are gathered back into the natural world:

The numberless stars out of heaven
Look down with a pitiful glance;
And the lilies asleep in the forest
Are closed like the lilies of France.

(1973)

NOTES

[1] Richard Hengist Horne, *Orion*, 10th ed. (London: Chatto & Windus, 1874), p. v.

[2] Archibald Lampman, *Lyrics of Earth: Poems and Ballads*, edited and with an Introduction by Duncan Campbell Scott (Toronto: Musson, 1925), p. 8.

[3] John Sutherland, "Edgar Allan Poe in Canada," *Archibald Lampman*, ed. Michael Gnarowski (Toronto: Ryerson, 1970), 159-78; Roy Daniells, "Lampman and Roberts," *Literary History of Canada*, ed. Carl F. Klinck (Toronto: University of Toronto Press, 1965), pp. 389-98.

[4] F. W. Watt, "The Masks of Archibald Lampman," *Lampman*, pp. 205-6.

[5] *Ibid.*, p. 206.

[6] Arthur S. Bourinot, ed., *Archibald Lampman's Letters to Edward William Thomson, 1890-96* (Ottawa: A. S. Bourinot, 1956), p. 33.

[7] "Copy of a Letter to Ralph Gustafson," *Lampman*, pp. 154-58.

[8] Scott, *Lyrics of Earth*, p. 38; Gnarowski, *Lampman*, p. xxiv; Bruce Nesbitt, "A Gift of Love," Canadian Literature, No. 50 (Autumn 1971), pp. 35-40.

[9] Lampman, *Lyrics of Earth*, p. 23.

[10] Bourinot, *Letters*, p. 18.

[11] Lampman, *Lyrics of Earth*, pp. 31-32.

A GIFT OF LOVE

Lampman and Life

Bruce Nesbitt

ARCHIBALD LAMPMAN is rightly remembered for the few nature poems illuminated by his personal "small clear flame". Unfortunately we are still waiting for a definitive biography to deal with all that annoying ash, those refractory clinkers that have to be swept away without putting out the fire. A tantalizing clue to the most important and disturbing single influence in Lampman's life, for example, was not made public until 1959, when Arthur Bourinot published some correspondence between Duncan Campbell Scott and E. K. Brown. These letters reveal the connection between a manuscript copy-book of Lampman's poems — acquired by the University of Toronto Library in the 1940's — and a Miss Katherine Waddell.

This copy-book is in fact one of five in which Lampman transcribed his poetry as he wrote it, and was presented by him (probably in 1893) as a gift of love to Miss Waddell. The volume, tentatively titled "Poems" (1889-1892) is the second of four that follow in a definite chronological sequence from 1883 to 1894. As well as containing 129 of the nearly 3,500 lines of Lampman's poetry that remain unpublished, it also affords an interesting commentary on the effects of what Duncan Campbell Scott tactfully called in 1925 "an intense personal drama" concerning his friend Lampman. By 1943 Scott felt free enough to publish "A Portrait in Six Sonnets" in *At the Long Sault and Other New Poems* as "the record of a friendship strong in affection, and, to judge by the last Sonnet, high in emotional value." But to whom do these infuriatingly oblique glances refer?

142

Katherine Thompson Waddell was twenty-one, four years younger than Lampman, when she joined his office in the Post Office Department on 18 January 1887. According to Scott, whose impressions were recorded by E. K. Brown in a private memorandum, their "love began in the early nineties and was still a powerful thing at the end of Lampman's life."[1] His sole confidant during these stormy years was E. W. Thomson, who was having an affair in Boston at the same time. Scott must have been less a friend to Lampman than he thought, for he only learned what happened from W. D. Le Sueur, Lampman's office chief, after the poet's death.

Part of the cause of their entanglement, Scott suggests, was devastatingly simple: Lampman "found his wife unsympathetic to poetry although she was very devoted to his study and practice of it — and thought that in this girl he would find a spiritual mate. The idea of spiritual affinities was very important to Lampman. . . . His wife was not such an affinity." Although Lampman was sure that Katherine was a soul-mate, she was apparently unresponsive.

In a (mercifully) unpublished and untitled poem written in September 1893, Lampman expressed a quaintly ambiguous and tepid passion:

> I may not love you dearest
> And you may not love me
> Tho' one in truth and nearest
> I think our hearts must be
>
> And so from fear not knowing
> What advent, what surprise
> Might bring the overflowing
> We meet with coldest eyes
>
> For fear of things sincerest
> We pass and let it be
> I may not love you dearest
> And you may not love me.

By the following February it is clear that Katherine was determined merely to be polite, while her less than ardent suitor plunged himself in misery:

> Couldst thou but know my secret heart
> The sorrow that I dare not tell
> The passion that with bitterest art
> I hide so well . . . .
>
> Ah couldst thou know this and descry
> The sorrow and the dull despair

> Wouldst thou but smile and pass me by,
> Or wouldst thou care?

Scott firmly attests that Lampman failed to circumvent the moral propriety of Ottawa and Miss Waddell; the affair remained "spiritual", since at its height Lampman's wife bore him a son and apparently remained a good friend of Katherine. Although Scott was a very coy witness concerning his friend, another unpublished poem that Lampman confided only to his scribbler in 1895 suggests that Scott was right:

> Sweeter than any name
> Of power or blessing, tumult or of calm,
> The pride of any victory with its palm,
> Than praise or fame —
> The love we bear to women in our youth
> When ardour cleaves to ardour, truth to truth,
>
> When Beauty cuts her sheaf
> And flings its loaded ardour at our feet
> But bitter, bitter! even as this is sweet
> The gathering gulf
> Of passionate love misplaced, or given in vain
> The love that bears no harvest save of pain.

While it would be unsound to imply that Lampman's poetry was profoundly affected by his friendship with Miss Waddell, it is clear that his inability to resolve his personal conflicts, and particularly his love for Katherine, heightened his instability to the point of creative breakdown. There exists positive documentary evidence, moreover, to indicate that at this time his vaguely humanistic sentiments were being sharply focussed into poems of social protest. Lampman's letters to E. W. Thomson describe his "spiritual revolution; the manuscript book he presented to Katherine reveals some of the results of this disturbance.

In the manuscript version of "Winter-Store", written in December 1889, Lampman had simply declaimed the joys of recollecting summer's fruits in the tranquillity of winter. In the version published in *Lyrics of Earth* (1895), however, he dropped this view, together with the opening twenty-eight lines, to substitute a bitter poem first published in the Toronto *Globe* for 19 November 1892. The "time of songs" of the original version became, through the rearranged stanzas of "Vision" from the *Globe*, a time of spiritual desolation as intense as the "nameless hunger of the soul" that seized the poet at the end of the poem. When

Lampman suggested that we must stop "refashioning what was once divine", he was speaking of man, not Gatineau timber-farms.

At the same time Lampman had long been "constitutionally sensitive to a morbid degree", and it might be difficult to ascribe the tone of his unpublished "Individual Duty" (alternatively titled "Life") to Miss Waddell's influence, much less Poe's. Although it is the opening poem in the manuscript book he presented to her, it was possibly written before she rejected him:

> Housed in earthen palaces are we
> Over smouldering fires,
> When through the flames creep witheringly,
> Doubts and hot desires,
> And our souls in that dense place
> Lose their grace.
>
> Some forever grope and climb
> Toward the outer air,
> Some into the nether slime
> Slip and stifle there,
> Others with alternating mind
> Wander blind.
>
> Yet each palace — this we know —
> Hath one central tower,
> Round about it breathe and blow
> Winds for every hour,
> And its spire through ether driven
> Enters heaven.
>
> At its base a narrow slit
> Gleams and that is all;
> And the daylight slants through it
> Like a solid wall.
> Enter lest thou find that door.
> Nevermore.

It is no accident that the spire of each palace enters heaven, for Lampman could always see beyond the "vast seething companies" of frustrated mankind to "the banner of our Lord and Master, Christ". He was less certain of the role of a Church he regarded as corrupted. In "The King's Sabbath", probably written as early as 1884, the King replies to a priest's petulant reminder that it is Sunday by holding the burning bush in his bare hands. By the 1890's in an untitled piece in the Toronto manuscript Lampman is rather more direct:

How dealt the world, Oh Christ, with thee,
　　Who shrank not from the common rod,
Whose secret was humility?
　　They mocked and scourged, then hailed thee God!

And built out of thine earnest speech,
　　Whose gift was for the simplest needs,
Whose meaning was in all men's reach,
　　The strangest of phantastic creeds.

While Lampman's more bitter and despondent poetry may usually be termed poetry of social protest only by broad definition, it is significant as an early contribution to that thin stream which is as figuratively seasonal as the Canadian economy. We might also take it nearly as seriously as Lampman himself did, if we accept his statement written three years before his death:

> We form an ideal of ourselves and claim what seems to be due to that ideal. The ideal of myself is entitled to love and approbation from my fellow creatures — but the love and approbation does not appear and I feel and abuse the constitution of things. To the ideal of myself money and power and practical success are no doubt due, but they do not come and again I abuse the constitution of things.

Lampman's letters and unpublished work suggest that Katherine Waddell's "love and approbation" came to be his greatest hope, and their denial his most frustrating disillusionment. It is scarcely surprising, then, to discover that with three possible exceptions — "The Vagrant" (still unpublished), "The King's Sabbath", and "Freedom" — his poetry of social protest was written during and after his "crisis" over Katherine.[2] We may properly suspect that Canadian literature lost no great poet of social protest at Lampman's premature death in 1899. Nevertheless as one of those "poor shining angels, whom the hoofs betray", both in his poetry and his semi-tragic life, Lampman continues to typify an aspect of that curiously thwarted radicalism which every Canadian appears to carry within him.[3]

(1971)

NOTES

[1] E. K. Brown Papers, Public Archives of Canada. The following three poems are also transcriptions in the Brown Papers made by E. K. Brown from Lampman's notebooks.

[2] See Library of Parliament, Ottawa, four holograph MS copy-books by Lampman entitled *Miscellaneous Poems, Alcyone, David and Abigail,* and *The Story of an Affinity.*

[3] Remaining unpublished poetry from the Toronto MS is: an untitled four-line fragment, and the four-line stanza originally concluding "The Land of Pallas" (called in the MS "The Happy Land" and, in the identical version in the *Alcyone* MS, "The Country of the Ought-to-be"), both noticed by F. W. Watt in his "The Masks of Archibald Lampman," UTQ, 27, (January 1958) ; a complete 54-line poem "The Old Berserker," dated October 1889; and seven lines from "After Rain," originally the third stanza. The stanza appearing in the Memorial Edition of Lampman's poems was written on 27 April, 1895, and appears as a revision of f. 7ᵛ of the MS.

PIPER OF MANY TUNES

Duncan Campbell Scott

Gary Geddes

WㅤHAT STRIKES ONE most forcibly about D. C. Scott is
his versatility, his wide range of ability and interest; he is, in fact, the one breath
of fresh air escaping from the mixed bag of Confederation poets. Scott not only
has a deep response to nature, like his contemporaries, Roberts, Carman and
Lampman, but he has also added to this a genuine appreciation of the savage, a
Browningesque monologue, and a sophisticated sense of form and mission. And
yet, in spite of this diversity, there is an unexpected narrowness in the way in
which critics have discussed his poetry. In his own time, Scott complained about
"the cant of the more careless critics to keep dinging away that all Canadian
poets are nature poets".[1] Half a century later, his public image is equally distorted: Pelham Edgar has found it necessary to rationalize Scott to the twentieth
century by singling out Scott's "original response to the wilder aspects of the
Canadian scene".[2] Recognition of his primitive verse was necessary and justified,
but what began with Edgar as a special emphasis has become in the intervening
years an institution. It is now possible, for example, for Professor Daniells, in
the *Literary History of Canada*, to conclude that Scott's reputation rests ultimately on a small group of poems, such as "Night Hymns on Lake Nipigon", and
that "*only nature* [italics mine], and preferably nature in her most primitive and
untamed aspect, is capable of releasing Scott's powers as a poet."[3] This one-sided
view of Scott's poetry indicates a failure to see him within the context of the
nineteenth century, where most of his best verse belongs; furthermore, the attempt
to modernize Scott obscures his larger significance. Scott was already sixty when
"The Wasteland" was published and he was too firmly rooted by age and temperament in the nineteenth century to respond favourably, no less creatively, to

the prophecies of Yeats and the arid, shifting sands of the twentieth century. To expect Scott to be concerned with imagistic modes, cross-fertilization of metaphor, and so on, would be tantamount to expecting the later Milton to have written neoclassical satire. If evaluation of his poetry is to have any meaning, Scott must be reclassified; he must be seen alongside not his temporal but his spiritual mentors — Coleridge, Tennyson and Arnold. In what follows, then, I have tried to approach Scott's poetry through the medium of his published letters, with a view to dispelling a number of misconceptions concerning his aims and achievement; at the same time, I have been tempted to look freshly at some old favourites, especially "The Piper of Arll".

To reclassify Scott as a nineteenth-century poet is less seriously limiting than one might think. "Give me some credit for logic as applied to aesthetics," he wrote in 1905, "for I declare that I value brain power at the bottom of everything. If you call *me* a nature poet you will have to forget some of my best work."[4] These are not the words of a man denying his artistic destiny, but rather the sincere expression of a desire to be seen in the right perspective. Scott fully understood the place of nature in his poetry, but he believed that some of his best work derived its stimulus from elsewhere — from man and from the life of the imagination itself. I would like to discuss his poetry from these three points of view — nature, man, and the life of the imagination. This plan is not meant to provide a rigid tripartite division of Scott's poetry or to suggest arbitrary pigeon-holes for poems having an integrity of their own; on the contrary, it is a more fertile and flexible way to approach Scott, and one which is at least consistent with his expressed views of his poetry.

Scott responded to nature in the best traditions of romanticism — appreciation without prostration. While unwilling to prostitute himself emotionally and artistically to the enchanting elements and terrain of Canada, Scott nevertheless recognized their imaginative possibilities. "The life of nature", he declared, "is as varied and complex as the life of the spirit and it is for this reason that man finds in nature infinite correspondences with his spiritual states."[5] Fundamental to this impressionism, however, is the understanding that nature is not a repository of "truth", but rather the means by which man's own important sensations are elicited and activated. Nature remains subordinate to man, a vast reservoir from which he draws at will; it is but one of the means by which man may penetrate to the truth of his own sensations. Scott quoted Amiel's statement that "landscape is a state of soul," insisting that "in the apprehension of some such truth lies the sole excuse for poetry in which nature is described."[6]

In "The Height of Land", his most philosophical poem, nature becomes an incentive to reminiscence and reflection. The poet stands on the uplands in the serenity of evening, brooding about the lives and ideals of men. His senses sharpen to the hush of wind and the play of moths around a low fire, so that he can almost hear the "gathering of rivers in their sources". As he surveys the land in this hyper-sensitive state, a mysterious "Something comes by flashes/ Deeper than peace", as unexpectedly quiet and intriguing as the calm at the eye of a hurricane.[7] At that moment the state of the land may be said to reflect exactly the state of the poet's mind. The symbiosis is prelusive to finding a "deeper meaning" than is written on the surface of things. The poet's emphasis is centred not on the details of the physical scene, but on the impression which it fixes on his mind; thus, it may be seen, his reflections on life constitute a somewhat higher level of participation in nature — that is, a philosophical rather than a purely descriptive involvement.

Scott's insistence, that nature can only provide correspondence to man's spiritual states, is perhaps more rigorous than his practice justifies. In the same poem, for example, a significant change of pace occurs. Suddenly the smell of charred ground transports the poet back in time to a bush-fire he has experienced:

> Then sudden I remember when and where, —
> The last weird lakelet foul with weedy growths
> And slimy viscid things the spirit loathes,
> Skin of vile water over viler mud
> Where the paddle stirred unutterable stenches,
> And the canoes seemed heavy with fear,
> Not to be urged toward the fatal shore
> Where a bush-fire, smouldering, with sudden roar
> Leaped on a cedar and smothered it with light
> And terror.

There is something more instinctive than rational in the way this image is presented. Although the landscape is technically a state of soul, the image of the predatory bush-fire seems rather to have been dragged up involuntarily from the poet's subconscious than to have resulted from a conscious search for secondary correspondences. The sheer force and immediacy of the experience clearly indicates that Scott's response to nature was, at times, stronger than his theory suggests. Certainly this passage supports the emphasis that Daniells and Edgar place on Scott's susceptibility to the more turbulent aspects of his environment.

Similar spontaneous responses to nature occur in "September" and "In Winter", but Scott is at his most lyrical and unrestrained in "Ecstasy". Witnessing the upward flight and the jubilant morning song of the shore-lark, the poet is moved to ecstasy:

> The shore-lark soars to his topmost flight,
> Sings at the height where the morning springs,
> What though his voice be lost in the light,
> The light comes dropping from his wings.
>
> Mount, my soul, and sing at the height
> Of thy clear flight in the light and the air,
> Heard or unheard in the night in the light
>   Sing there! Sing there!

Coming in the wake of Shelley's "To a Skylark", "Ecstasy" invites comparison. As Dr. Johnson would have observed, Shelley's imagination soars higher and is longer on the wing; his intellectual and artistic powers equip him for a more profound and sustained flight. "Ecstasy" does not pretend to be profound or philosophical. Whereas Shelley uses the flight as a sustained metaphor, Scott keeps to its simpler, more immediate appeal. Less ambitious in scope, "Ecstasy" is nonetheless skilfully contrived; it is also free from the undue strain which length and poeticality place on Shelley's poem. With an almost breathless rhythmical sweep, a pronounced absence of simile and poetic diction, a predominance of crisp consonants and light palatal vowels, Scott captures the upward flight of the shore-lark. And this is no small accomplishment with a lark of the less sophisticated, Canadian, shore-bound variety!

From the poems already mentioned, it would not be difficult to equate Scott's rejection of the "nature poet" label with Wordsworth's *post facto* denial of his own phrase, "worshipper of nature". No doubt both poets do protest too much. At the same time, however, Scott was too classical in his tastes to countenance an over-abundance of feeling and a deficiency of art. Nature poetry, characterized in his mind by excesses of emotion and description, stands here opposed to "brain power" and "logic as applied to aesthetics". As such it is below the dignity of serious poets. "One of my faiths is expressed by Ben Johnson [sic]," Scott said, " 'It is only the disease of the unskillful to think rude things greater than polished.'"[8] Like Jonson himself, Scott was a careful craftsman. "You could find plenty to say about metre and I have invented not a few new stanzas," he insisted. "I have not been self-conscious in practice; my desire was to make the thing under my hands as perfect as I could make it."[9]

Scott was pleasantly surprised to have pointed out to him by E. K. Brown the "intensity and restraint" in his poetry.[10] Consciously or unconsciously, Scott had long been pursuing this elusive goal. In his introduction to Lampman's *Lyrics of Earth*, he quoted Coleridge's famous statement: "In poetry it is the blending of passion and order that constitutes perfection."[11] Scott's respect for the guiding and restraining influence of traditional forms and metres parallels Coleridge's claim that metre originates psychologically, "to hold in check the workings of passion".[12] Control is the standard for both art and life. In "Ode for the Keats Centenary", Scott praises Keats,

> Who schooled his heart with passionate control
> To compass knowledge, to unravel the dense
> Web of this tangled life.

"The Woodspring to the Poet" describes the "vast wave of control"; "In a Country Churchyard" asserts the "moderate state and temperate rule".

THE CLASSICAL BALANCE between passion and order, which Scott shared with Coleridge and Arnold, is best illustrated in "At Delos", a poem which is unexplainably absent from Brown's edition of the *Selected Poems*, but included in A. J. M. Smith's *The Book of Canadian Poetry*:

> An iris-flower with topaz leaves,
>   With a dark heart of deeper gold,
> Died over Delos when light failed
>   And the night grew cold.
>
> No wave fell mourning in the sea
>   Where age on age beauty had died;
> For that frail colour withering away
>   No sea-bird cried.
>
> There is no grieving in the world
>   As beauty fades throughout the years;
> The pilgrim with the weary heart
>   Brings to the grave his tears.

"At Delos" illustrates finely the meeting and mingling of the classical and the romantic in Scott; it is a beautiful and delicate rendering of a romantic grief at the passing of beauty, handled not subjectively but impersonally, and with classical restraint.

While admitting the influence of nature in his poetry, Scott hoped to make clear that his main interest and stimulus was in man. "It is inevitable that we should deal with nature and somewhat largely," he wrote to J. E. Wetherell in 1892, "but I think it will be found that much of this work rises from and returns again to man and does not exist from and to itself." [13] Even his impressionism, which asserts the superiority of the impression to the object, reflects Scott's humanism. Similarly, he despised all types of artistic escapism and obscurantism as much as he despised the mindless veneration of nature, because both led away from the proper study of mankind. He had only contempt for Yeats, who required a "fund of Irish legends to set imagination aglow".[14]

In "Ode for the Keats Centenary", Scott lamented the loss of beauty from life — "Beauty has taken refuge from our life,/ That grew too loud and wounding" — but his Indian and habitant poems reveal that he discovered beauty again in the very noise and wounds he had lamented, in the beauty of human suffering. In "The Height of Land", Scott paused to "Brood on the welter of the lives of men", but he did not pause long; he plunged beneath the surface of beaver-skins and tail-feathers into the dark recesses of the human heart. And the raw life he found there is quite distinct from anything outside of Pratt in anthologies of Canadian poetry. The tragic killing of Keejigo in "At Gull Lake: August, 1810" is a dramatic *tour de force*:

> At the top of the bank
> The old wives caught her and cast her down
> Where Tabashaw crouched by his camp-fire.
> He snatched a live brand from the embers,
> Seared her cheeks,
> Blinded her eyes,
> Destroyed her beauty with the fire,
> Screaming, "Take that face to your lover."
> Keejigo held her face to the fury
> And made no sound.
> The old wives dragged her away
> And threw her over the bank
> Like a dead dog.

The strength here is not descriptive but dramatic; Scott combines the economy of the ballad, the human interest of the drama, and the suspense of both.

The difficulty Scott had in subduing his subjective and descriptive impulses was largely dispelled when he embraced the human drama. In "At the Cedars", a fascinating dramatic monologue, the narrative is exceedingly stark — boiled right down to the skeleton. Bones, at any time, are provocative, and these are no exception; consequently, the temptation to find allegory in the suggestive names — Isaac, Baptiste and Virginie — and the *diabolus ex machina*, is subdued only by the rapid pace and intensity of the narrative. As in the ballad, much of the success of "At the Cedars" depends on what is left unsaid; the poem gains considerably by the indefiniteness of the motives in the suicide of the nameless sister of Virginie:

> There were some girls, Baptiste,
> Picking berries on the hillside,
> Where the river curls, Baptiste,
> You know — on the still side;
> One was down by the water
> She saw Isaac
> Fall back.
>
> She did not scream, Baptiste,
> She launched her canoe;
> It did seem, Baptiste,
> That she wanted to die too
> For before you could think
> The birch cracked like a shell
> In that rush of hell,
> And I saw them both sink.

To call Scott a poet of nature in these poems can only be justified if one means what Dr. Johnson meant when he applied the same label to Shakespeare — *human nature.*

While responding creatively to man and nature, Scott also rejoiced in the fervid life of his imagination. "The life of poetry is in the imagination," he insisted, "there lies the ground of true adventure and though the poet's mind may be starved and parched by the lack of variety in life, he persists nevertheless to make poetry out of its dust and ashes." [15] Much of his poetry finds its life not in external stimuli but in an internal compulsion, in the "volcano", as Scott called the imagination.[16] And it is there — in the heat of imagination — that one of Scott's finest poems arose, Phoenix-like from the ashes. "The Piper of Arll" stems from, and is itself a poem about the life of the imagination.

"The Piper" has had a poor press; critics seldom fail to mention it, but always for the wrong reasons. John Masefield, the poem's most vigorous supporter, no doubt began this negative reinforcement. Faced with the challenge of defending "The Piper" against a charge of meaninglessness, Masefield side-stepped the issue: "let it escape", he said of the symbolism, the "romantic mood and the author's dream may be of deep personal significance and joy, even if the author's thought eludes us." [17] Criticism of this sort we can do without. Indeed, nothing could have been more damaging to the poem's reputation at a time when wit and intellect in poetry were at a premium. Subsequent criticism reveals quite clearly that Masefield unwittingly closed the doors on serious study of "The Piper": Pelham Edgar, for example, praises the poem as "musical incantation"; W. J. Sykes asserts that it seems "too tenuous, too unsubstantial to induce that 'willing suspension of disbelief' " and lacks "concrete meaning"; Daniells also notes that "Even the often quoted 'Piper of Arll' is lacking the compulsion of true magic"; even E. K. Brown, whom the meaning does not elude, nevertheless finds the poem a "mass of suggestions which do indeed lack definiteness".[18]

Criticism of "The Piper" seems based on the mistaken assumption that meaning and indefiniteness are mutually exclusive. That the poem is intentionally vague and mysterious there can be little doubt. "At the root of everything is mystery," Scott wrote. "Poetry illuminates this mass of knowledge and by inspiration will eventually reach the core of the mystery." [19] He preferred the poetry of Maeterlinck, who was "endeavouring to awaken the wonder-element in a modern way, constantly expressing the almost unknowable things we all feel".[20] To convey the mystery and wonder surrounding our daily lives, the poet requires a special vocabulary. As Scott says in "Meditation at Perugia": "Our common words are with deep wonder frought." Scott laboured, of set artistic purpose, to leave "The Piper" indefinite and suggestive; he aimed at a fusion of form and content. "He may not care for the mystical," Scott said of his critic, Sykes, "but there is more in 'The Piper of Arll' than he seems to have discovered." [21]

"The Piper" may be seen on one level as an allegory of the artist. Living in harmony with his idyllic environment, the artist is confronted with a vision of loneliness to which he responds creatively. When the vision passes and inspiration dies, his remorse drives him to such distraction that he abuses his powers of compassion and communication:

> He threw his mantle on the beach,
> He went apart like one distraught,

> His lips were moved — his desperate speech
> Stormed his inviolable thought.
>
> He broke his human-throated reed,
> And threw it in the idle rill;
> But when his passion had its mead,
> He found it in the eddy still.

Through conscious self-renunciation the artist begins to heal and he resurrects out of the ashes his initial heart-felt response to the vision. When this is accomplished, in a burst of selfless creative energy he pours out his soul in perfect harmony with the world and is reunited with his dream-vision in a beautiful immortality.

The nature of the poetic experience, thus oversimplified, is essentially religious, and it is almost certain that Scott intended the parallel to run throughout the poem. Given his desire for indefiniteness and suggestiveness, it would be trite to observe that the image of the three pines in "The Piper",

> There were three pines above the comb
> That, when the sun flared and went down,
> Grew like three warriors reaving home
> The plunder of a burning town,

is less obviously and less effectively symbolic than the similar image in Eliot's "Journey of the Magi". Scott's simile works well as a symbolic pre-figuring in nature of the piper's experience: as the image of the plunder-laden warriors comes at sunset, is lost in the night, and then returns, so also the piper receives, loses, and then regains his artistic "loot" — his inspiration — from the vision ship. The problem of the loss of inspiration is stated more explicitly in "Prairie Wind":

> But the vision you found in the twilight,
> You could never again recapture,
> It was lost in one careless impulse
> In the first wild rush of the rapture.

The piper's loss, however, is not so permanent; he is able to recapture the fleeting vision:

> He mended well the patient flue,
> Again he tried its varied stops;
> The closures answered right and true,
> And starting out in piercing drops,

> A melody began to drip
> That mingled with a ghostly thrill
> The vision-spirit of the ship,
> The secret of his broken will.

The "secret of his broken will" may mean simply the necessary conversion of inspiration to elbow-grease which all serious artists learn, or it may refer to what Eliot calls "depersonalization" — "a continual surrender . . . to something which is more valuable. The progress of the artist is a continual self-sacrifice, a continual extinction of personality." [22]

The poem does support a religious interpretation of the image of the three pines. The piper responds to God as the bay responds to the ocean's tides. The vision-ship comes with an angel at the bows, who departs just as the piper achieves his immortality. The piper's broken will corresponds, of course, to the Christian paradoxes of life in death, fulfilment in self-sacrifice and knowledge through child-like faith. At the moment of his mastery over passion and power, the piper is standing at the foot of the three pines, "Immortal for a happy hour". The piper must learn the lesson which the woodspring teaches in "The Woodspring to the Poet": "Give, Poet, give!/ Thus only shalt thou live./ . . . Give as we give unbidden." This responsiveness or sympathy cannot be achieved otherwise than by instinctive humility, by an unconscious giving of self. This achieved, the piper's powers are restored:

> He, singing into nature's heart,
> Guiding his will by the world's will,
> With deep, unconscious, childlike art
> Had flung his soul out and was still.

He has experienced the reconciliation which was achieved by the Ancient Mariner when he blessed the water snakes unawares.

The intriguing conclusion of "The Piper", in which the intimations of immortality are realized, is the artistic equivalent of Elijah's translation:

> And down she sank till, keeled in sand,
> She rested safely balanced true,
> With all her upward gazing band,
> The piper and the dreaming crew.
>
> And there, unmarked of any chart,
> In unrecorded depths they lie,
> Empearled within the purple heart
> Of the great sea for aye and aye.

Their eyes are ruby in the green
Long shafts of sun that spreads and rays,
And upward with a wizard sheen
A fan of sea-light leaps and plays.

The *Tempest*-like sea change implies a concept of art as stasis. Life, in Scott's poetry, is a movement towards eternal rest, a rest which is common to all men — the poet, the religious and the oppressed of every kind. Even the violent death of Keejigo in "At Gull Lake" becomes a release from suffering, a final, beautiful merging with the natural cycle of the universe. The accompanying storm brings the rainbow; the moon changes its shade for the perfect glow of the prairie lily. Her death is a victory, a final reward: "After the beauty of terror the beauty of peace". Like Keejigo, the piper achieves his rest; first his will and then his body merge with the harmonious cosmos.

So much for the lack of meaning in "The Piper". Most of what is best in poetry, as Frost suggests, is lost in the translation. While a too extensive explanation of "The Piper" would destroy a good deal of its magic, existing criticism deserves to be challenged. What is important in the present discussion is that the poem be reconsidered as fundamental to an understanding of Scott's poetic achievement. These remarks are a suggestive rather than an exhaustive step in that direction.

NORTHROP FRYE has cited Scott's poetry as a prime example of what he calls the "incongruous collision of cultures" — the primitive and sophisticated — to be found in Canadian literature.[23] To be accurate one would have to add classical and romantic, natural and mystical. And yet the results are neither incongruous, nor a collision. Scott does not jar by throwing his various interests together pell-mell into a single poem; "On the Death of Claude Debussy", "At the Cedars" and "The Piper of Arll" have an integrity of their own. Scott's many-sidedness stems not so much from his wide areas of interest as from his conception of the function of poetry.

The responsibilities of the poet are outlined in "The Woodspring to the Poet", Scott's poetic manifesto. The woodspring presents himself as an exacting master. He counsels the poet to cultivate flexibility (a good Canadian virtue!), to be all things to all men, a sort of general practitioner whose task it is "To charm, to comfort, to illume". To fill this colossal order the poet must write poems of every kind: he must write those which will guide and inspire youth, "Till over his spirit shall roll/ The vast wave of control"; he must nurture the creative spirit with poems like "The Piper of Arll" —

> Give them songs that charm and fill
> The soul with an alluring pleasure,
> Prelusive to a deeper thrill,
> A richer tone, a fuller measure;

and, finally, he must administer to the dead souls of academe and the market-place a particularly metaphysical cure:

> Helve them a song of life,
> ... Proud pointed with wild life,
> Plunge it as the lightning plunges,
> Stab them to life!

This broad view of the function of poetry beggars the notion that Scott was only a nature poet. Whatever his creative stimulus — whether nature, man, or the life of the imagination — Scott directed his various melodies to the needs of the human heart; and if his poetry has a wide-spread appeal, it is because Scott was a piper of many tunes.

(1968)

NOTES

1 A. S. Bourinot, ed., *More Letters of Duncan Campbell Scott* (2nd Series) (Ottawa: A. S. Bourinot, 1960), p. 68.
2 Pelham Edgar, "Duncan Campbell Scott," *Leading Canadian Poets* (Toronto: Ryerson, 1948), p. 213.
3 Roy Daniells, "Crawford, Campbell and Scott," *Literary History of Canada*, ed. Carl F. Klinck (Toronto: University of Toronto Press, 1965), p. 421.
4 A. S. Bourinot, ed., *Some Letters of Duncan Campbell Scott and Others* (Ottawa: A. S. Bourinot, 1959), "Autobiographical Note."
5 D. C. Scott, ed., "Introduction," *Lyrics of Earth*, by Archibald Lampman (Toronto: Musson, 1925), p. 44.
6 *Ibid.*
7 All citations from Scott's poetry, unless otherwise indicated, are from *Selected Poems* (Toronto: Ryerson, 1951), and *The Poems of Duncan Campbell Scott* (Toronto: McClelland and Stewart, 1926).
8 Bourinot, *Some Letters*, "Autobiographical Note."
9 *Ibid.*, p. 30.
10 E. K. Brown, *On Canadian Poetry* (Toronto: Ryerson, 1943), p. 122.

[11] Scott, *Lyrics of Earth*, p. 45.

[12] S. T. Coleridge, *Biographia Literaria, II*, pp. 49-50.

[13] Bourinot, *More Letters*, p. 68.

[14] *Ibid.*, p. 25.

[15] Scott, *Lyrics of Earth*, p. 37.

[16] Bourinot, *Some Letters*, p. 29.

[17] Quoted in Brown, *On Canadian Poetry*, p. 124.

[18] Edgar, "Duncan Campbell Scott," p. 217; W. J. Sykes, "Duncan Campbell Scott," *Queen's Quarterly*, XLVI (1939), p. 60, 52; Daniells, "Crawford, Campbell and Scott," p. 418; Brown, *On Canadian Poetry*, p. 124.

[19] Bourinot, *More Letters*, p. 28.

[20] *Ibid.*, p. 25.

[21] Bourinot, *Some Letters*, p. 47.

[22] T. S. Eliot, "Tradition and the Individual Talent," *Selected Essays* (New York: Harcourt, Brace & World, Inc., 1960), pp. 6-7.

[23] Daniells, *Literary History of Canada*, p. 825.

THE WOUND UNDER THE FEATHERS

Scott's Discontinuities

Glenys Stow

K̲EEJIGO, STAR OF THE MORNING, victim of the battle between the instinctive and the cerebral worlds, is perhaps the most striking emblem of the tension which gives dark power to the best of Duncan Campbell Scott's work. "At Gull Lake: August 1810" was published in the poet's old age;[1] but it is a tale set in the prairie country which he explored with the painter, Edmund Morris, in 1906, and it represents not a falling away from vigour but a resurgence of the energy of "those great journeys".[2] All the typical images of the Scott landscape come together forcefully in this poem. The peaceful lake and serene heavens are rent by storm. The girl, innocent yet barbaric, her face painted with exotic patterns, stands between the tents of the corrupt white trader and the savage, revengeful chief of her people, longing for love, and rejected by both men. Daughter of a white hunter and a native woman, Keejigo calls for a reconciliation of warring worlds in her love lyric, at an emotional level which seems far beyond the capacity for comprehension of the embittered Scotsman who is the object of her passion. She is herself the divided world, delicate yet powerful, the star of the storm, "the wind and the flower". Like the crane she hides in fear, yet suffers the destructive power of the wolverine and the trap. The "wound under the feathers" can only be healed, the trapped foot released, by the love for which she will shortly be killed. The peace which heals the wound can come only when death extinguishes the possibility of love. The bitter old women of her tribe torture her. Her face is branded by the husband whom she has shamed. But now the mood changes, for "After the beauty of terror/Comes the beauty of peace." The wilderness of which she is a part takes her back and hides her, so that "Only the leaves of autumn, the snows of winter/Knew where she lay."

The serenity which marks the ending of this poem, where the protagonist surrenders herself to the protection of her mother the earth, is present in only a few of Scott's verses, spaced rather widely through his literary career. Perhaps only "The Forsaken" (1905) and "Lines in Memory of Edmund Morris" (1915) conclude on a comparable note of resolution. A larger body of his work is worth examination, much of it concerning native characters or legends, but in many of these poems the conclusion is melancholy, and the persona's division left unhealed. Given the haunting quality of his handful of effective lyrics, it is strange that Scott has been, in terms of critical evaluation, the most neglected of the "Confederation poets". His name has appeared, musically but with a dying fall, at the end of the familiar catalogue, following Roberts, Carman, and Lampman with a monosyllabic finality which seems to close the door on the nineteenth century and the "Maple Leaf" school. He is remembered as a wilderness poet, as a painter of striking Indian word-portraits, as the fanciful creator of "The Piper of Arll". E. K. Brown, Desmond Pacey, A. J. M. Smith, and Douglas Jones have noted the demonic or tragic power in some of his verse and short stories, but few critics concern themselves with the bulk of the work of this prolific writer. Their decision is not surprising; much of it is traditional, popular and bland. It is in the contrast that the question lies. The stark malevolence of the medicine man Powassan etches its way into the reader's mind with puzzling insistence. Why did the poet who produced by the innocuous dozen such lyrics as "November Pansy" and "Lilacs and Humming Bird" rise at times to heights of melodramatic tension? And having reached them, what were the compelling polarities which almost always prevented him from resolving the tension into "the beauty of peace"?

It is worth observing first that Scott's presence in the nineteenth-century catalogue is misleading. At the date of Confederation he was only five years old; he began publishing in 1893 and continued until 1947. While his political thinking tended towards paternalism and his social life was that of the golden Edwardian afternoon, he experimented in his better verse with a number of the techniques used by later twentieth-century poets. As a pre-Freudian, he did not consciously express psychological conflict in symbolic terms, but his most effective work contains a striking array of repeated images which are worth examination beyond the denotative level. His protagonists engage themselves in an often ferocious relationship with the primitive elements of earth, air, fire and water. A series of opposites is explored; light and darkness, joy and hatred, action and powerlessness, terror and peace, form tensions which begin to be felt in his earliest poems, and which reappear in various guises, seeking their resolution, throughout his fifty-four years of writing.

Of the mass of varied material contained in Scott's nine major publications, only sixteen poems and a few essays and short stories are directly based on Indian material or contain relevant references. It is within this small body of verse and prose, however, that most of his imaginative power is concentrated. His first collection, *The Magic House* (1893)[3] included reflections on nature, melancholy meditation, nostalgic love poems, descriptions of Quebec and Ontario scenes, and some melodramatic action, but no native themes. In his second volume, *Labour and the Angel* (1898),[4] the first sombre tones of racial disquietude were sounded in his pages, embodied in characters notable both for their vitality and their anger. In "Watkwenies" and "The Onondaga Madonna" the dark, brooding, suffering woman of an alien blood first took visible form in Scott's work. The portrait in the second poem is familiar, of the young woman rebellious at the destruction of her tribe, defending by her hostile stance the power and cohesiveness of her past, yet contributing to her people's disintegration by giving birth to a young warrior "paler than she" and burdened with an instinctive knowledge of his own division. The old woman of "Watkwenies" was once the embodiment of the vengeance which the Onondaga Madonna longs for. In her youthful strength as one of the "triumphant Iroquois" she stabbed and drowned a white sentry, glorying in the blood dripping from her wrist. In old age her strength has gone, and her final end is a degrading one, since the hand that once held a dagger now fondles the white agent's treaty money.

These matching sonnets have little originality of technique, but they outline vividly a subject of great importance to the poet, the portrait of woman divided. This fission cannot be solved by courage and endurance, though both protagonists possess those qualities, for the force opposing them is not environmental savagery or the callousness of their own people. It is the development which Scott saw as the doom of this "weird and waning race", the power of white commerce and custom. Indian values dwindle before this force, as the war-whoops of the Iroquois have dwindled into the cries of boys playing snow-snake in the winter cold.

On the rational surface of his mind Scott approved of this change from the old ways. His reason rejected violence; he held classical calm and restraint as an ideal, and he labelled passionate action "savage" or "pagan". This attitude was to be expected in a man who held for fifty-three years a position in the federal civil service, and who rose to become Deputy Superintendent General of the Department of Indian Affairs. Addressing the Fourth Biennial Conference of the Institute of Pacific Relations at Hangchow in 1931, he mentioned with admiration the progress which Indian people had made in education, health, military service, the professions and trades. He described the Canadian Government's efforts to hasten this progress, and spoke hopefully of the day when "the Indians progress into civilization and finally disappear as a separate and distinct people, not by race extinction, but by gradual assimilation with their fellow citizens."[5]

The sombre mood of Scott's verse, however, projects little optimism over the advantages of the new culture. The Agent in "Watkwenies" brings only money for the old woman, and no more lasting values; the young madonna has been used by some vanished white man for his own pleasure, and is left to bear the resulting physical and mental burden alone. The "savage" qualities which the rational mind would eradicate bear in the poetry a power which excites a reluctant admiration. The pride of the revenger as she stands over her drowning victim, the "pagan passion" which burns and glows in the face of the tragic young mother, are not negligible qualities, though outside the Protestant ethic in which the poet had been raised, and the European cultural tradition to which he was intellectually committed. Scott's professional and social life conformed to the latter patterns; he was a dedicated civil servant, lived peaceably in a city house, and numbered many contemporary artists and scholars among his friends. The wilderness people over whom he had administrative control, however, assumed increasing importance in his mind as he took, at intervals from about 1883 onwards, a series of canoe journeys into the North. First with his close friend Archibald Lampman and later with Edmund Morris and Pelham Edgar, he came to know the contour and nature of the land and some of the characteristics of its primitive inhabitants while listening to tales told by traders and guides, narratives as sinister and melodramatic as the French Canadian legends which had excited him as a child.

IN THE GROUP of poems on the wilderness life contained in *New World Lyrics and Ballads* (1905),[6] we can detect the uncertainty about cultural values which Scott felt during these journeys. Some lyrics, such as "Roses on the Portage" and "Night Hymns on Lake Nipigon" convey the beauty of landscape evocatively, but present native skin colour and speech as uncouth and ugly. In places the imagery seems deliberately weighted in favour of the European mode. The Indians of the first poem are blessedly incapable of noticing the beauty of flowers, for if the "swarthy Arcange" were to pluck a rose, she would only be filled with sadness at her own comparative crudity. The choice of a rose as the item of comparison suggests the poet's detachment from the real nature of his subject in this instance. The legends of the Ojibwa, in whose land he was travelling at the time of composition, show an intense awareness of natural phenomena, and indigenous flowers such as the trillium or jewel-weed are woven into the tales with delicate and particular observation. In using the rose, however, Scott is appealing to the European mind and suggesting a simple solution to the choice between North American darkness and barbarity and the delicate culture of the old world. A parallel imbalance is implied in "Night Hymns", where the ancient, serene values of the Christian world, exemplified by the Latin hymn "Adeste Fideles", are ranged against the sad, harsh, unhistoric sounds of the "long-drawn Ojibwa". White prejudice seems triumphant within the poet; yet while his reason patronizes the native people, his emotions are powerfully drawn to the scene of which they are a part, to its passionate contrasts, its rhythmic sounds and silences, its lightning and darkness. The mingled syllables of the two languages echoing above the lake unwittingly convey Scott's own ambivalence. The unknown now repels, now attracts. In "Indian Place Names" he changes ground, celebrating the musical quality of the native cadences. Of Restigouche and Mirimichi, Manowan and Kamouraska, he says: "All the land is murmurous with the call/Of their wild names." Wildness was the intrinsic nature of the land which Scott came to love, yet fear, the wildness of the mallard and the wolverine, of the lonely waterfall and the frozen lake. It was also the nature of the people who stood uncertain on the border between old and new ways, and who simultaneously fascinated and appalled the poet by their symbolic representation of a division not only their own, but his.

In the two poems concerning native journeys to a mission settlement, the choice between two cultures again presents itself. In the poorer example, "The Mission of the Trees", a Christian father and child are cast out by their tribe in the hungry depths of winter. The father staggers through the storm, bearing his son's dying body, while the boy experiences a vision of the mission chapel awaiting him like Paradise. Both perish in their agonizing effort to reach civilized serenity. In "On the Way to the Mission" Scott is not so sanguine about the advantages of white culture. Here the Indian protagonist is a heroic figure, his face calm, his eyes "jewels of content,/Set in circles of peace"; but his heart is filled with sorrow as he pulls a toboggan heavy with the body of his dead wife. He is taking her to the Christian mission for burial; but to cut him off from European value comes European greed, in the shape of two ruffians eager for what they believe to be a load of furs, who destroy him before his journey's end. As he falls across his wife's corpse "on a shield of moonlight", he takes on a chivalric nobility which stands in striking contrast to the corruption and cowardice of his white murderers. When they tear away the covers and find what lies beneath, the tableau achieves a Tennysonian elegiac quality, as the moonlight gleams on the ivory features of the Montagnais woman, and on her braided hair. The tension between good and evil is graphically and melodramatically conveyed, and this time there is no doubt about the intrinsic value of the native character. One is reminded of a passage in "The Last of the Indian Treaties", where Scott describes a young man making his occasional contact with the fringes of white settlement:

> He seemed about twenty years of age, with a face of great beauty and intelligence, and eyes that were wild with a sort of surprise —. . . . There was the Indian at the best point of a transitional state, still wild as a lynx, with all the lore and instinct of his race undimmed, and possessed wholly by the simplest rule of Christian life, as yet unspoiled by the arts of sly lying, paltry cunning, and the lower vices which come from contact with such of our debased manners and customs as come to him in the wilderness.[7]

The doubtful influences of the invading civilization here outweigh the advantages of assimilation. Left alone, the native as Scott sometimes sees him possesses a dignity and skill which allow him to affirm his place in the environmental pattern. The writer's psychic dilemma is perhaps most effectively stated, and for the moment solved, in his most familiar poem from *New World Lyrics and Ballads,* which shows a native woman cut off from outside help or injury, fighting an elemental battle alone. Scott never describes the values of middle-class white life with the persuasive empathy which he brings to the stark northern landscape of "The Forsaken". In its narrative balance, accurate sensory detail, simple language and fluid line structure the poem represents the peak of his technical skill; while philosophically the bitter tensions seen elsewhere in his verse, all potentially present in those events, resolve themselves into an unprecedented peace and acceptance.

The two episodes of "The Forsaken", each relating a crucial experience in the protagonist's life, take place in winter. In each she is alone, with no aid but her own ingenuity and endurance, facing a killing storm. In the first part she is young, isolated on a frozen northern lake, far from human help either red or white, and having dependent on her a starving infant. The short dactylic-trochaic lines reflect her youthful vitality, the strong heart beating, perhaps the memory of distant tribal drums. Powerful rhythm and harsh onomatopoeic word choice convey the violence of the storm, as the lake-surface "Stream(s) with the hissing/ Of millions of iceflakes/Hurled by the wind." Her reaction to the challenge is vigorous. With concrete and accurate detail Scott describes her skilled use of native tools, the rabbit-bone hook, the twisted cedar-line, with which she fishes for food for herself and hence milk for the "young chieftain" whom she is nursing. Her courage is stronger than cold and hunger, stronger finally than the pain of mutilation, as she pays for success by baiting the hook with her own flesh. The storm slackens, the rhythm slows, but only into a tramp of endurance three days long, which at last brings her to the protection and smoky peace of the white man's fort.

The mood, tone, rhythm and language of the second section are in strong contrast to those of the first. The woman has grown withered and old. Now the long journey is retraced, not with a small child, but with the whole family group, the companions of a lifetime. Once more she is abandoned, not by accident now but deliberately, and by the son and the son's sons to whom she gave existence. Her vigour has gone; she is a splintered tool. Gathering up their more useful gear, the family members quietly disperse, leaving behind them this "paddle broken and warped". Long meandering irregular lines imply her loss of power, but repetition of a short strong phrase from Part I, "valiant, unshaken", tells us that this loss is not defeat. The long lines acquire a Biblical sonority and impressiveness as the old woman, "her breasts spent with the nourishing of children", begins to merge herself into the tranquillity of the landscape. The vigour and activity of her youth are translated into peace and acceptance, without pain or fear. Now the storm comes, not with hissing violence, but with benediction. On the third day, where once long ago she had reached the peace of the fort, she is covered deep and silent with a shroud of snow, with only a wavering column of breath, persisting till set of sun, to tell of the unresisting ebb of her spirit, "gathered up by the hand of God".

"The Forsaken" repeats a number of the motifs noticed in Scott's other verse; isolation, faced with endurance in a hostile landscape; the sufferings of a woman, caused as so often by a man or group of men; mortal conflict, conveyed symbolically by a storm resolving itself into a peace and acceptance which means death for the protagonist. In this poem, however, the result of the battle is not ambiguous. At the appropriate time, human skills prove their survival value; but, her function ended, the central figure can willingly melt back into the landscape which nurtured her, without any sense of futility, anger or waste.

Very few of Scott's women achieve this kind of serenity. In the only other collection of verse made before the hiatus in his publishing from 1907 to 1916, we see again the figure of a woman as the object of tension between two life-styles. In "The Half-Breed Girl", first published in the brochure *Via Borealis* (1960),[8] the Indian daughter of a Scottish father is torn by subconscious longings for "The gleam of loch and shealing,/The mist on the moor", a torment which she may resolve only by thoughts of suicide. Again the writer's uncertainty emerges in symbolic form.

Elsewhere in the same volume he tries to solve the dilemma. "Spring on the Mattagami" describes the poet's love for a European woman, but also conveys his sense of the enervating corruption of her environment, all "fraud and fame and fashion". He longs to bring her to his land of "quintessential passion", where the interplay of light and darkness, storm and peaceful aftermath, will awaken her to more significant life. The language, dramatic situation and philosophical content of this derivative poem are uniformly distressing, but the central event reflects Scott's conflict rather effectively. His best verse presents the violence and passion of natural man, but he continually persuaded himself that he was a writer of classical rationality and balance. In letters he stated that intense emotion needed the restraints of conscious craftsmanship and rigorous thought. Despite his interest in local folk-tales, he expressed scepticism about the symbols, allusiveness and fluid and remote legend[9] which he saw in Yeats' work. Image and feeling were, so he said, merely "circumstances for the process of thought".[10]

THE RESULTS of his conscious craftsmanship can be seen in the bulk of his verse. Most of it is formally patterned, expressing all the repectable nine-teenth-century attitudes towards nature and man, tediously derived from Arnold, Tennyson, and Rossetti. This is work drawn from the level of sensibility which made him rate Bridges a more genuine artist than Yeats. It includes sonnets and ballads, dramatized narratives and tableaux, eulogies on landscape, and romantic melan-choly tales. Literary borrowings are fairly frequent. "In a Country Churchyard", in memory of his father, has its obvious antecedent. "Avis", the tale of a languish-ing maiden in a tower, is only one of the many versions of "The Lady of Shalott" which Scott attempted. His later work includes patriotic verse ("To a Canadian Lad Killed in the War"), commemorative poems on European artists such as Keats and Debussy, and that odd experiment, "Variations on a Seventeenth Century Theme", which is written partly in pseudo-medieval diction and partly in dramatic dialogue. Little of this verse, so much greater in quantity than his Indian material, has any verbal or emotional impact.

Occasionally in his non-Indian work, however, the classical bonds slip loose, and images congregate in passionate and grotesque confusion. In a letter written late in his life to E. K. Brown, he revealed that one poem at least, "Amanda", was based on a dream experience,[11] and it seems likely that some similar form of sub-rational activity may have been the basis for a number of works in which the imagery is compelling but difficult to assess intellectually. A study of these images suggests that Scott's divided outlook was the result of tensions more personal and deeply felt than a merely cultural clash. "Amanda" itself, published in 1947, but dreamt, as the letter tells us, many years earlier, is a chilling tale of a young girl engulfed in a dark pool which has been created for the express purpose of destroying her, and which disappears after her death. Engulfing and destructive water, negating its natural life-giving properties, is a non-rational image repeatedly found in Scott's verse. It appears early, in his first volume, in a poem which foreshadows much of his later power, "At The Cedars". When Baptiste leaps exultantly above the battling logs, only to be caught by them, crushed, and drowned in the rushing torrent, active and joyful virility is quenched by the force which should represent life. When the girl to whom this wilderness spirit kisses his hand launches her canoe, the first of Scott's women to accept the power and violence of the Canadian environment comes into vital existence. Yet the water, symbol of fertility, destroys them both. Love celebrates life only at the point of death. This poem, like "The Piper of Arll" in the same volume, shows Thanatos quenching Eros with a completeness which leads D. G. Jones in *Butterfly on Rock*[12] to comment on the intensity of Scott's struggle to recover the dynamic life buried within himself and his environment.

Stifled instinctive forces project themselves in a variety of oblique images in some of the lesser verse. *The Magic House* contains at least two poems of puzzling aspect. "By the Willow Spring" is a Tennysonian variation on a well-known fairy tale motif. A "fragile daughter of the earth", changeable in mood as the seasons, loves to sit and watch beside a magic pool. She lays flowers beside it each day, but evokes no response. She has no golden ball of fruitfulness to offer, and in this spring there is no enchanted prince to rescue it and become transformed by her love. Beside the sterile waters she withers and dies, like the flowers. It is a slight and dated tale; yet how consistently Scott's lesser women fade. "In the House of Dreams" in the same volume assembles a much more incongruous but suggestive collection of images. The Lady Lilian, waiting before an arbour, contemplates a number of vertical objects; sheaves of barley, a blade of gladiolus, a poplar, a fountain poising aloft a golden ball and a frosted serpent protecting the fertile water and the female symbol. Anon comes "a little naked lad" who proceeds to demolish the gladiolus, and, after much struggling with the "ponderous thing", to smite the snake, meanwhile calling a magic name. (Scott does not elaborate. . . .) One can hardly make sense of this very bad poem in any other way but as a dream sequence embodying sexual imagery. In the last stanza, as the snake is cut in two, the garden explodes into an orgasmic storm, leaving the reader a little more cheerful about the fate of the Lady Lilian than about the maiden by the willow spring. Scott's storms so often destroy, however; if Lilian does not fade through lack of love, she is probably mutilated by her psychic experience, like the vivid Keejigo (in "At Gull Lake: August, 1810") of whom she is a flimsy preliminary sketch.

Male-female tensions and longings seem to provide, probably unconsciously, much of the energy which drives Scott's verse. Men and women are either consumed by their passions or annihilate each other. In the title poem of the 1898 volume, "Labour and the Angel", the central figures are a blind man and the golden-haired girl who leads him up and down a farm field on the treadmill of his grim and oppressive toil heaping "dark coloured beets" row upon row into a barrow. The girl is the angel, loving and protective, yet her cry to the man is "Effort!" and the cheek which she fondles is scarred. Sightless amid images of castration, the man can experience nothing but grinding labour and the agony of storm, followed by a peace which represents only pity. In his Oedipal blindness, man can expect little joy from his relationship with woman, except when she is held at an idealizing distance; closer up, she will smother or emasculate him. The protagonist of "The Dame Regnant" in the same volume shows how viciously formidable the female can become, "Personed like a regnant queen/Cold as pole-ice, hard as quartz". In "Night Burial in the Forest" from *Via Borealis*, she brings death to the power and beauty of man, and the landscape is instinct with horror, expressed characteristically in a macabre flame/darkness contrast:

> Let the birchbark torches roar in the gleam
> And the trees crowd up in a quiet startled ring. . . .

As betrayer of love, or as smothering mother figure, woman can stifle man, as the emotions may stifle the reason. Man in the early poems is the lost wanderer, the blind and impotent labourer, or the helpless infant at the breast. Only once in a while, as in "At the Cedars", is he free and virile. Even more often, though,

it is the woman who is cast in the role of victim, torn in two by unresolved longings, suffering physically, fading or exploding into death. If man and woman
meet, they can achieve a loving union only in common annihilation. Water, the
life and fertility symbol, consistently destroys.

What circumstances in Scott's personal life might predispose him to such a
bleak subconscious view of heterosexual emotion? Like many other nineteenth-
century Canadian intellectuals, he was the son of a minister, who in Duncan's
childhood served on a Methodist circuit in the Eastern townships and the Ottawa
Valley, but who had in earlier years been a missionary to Indian tribes on the
Lake Huron area. William Scott was fifty years old when the poet was born.
Isabella Campbell MacCallum was his second wife, and his first family was
already grown. Scott spoke warmly of his happy childhood and indulgent parents,
who surrounded him with the best examples available to them of letters, music
and art.[13] Along with this, however, he was taught the controlled behaviour
expected of a minister's son; and as the only boy in this second family of girls,
with a father necessarily somewhat remote through age and occupation, he must
have been continually aware of female values. The protective pastoral charm of
his childhood surroundings is conveyed in many of his short stories about the
area, published in *In The Village of Viger*[14] and *The Witching of Elspie*;[15] but
these tales also vibrate with other qualities that fascinated him in peasant life,
and which were almost certainly hooded and repressed in his own home. Figures
of power and violence appear in his pages. Isolation, melancholy and madness
occur often, and some characters are terrifyingly grotesque. Such a one is "The
Pedler", an object of mystery and fear to the village people, who in anger tears
off his protective goggles to reveal, not the rapacious eyes of a demon, but the
"seared fleshy seams where those eyes should have been". Blindness and impotent
frustration are close to demonic violence, both in this tale and in the title story
from *The Witching of Elspie*, where an old man's perverse passion for a young
and beautiful girl is the motive force behind a plot of chilling suspense. The man
is a "loup-garou", a were-wolf who can represent himself in the girl's eyes as
handsome and virile and enchant her spirit away from her real lover. His power
can be exorcized only by branding his body with red-hot metal shaped into the
sign of the cross. By this means the child is saved and the seducer driven out.
The unresolvable tension between desire and propriety forces him into the
seclusion of a monastery, where daily physical torment distracts him from the
agony in his mind.

Gentleness and violence, controlled rationality and explosive passion, form polarities between which Scott oscillates continuously. Culture and affection tie him to the quieter patterns of life; yet while he fears the wilder powers, they attract him irresistibly. His masculinity seems to be crying out for expression. His better writing is filled with urgent emotion, with suffering characters both male and female, longing for release.

Is this the same poet who wrote such lyrics as "Hill Path" ("Gently, gently, little wind" — the storm restrained by good manners.)? Does the moral ending of "Madonna with Two Angels" (a white Madonna now, tranquilized and passive) represent the major tenor of Scott's thought?

> Ponder here in the orchard nest
> On the truth of life made manifest:
> The struggle and effort was all to prove
> That the best of the world is home and love.

A comforting bourgeois ethic; but how intrinsically false to the conclusions of his more lasting work. The civilized pole of his psychic world, so conscientiously served by the bulk of his verse and by his daily work, has none of the hypnotic force that its passionate opposite exerts on him and on his readers. On his strenuous canoe journeys to visit northern tribes, made at intervals over a period of about twenty years, he lived more intensely, though more bleakly, than in most of the rest of his long life. Here he encountered the objects which dominate his more powerful and divided verse, the rapids and lakes, the granite rock face and the tempest, and the native people, torn between past and present. Nothing could form a greater contrast to the pleasant but restricted correctness of his parental home and the serene and balanced values which his rational mind believed in.

Yet while even some of his early poetry spoke of escape, in practical affairs he made little attempt as a young adult to break with his home restrictions. He took a safe job and married respectably; but it is interesting to note that his marriage to a rather well-known American musician antagonized his mother and sisters to such an extent that with his mother the breach was never healed. If his family was possessive, and his marriage an attempt to escape female domination, he was unfortunate in his choice of a wife. Belle Warner Botsford was a strong-willed woman of superior gifts who did not help her introspective husband to express or resolve his conflicts. Before long his emotional life seemed centred on his only child Elizabeth. When she died suddenly in 1907, aged twelve years, and he received the news in a brutal telegram, "Elizabeth morte", he wrote to Pelham Edgar, "We have both suffered too much: I think every fibre of our souls was ingrown and tangled with hers. In no merely rhetorical way I say it seems impossible for us to go on. . . . If I might be there now by one of those still deep lakes with my friend, as it was last summer, I might get some rest."[16] He published no more for nine years. Even his handwriting became shaky and indecipherable. One of the two well-springs of his emotional life had been tragically quenched, in ironic mortal enactment of the virginal deaths so often portrayed in his verse.

After the long hiatus caused by this sorrow, his other source of imaginative strength, the northland, was again to serve him well. As he gradually resumed writing and gathered the results in *Lundy's Lane*,[17] the northern landscape once more became, in his better work, the symbolic geography of his psychic explorations. In "The Height of Land" he stands on the ridge of ancient rock dividing the civilized but corrupt southland from the wilderness and plays out another act in the drama between culture and freedom. Storm-clouds dominate the sky. The bushland is beautiful but dangerous. Douglas Jones has noted the horrifying intensity of the swamp verse,[18] where the "skin of vile water over viler mud" presents no escape from the fierce power of the fire on shore, which ". . . with sudden roar/Leaped on a cedar and smothered it with light/And terror." Life-giving water and light, like fertile and loving woman, have again become sinister and foul. Yet, on the other hand is only confusion, "The crowded southern land/ With all the welter of the lives of men"; and the wilderness gives peace and natural beauty as well as horror. The poet, "Wrapped in his mantle on the height of land", searches for an answer. Arnold and the American transcendentalists contribute much to his posture and his conclusion. Now his resolution is not death, but an escape upwards into realms of intellectual joy far above the battling waters, where light is free-flowing and radiant.

The same philosophical escape, the Platonic expression of pure mind, appears in "The Eagle Speaks", published in *Beauty and Life* (1921),[19] where passionate instinct, significantly in the shape of an Indian warrior, is brutally blinded, scalped, and dashed to the ground by the triumphant bird, who proceeds to soar above the snarls and bickerings of lower forms of life . . .

> Into the region where, after vivid action,
> Thought rises the immortal ghost of action,
> Above the orb where space assembles silence,

> Where all the ache and effort of this petty life
> Are quieted with silence.

Such a resolution is of doubtful validity, as is the poetic quality of the verse. Scott is now more clearly attempting to express masculine values of physical strength and competence, independence and intellectual detachment, but the male protagonist in this poem is arrogant and brutal, enjoying the fight more than the conclusion, which leads to a large void. Violence is still more powerful than peace. The transcendental leap is here a failure.

In "Powassan's Drum", added to the collection *Poems of Duncan Campbell Scott*[20] in 1926 and written the previous year, brutality and hate are triumphant. The drum beats which called the young woman home in "The Forsaken" are calling here too, but with sinister intent. Age and vindictive power, in the shape of Powassan the medicine man, seem to dominate all nature, and even to be the heart of it, the "pulse of being". As he crouches in his bark shelter, his eyes burning through the ancient worn eyelids, Powassan waits balefully for his victim, and the world waits with him from the rise of the morning star to the time when the sun draws in his net full of stars like flashing fish to the shores of night. The sky is tense like a blue-grey bubble with waiting; the hand of a storm-cloud, with a bracelet of bright fire "sharp as pain", gropes across it. The scene is set for a characteristic explosion: but first appears the terrible object of this venom, called up by the incessant throbbing of the drum. A canoe glides into sight, in which sits a warrior, young, powerful — and headless. The severed head trails through the dead water, its hair grasped in nerveless fingers. The man is the personification of masculine strength, but he has been struck impotent. The unquenched eyes burn up through the water, towards their "throne on the shoulders of power". Male vigour and independence are destroyed by blighting, instinctive evil, and the dark waters engulf the corpse as the inevitable storm applauds in its wild vortex the triumph of the old man's magic.

This poem is probably based on an Indian legend, as was "The Forsaken". Most tribes tell tales of supernatural horror, of headless men or severed hands, or of the blood-thirsty Wendigo or Tsonoqua who devour men. These tales are only part of the native folklore canon; humour, whimsy, sentiment, explanations of natural and cultural phenomena, and proverbial history, wisdom and mortality are also the basis of much story-telling. To Scott, however, the macabre was of overwhelming importance, and in this strange but gripping poem the central situation is once again powerlessness. The slaughtered Indian seems to suggest humane values, but he is eliminated, and the serene heavens are blackened into chaos.

Powerlessness also pervades "A Scene at Lake Manitou", published in *The Green Cloister* in 1935. This is a documentary scene rather than a wild nightmare and shows a tribe confused and diminished by the acquisition of white possesssions and religious ideas. The passionate energy usually present in the Indian verse is missing here, but the persona is worth noticing. She is an old woman who, having lost her husband, attempts to save her son's life by magical prayer, first to the white deities, Jesus and Mary, and then by sacrifice to the Manitou of the lake. Both fail her. The boy dies. The two cultures are alike in their impotence.

It would seem at this juncture as though Scott was able to do little in his verse but express repeatedly, with female imagery or with male, his psychic conflict. In 1905, however, in "The Forsaken", he had reached his first reconciliation of warring elements, and in 1915, in a poem written during his "silent" period, he came to a similar conclusion. The loss of his daughter was perhaps too deeply felt to yield itself to memorable expression, as his lyric series, "The Closed Door", suggests; but in his elegy to a friend he speaks of death in a calmer voice. "Lines in Memory of Edmund Morris" was another result of the climactic 1906 journey to the north-west. Written after Morris was drowned in 1913, the poem is an imaginary letter to the painter, Scott's close friend and travelling companion. It describes the virginal stillness of the pre-dawn prairie which they crossed together, the shifting colours of dawn and sunset, and the spare intense sensory life of the Blackfoot teepees. Scott recalls the death of one of the oldest warriors, once vigorous and fleet of foot, now in his old age blind and spent, creeping along a rope in the warm sun. Before his death comes a sudden resurgence of power. Akoose, with "all his instincts cleared and quickened", leaps from a withered old age to re-enact in a brief entranced episode the life of hunter and warrior, before sliding from his pony in the shelter of a bluff, to become more fully in death a part of the timeless natural world. He sleeps beneath the poplars, as much part of the land as its prehistoric inhabitants "clamped in their rocky tombs".

> Who shall count the time that lies between
> The sleep of Akoose and the dinosaurs?
> Innumerable time, that yet is like the breath
> Of the long wind that creeps upon the prairie
> And dies away with the shadows at sundown.

In the deaths of Akoose and Keejigo, as in that of the woman in "The Forsaken",

Scott seems to reach a reconciliation of his warring elements, and an acceptance of both his instinctive and his cerebral drives. Although the "wound under the feathers" is not apparently healed either by passion or by the achievement of civilized serenity, yet these three protagonists find their peace at last in their native earth. Keejigo's passion, moving so rapidly from serenity to violence and back again, is natural to the land which she resembles. The fluctuation of energy and peace is the motive pattern of all three poems. Scott's fluctuation, too, as he expresses a cultural division, and beneath that a personal division common among those raised in his particular milieu, is perhaps more closely in touch than at first seems evident with the duality of the land which nurtures both tribes and individuals. In him, as Layton puts it, "nature's divided things have their fruition."[21] His lyric energy is that of the violent, changeable climate, the thrusting green growth, the luminous treacherous waters of the wilderness, and in his better work he can accept the consequences of this untamed power. The waters of fertility and spontaneous life had in much of his verse been too threatening for him to accept; they darkened into quenching pools or vicious storms. The forest fire of passion brought terror and destruction. The upper air of rational philosophy promised a deceptive serenity which dissolved into emptiness. When the protagonists are received by the protective earth, however, the tensions are resolved, ending the battle between man and woman, joy and hatred, light and darkness, action and powerlessness, calm and storm, reason and passion. It is in these characters, the woman in "The Forsaken", Akoose and Keejigo, that "the wound under the feathers" is healed.

Scott achieved in his second marriage in 1931 an emotional stability unknown in his earlier life. His range of friends and interests widened, and his last publication is entitled *The Circle of Affection*.[22] E. K. Brown recalls him in his old age speaking of the arduous canoe trips long ago, and describes him, quoting Pater's words from *Marius the Epicurean*:

> It is the one instance I have seen of a perfectly tolerable, perfectly beautiful old age ... in which there seemed ... nothing to be regretted, nothing really lost in what the years had taken away. The wise old man ... would seem to have replaced carefully and consciously each natural trait of youth, as it departed from him, with an equivalent trait of culture.[23]

In the conclusion of "Lines in Memory of Edmund Morris" Scott relates physical and spiritual life together in the image of a sun-ripened fruit which, splitting, looses a golden kernel to the ground to complete the life-cycle. It is a symbol of his own desire for completion. The world, and man within it, ripening, will set free a platonic essence where opposites blend and reconcile:

> Where the appearance, throated like a bird
> Winged with fire and bodied all with passion
> Shall flame with presage not of tears, but joy.

(1974)

NOTES

[1] D. C. Scott, *The Green Cloister* (Toronto: McClelland and Stewart, 1935), pp. 54-58.

[2] E. K. Brown, "Memoir," in *Selected Poems of Duncan Campbell Scott* (Toronto: Ryerson, 1951), p. xxviii.

[3] D. C. Scott, *The Magic House and Other Poems* (Ottawa: Durie, 1893).

[4] D. C. Scott, *Labour and the Angel* (Boston: Copeland and Day, 1898).

[5] D. C. Scott, "The Administration of Indian Affairs in Canada" (The Canadian Institute of International Affairs, Aug., 1931), p. 27.

[6] D. C. Scott, *New World Lyrics and Ballads* (Toronto: Morang, 1905).

[7] D. C. Scott, *The Circle of Affection and Other Pieces in Prose and Verse* (Toronto: McClelland and Stewart, 1947), p. 122.

[8] D. C. Scott, *Via Borealis* (Toronto: Tyrell, 1906).

[9] A. S. Bourinot (ed.), *More Letters of Duncan Campbell Scott* (2nd Series) (Montreal: Quality Press, 1960), p. 24.

[10] Brown, "Memoir," p. xxvii.

[11] Bourinot, *More Letters of Duncan Campbell Scott,* (2nd Series), p. 86.

[12] D. G. Jones, *Butterfly on Rock* (Toronto: University of Toronto Press, 1970), p. 20.

[13] Brown, "Memoir," p. xii.

[14] D. C. Scott, *In the Village of Viger* (Boston: Copeland and Day, 1896).

[15] D. C. Scott, *The Witching of Elspie* (New York: Doran, 1923).

[16] Bourinot, *More Letters of Duncan Campbell Scott* (2nd Series), pp. 34-35.

[17] D. C. Scott, *Lundy's Lane and Other Poems* (New York: Doran, 1916).

[18] Jones, *Butterfly on Rock*, p. 106.

[19] D. C. Scott, *Beauty and Life* (Toronto: McClelland and Stewart, 1921).

[20] D. C. Scott, *The Poems of Duncan Campbell Scott* (Toronto: McClelland and Stewart, 1926).

[21] Irving Layton, *A Red Carpet for the Sun* (Toronto: McClelland & Stewart, 1959), no. 58.

[22] Scott, *The Circle of Affection and Other Pieces in Prose and Verse.*

[23] Brown, "Memoir," p. xii.

CARMAN
AND TRADITION

Donald Stephens

It is amazing, though not surprising, what Bliss Carman means to a majority of Canadians. They think back to school days, hesitate, and mention "Low Tide on Grand Pré", falter over whether or not he wrote "Tantramar Revisited", muse over "Vestigia" ("I took a day to search for God"), and lapse into memories of other school days in other times. For the people in the Maritimes, things are different, but not much. Thanks to the New Brunswick Tourist Bureau, Fredericton is called the Poet's Corner of Canada, with the elms —some decayed—magically reminiscent of the vaulted ceilings of the other Poet's Corner in Westminster Abbey. At the University of New Brunswick there is a plaque dedicated to Carman, Roberts and Sherman, and a bronze bust of Carman in the foyer of its library whose much needed haircut receives jibes from students and professors alike. Once a tree was planted at Carman's grave ("Let me have a scarlet maple for the grave-tree at my head") but that was twenty-five years after his death, and was brought to the attention of the university by an American tourist, and the university succumbed in an anniversary mood. People mumble about Carman, and are proud. His poems are not fondly remembered; rather, there is an apathy, a superficial awareness that a poet once roamed the New Brunswick fields, wrote a few poems, was a nice boy, but died.

And perhaps this attitude is right after all. For was Carman a poet to be proud of? There is pride here, but is it not superficial? There is the bronze bust, the rusted plaque, the grave-tree; but is there anything more? Should there be? Is it worth mentioning if there is? Is this shallow reverence in the Maritimes an acknowledgement of a kind of gift which flourished with the maritime air, and was stilled? Is there greatness here?

Carman wrote some fine regional poetry, and his knowledge of the maritime scene is authentic and clear. But does regionalism make a good poet? Because a poet is remarkably Canadian, and captures the Canadian mood, does this make him great? Surely a poem which would be understood and appreciated everywhere is called great. Where is Grand Pré? The autumn colours may be scarlet and golden, the hills may be ablaze with colour, but does that picture appear real to a resident of Hawaii, or to one who lives on the Canadian prairies, for that matter? Regionalism does not make a poet great, though to listen to some Maritime scholars, one would certainly think so. What about the poetry, then?

The most remarkable thing about Carman's poetry—if not remarkable, at least it is the most noticeable—is that it is so highly imitative. Desmond Pacey says:

> The fact is that Carman is one of the most 'derivative' poets who ever lived. This is as true of his best poems . . . as of the inferior works.

Even the kindly James Cappon says the same thing:

> Everything in Carman's training and temperament tended to attach him to the older tradition in literature . . . even his style and methods of composition when they have the most individuality show respect of the standards of older literature.

Any reader can agree with these men. There abounds in Carman's poetry a great deal of conscious, and at times, unconscious, borrowing from the poets whom he admired. And he admired a great many. At times this was done skilfully; at other times the blatant borrowing is stultifying to the reader.

The most obvious pattern in Carman's poetry is one that is essentially romantic in character and tone. From the publication of *Low Tide on Grand Pré* (1893), through the *Songs of the Sea Children* (1904) and *April Airs* (1916), and in the *Later Poems* (1921), there is the always present romantic tone. Carman, like his Canadian contemporaries, was much attracted to the beauty and magic of the songs of Wordsworth, Coleridge, Byron, Shelley, and Keats. He sang of nature as Wordsworth did, with the same attitude of child-like fascination. From the *Lyrical Ballads* he learned that simple diction was the best method to describe nature. It was easy to imitate Wordsworth; there was the similar environment. Carman was a young man with wild nature all about him, and one whose memories were deeply rooted in New Brunswick's wind-swept marshes and rocky coast-lines when the nature poetry of Wordsworth with its lyrical magic took possession of his verse.

Carman's haunting lyricism is best when he writes about nature:

179

And there when lengthening twilights fall
As softly as a wild bird's wing,
Across the valley in the dusk
I hear the silver flute of spring.
("The Flute of Spring")

Like Wordsworth, Carman revelled in the physical beauty of external nature; he worshipped the vivid loveliness of a budding tree, a blooming flower, and the restless inimitable sea. He attempted, as Wordsworth did, to liken man to nature and its phenomena:

Was it a year or lives ago
We took the grasses in our hands,
And caught the summer flying low
Over the waving meadow lands,
And held it there between our hands?

The while the river at our feet—
A drowsy inland meadow stream—
At set of sun the after-heat
Made running gold, and in the gleam
We freed our birch upon the stream.
("Low Tide on Grand Pré")

Here is Wordsworth's contemplation and music, mingled with his plaintive wistfulness. Carman adopted the Wordsworthian philosophy that nature was good. Both poets believed in the essential goodness of man and nature; and Carman saw God in nature:

I took a day to search for God
And found him not. But as I trod
By rocky ledge, through woods untamed
Just where one scarlet lily flamed
I saw His footprint in the sod.
("Vestigia")

But Carman cannot be called, like Sangster, a true Wordsworthian Canadian poet, for he was too conscious of symbols in his nature poetry. He saw himself as a part of nature and considered that he, too, was growing like a plant:

Between the roadside and the wood,
Between the dawning and the dew,
A tiny flower before the sun,

> Ephemeral in time, I grew.
>
>   ("Windflower")

Wordsworth used the flower as a symbol of nature, but his nature poetry was a summation of philosophy rather than true symbolism. Carman used nature, its growth and decay, as an inherent symbol, and he related his myth of man to nature and the seasons.

As did Coleridge and Shelley, Carman expressed his ideas in terms of physical sensations. He modelled his first ballads after Coleridge's "Rime of the Ancient Mariner"; the suggestive and pictorial metaphors are not always concrete and are often illuminated mystically as are Coleridge's. Many of his poems, and especially "The White Gull", suggest Shelley; there is the use of similes in great profusion and the restless spirit of Shelley:

> The gray sea-horses troop and roam;
> The shadows fly
> Along the wind-floor at their heels;
> And where the golden daylight wheels,
> A white gull searches the blue dome
> With keening cry.

But where Carman occasionally uses the fervid tones of Shelley, he sings most frequently in the autumn calms of Keats. The Keatsian love of beauty is manifest in all his work; every object to Carman was "a thing of beauty", and what was sordid he disregarded. By the use of exquisite diction, he tried to attain Keats' supremely natural utterance in order to create a poem that would be individual, spontaneous, and poignantly musical. He never attained the rapture, the joy, and the exuberance which Keats created, but at times he almost succeeded. With his classical training, Carman could equal Keats in subject matter, but the Keatsian atmosphere was unattainable. The influence of Keats is strongest when Carman uses metaphor and personification to give an excessively romantic character to his verse:

> Lo, now far on the hills,
> The crimson fumes uncurled
> Where the caldron mantles and spills
> Another dawn on the world.
>
>   ("A Northern Vigil")

Possibly, too, the undercurrent of melancholy in Carman's verse owes much to Keats. This note was originally heard in his first volume, *Low Tide on Grand Pré* (1893), and was to occur in most of his verse. He sang sad songs of absent women, of unrest, the futility of striving, and the Arcadian gardens where one would find love and dreams. His epitaph, perhaps, best exemplifies the melancholy of his poetry:

> Have little care that life is brief,
>   And less that art is long;
> Success is in the silences,
>   Though fame is in the song.

Keatsian metaphors seem to come naturally to Carman. In "At Michaelmas" there is the constant ability to find the right concrete image for his thought:

> Soon we shall see the red vines ramp
> Through forest borders,
> And Indian summer breaking camp
> To silent orders.

The images are specific; flowers, for example, are never merely flowers, nor trees mere trees; they are always definite species (a marigold, a daisy, a scarlet maple, a silver birch). The Keatsian qualities—those of predominant colours, love of beauty, the poignant melancholy—are obvious influences upon Carman's poetry. He recognizes this debt to Keats in one of his memorial poems:

> And so his splendid name,
> Who left the book of lyrics and small fame
> Among his fellows then,
> Spreads through the world like autumn—who
>   knows when?—
> Till all the hillsides flame.
>
>   ("By the Aurelian Wall")

CARMAN'S GREATEST DEBT was to the Romantics. His rural background in the Maritimes, and his home environment, produced a temperament which can in part be equated with that of the great Romantics. His education made their poetic values coincide with his own. All his life he was conscious of his own similarities to them, and he attempted to fuse their influences into his own poetry. He was separated by over half a century from them and limited by the standards of a different continent, but like the Romantics Carman was a poet whose main inspiration was nature; in this respect he fulfilled his desire to continue and enlarge the romantic tradition in Canadian poetry.

Woven into the pattern of Carman's poetry is one of the marked characteristics of the Victorian age—moral purpose. Carman was brought up in an environment which accepted the Victorian values, a society which demanded that any creative work should justify its own existence by having a definite moral significance. Carman was deeply aware of Tennyson, Browning, Arnold, Carlyle, and Ruskin—men who were definite teachers of society with faith in their message and a conscious purpose to uplift and instruct. But Carman did not have Tennyson's capacity for working out the flaws in his poems, either because he did not recognize them or because he was too impatient to make a satisfactory change. He did, at times, attain the Tennysonian quality of rhythm and musical cadence:

> Noons of poppy, noons of poppy,
> Scarlet acres by the sea
> Burning to the blue above them,
> Love, the world is full for me.
> ("Noons of Poppy")

If Tennyson was an inspiration to Carman's method of description and atmosphere, he was also the source for didacticism and moralism. Carman saw, as Tennyson had seen, that perfect man was a result of a reign of order. He was a traditionalist in politics and looked back to the past for an order which would come out of a faith in that past. He was sceptical about the progress of his own society and shared Tennyson's fear of democracy in politics:

> We have scorned the belief of our fathers
> And cast their quiet aside;
> To take the mob for our ruler
> And the voice of the mob for our guide.
> ("Twilight in Eden")

But if he learned to teach from Tennyson, it was more in the style of Browning and Swinburne that this teaching was established. He wrote to his mother from Edinburgh in 1893 that he had enjoyed reading Browning, and it is at that time that the Browning influence is strongest in his poetry. "The Wanderer", written the same year, shows Browning's optimistic vigour:

> Therefore is joy more than sorrow, foreseeing
> The lust of the mind and the lure of the eye
> And the pride of the hand have their hour of triumph
> But the dream of the heart will endure by-and-by.

Where the vigour is of Browning, the rhythm of the anapaest lines is of Swinburne, an influence which for a time was predominant in Carman's verse. In *Behind The Arras* (1893), which has the Browning joy in the challenge, Carman achieves a much different style and tone from the soft, elegiac strain of his previous volume, *Low Tide on Grand Pré*. Here the mould is more of Browning; he uses the brisk pace and the metrical device of a long line in sharp contrast with a short one, which was a favourite of Browning. He could not, however, be successful with the dramatic monologue, the frame of which was too vast for Carman's mind. He lacked the intellect to give it a clear and logical development, or any real artistic unity. He could not create a picture of life and retain the sharp flavour which characterized Browning's monologues. But, at times, it was easy for Carman to make Browning's manner his own. He recaptured Browning's vision and frequently the phrases have all the vigour of the master. Browning's narrative style, with its realistic and familiar scenes, is especially apparent in "The Man With the Tortoise" (1901) and in "On the Plaza" (1900):

> One August day I sat beside
> A cafe-window open wide
> To let the shower-freshened air
> Blow in across the Plaza, where
> In golden pomp against the dark
> Green leafy background of the Park
> St. Gauden's hero, gaunt and grim
> Rides on with Victory leading him.

Though the Victorian age is generally characterized as practical and materialistic, nearly all the writers, and especially the great poets, attacked materialism and exalted a purely idealistic concept of life. Carman saw Tennyson and Browning as exemplar poets fundamentally, since love, truth, brotherhood, and justice were emphasized by them as the chief ends of life. He agreed with their ideas, and their poetry had a rapid and far-reaching effect on his own verse.

One aspect of Carman's poetry which is practically ignored by his critics is his love poetry. Here, the influence of Rossetti is seen most strongly. His metaphors have the Rossetti qualities of picture and suggestion, and are often magically illuminated:

> In the cold of the dawn I rose;
> Life lay there from hill to hill
> In the core of a blue pearl,

As it seemed, so deep and still.
    ("XXVII", *Songs of the Sea Children*)

He followed Rossetti's extensive use of colour words to create mood. Though Rossetti's words are usually applied to physical descriptions or room furnishings, Carman applies the medieval colour words to external nature. He follows Rossetti in an over-indulgence in detailed descriptions. But often his many pictures are too heavy for his verse. In "Eyes Like Summer After Sundown" (1901), the tone is Rossetti, and the images have the concrete qualities which Rossetti gained in "The Blessed Damozel":

> Eyes like summer after sundown,
> Hands like roses after dew,
> Lyric as a blown rose garden
> The wind wanders through.
>
> Swelling breasts that bud to crimson,
> Hair like cobwebs after dawn,
> And the rosy mouth wind-rifled
> When the wind is gone.

The inanity of the image "hair like cobwebs after dawn" is Carman at his very worst, though it is not as bad, surely, as the image of Rossetti in "The Blessed Damozel":

> Her hair that lay along her back
> Was yellow like ripe corn.

But he does achieve greatness in "Bahaman":

> Where the gorgeous sunset yellows pour aloft
>   and spill and stain
> The pure amethystine air and the far faint
>   islands of the main.

Carman's poetry is only occasionally Pre-Raphaelite, and when it is, it is more a blending of Keats, Rossetti, and Carman's own distinctive application of the influences. From the Pre-Raphaelite Brotherhood, Carman assimilated a musical quality ("noons of poppy, noons of poppy"), a richness of colour ("Gold are the green trees overhead, and gold the leaf-green grass"), and a reaffirmation of the Keatsian love of beauty. The Pre-Raphaelites strengthened Carman's interest in the first Romantics and so, from the "last Romantics", Carman created a poetry which is for the most part romantic in style, thought, and tone.

Bliss Carman bridged the era between the last of the great Victorians, and the new writers who evolved the complexities of twentieth-century poetry. During this period no great major poet appeared on the literary scene: Yeats had not yet attained his greatness; the groupings of poets—the Rhymer's Club, the Georgians, the War Poets—never reached undebatable fame; Eliot was still extremely "avant garde" even toward the end of Carman's life. World poetry was in a state of fluctuation; there was no definite contemporary poetry.

Despite this, Canadian poetry flourished. The well-known Canadian poets— Carman, Roberts, Lampman, Duncan Campbell Scott—wrote at this time. None of them were innovators; most of them were imitators. Carman is typical of them in that his poetry is a restatement of certain nineteenth-century poetic values. These poets were greatly influenced by the writers in England, and tried to make Canadian poetry in the British tradition. Some poetry of imitation reaches beyond the teacher, but the verse of these poets does not. Rather, it is poetry which is reminiscent of English poetry, that vaguely refers to the Canadian scene, and poetry that is never completely successful. It is characteristic of Canadian writers to forget that to write in the English language is to compete with the best writers in Britain and the United States.

CARMAN IS THE MOST WELL-KNOWN of this flourishing in Canadian poetry, well-known mainly because his poetry is taught in Canadian schools for its strong resemblance to the great English poetry that is also taught. In both form and mood his strongest link is to the Romantic Movement. His predominant mood is one of sentimental emotionalism which his sincere and humble personality could accept without any strongly mature stabilizing factor of mind. This emotional quality has a certain charm and poignancy which was characteristic of the age and the result of the simplicity of his personality. He saw everything in terms of nature. The connecting link in his poetry is seasonal; he correlates emotion to either spring, summer, autumn, or winter. For the most part, spring and summer, with their awakening and youthful associations, have most attraction for him. His moods are always equated with some natural phenomenon: the budding of the trees, the falling of the leaves, the ebb and flow of the tide. This is Carman's one approach to originality. The seasonal and natural phenomena are present in almost every poem, and provide the central theme of his work, and also mark Carman's poetry as distinct from that of other poets. But it is not, after all, a very fresh idea.

His colours and imagery, too, are derived from this central theme. There is little classical, Christian, or literary imagery in his work. Even in the *Pipes of Pan,* the source of word-pictures and music is in the world of nature. Such word combinations as "gold-green shadows", "soft purple haze", "pale aster blue", are frequently present. His musical imagery, too, is derived from the same source. For him "music is the sacrament of love" and he is a "harpstring in the wind", aware of the subtle tonal effect in nature:

> Outside, a yellow maple tree,
>   Shifting upon the silvery blue
> With tiny multitudinous sound,
>   Rustled to let the sunlight through.
>   ("The Eavesdropper")

Like many poets, Carman uses colour and music, not so much for their own sake, as for the mood and atmosphere which their cumulative effect would produce. Words and images are used to create intense mood-atmosphere, and to evoke in the reader an emotional reaction by means of tonal effects. Romantic and Victorian poetry is an attempt to give a subjective interpretation of life, and so is Carman's.

The whole tone of Bliss Carman's poetry is that of the Romantic Movement. His poetry is the manifestation of all the basic assumptions of romanticism. He had the Romantic's faith in the creative imagination and the potentialities of the individual; the preoccupation with the particular rather than the general; an interest in the past; and a feeling of close companionship with nature and God. Since his was an emotional rather than an intellectual personality, Carman found reflections of his own attitudes and moods chiefly in the poetry of the Romantics and the Victorians, concerned as they both were with subjectivity. When Carman is influenced by the Victorians, the romantic elements of their work appear in his poetry. Carman brought nothing new to poetry as poetry—though it was new to Canadian poetry—and sought only to bring together his own favourite expressions in poetry which seemed to suit his limited view of life.

Carman's whole attitude to poetry was that of the devotee rather than a true creator. He worshipped at the shrine of poetry, but was unable to penetrate to the inner circle; his was a minor inspiration because of the narrow range of subject matter and mood. Had Carman been a truly original poet—in so far as any poet can be original—he would have shown a development toward a greater assurance of style and a deeper emotional and intellectual content. However, between the early Carman and the late Carman the differences are of minor tones and that, for a time, one idea is predominant over others. For a while one may believe that there is a development, but always he returns to something which he had pursued before. There is no sign of growth as in Keats, no strongly conscious change as in Yeats. Carman's outlook and attitude changed very little from the beginning to the end of his work.

In the Maritimes, the people worship at this shrine of Carman, as Carman himself worshipped at the shrine of poetry. Perhaps the lack of real knowledge about his work indicates that Carman contributed nothing to world poetry, but because he was at least a poet in a world of few poets there should be the bronze bust, the plaque, and the grave-tree. Perhaps, too, it is guilt on the part of the New Brunswickers who realize that Carman had to go to the United States to have his work published, and somehow the material tributes can recompense for this, and show gratitude to Carman's wish to be buried in Fredericton.

The myth persists. Should it persist? Everything that Carman said had been said before; it was only the monotonous effect which was characteristically Carman. He used the same styles and themes as had the Victorians and Romantics, but in Carman the original intensity was lost. There is about his work a pervading monotony of tone, a lack of strength, and a slightness of content. His diction and his ideas lack the vigour of a Shelley or a Browning. He was a poet who had very little to say; yet, there is a characteristic quality to his work, a tone showing a delicacy of expression, a haunting melancholy, and a musical lyricism. Within his own artistic limits he displayed a consistency of expression; he was always able to capture the melody of a mood, the tone of an atmosphere, the colour of a setting. And even though his themes are limited, he was able to give a spontaneous quality to his verse. But all this does not make him a great poet; neither does it put him into the category that critics often do, that of a "minor but good" poet, an excuse which the myth surrounding his name seems to demand. It is the quantity rather than the quality of his verse which gives him a place in a study of Canadian poetry. He brought to Canadians an awareness of poetry and poets, and also the knowledge that when good poetry is wanted, it is found in other places rather than Canada.

(1961)

TRANSCENDENTALIST, MYSTIC, EVOLUTIONARY IDEALIST

Bliss Carman, 1886-1894

John Robert Sorfleet

I T HAS BECOME a convention of Canadian criticism to hold that Bliss Carman's poetry, although containing some good lines and stanzas, is, as a whole, careless and confused, derivative and diffuse, philosophically obscure and incoherent. Development in the poetry is denied and aspersions are cast upon the poet's intellectual capacity. This downgrading of Carman's intellect is not substantiated by a close reading of his work, and it is the purpose of the present article to demonstrate that Carman's individual poems are philosophically coherent and that, in the body of his work, philosophical development is apparent. The discussion will concentrate on three major poems: "Low Tide on Grand Pré" (1886, described by Carman as his "first poem"[1] of any value), "Pulvis et Umbra" (1890), and "Beyond the Gamut" (1894). These three poems are chosen not just because they are philosophically significant but also because they treat, at four-year intervals, topics in some ways similar. As well as detailed discussions of these poems, brief background accounts of previous, intervening and subsequent stages in Carman's development will be supplied.

During his first twenty-five years, Carman's philosophy evolved to what can be described as a transcendentalism based upon life-long intimacy with nature plus extensive study of Emerson and Thoreau. This intimate relationship was characterized in childhood by a loving marvel at nature's beauty, in youth by a conscious pleasure at his kinship with her, and in adulthood by a transcendental cognizance of nature as infused with spirit, a part of the Emersonian Oversoul. The study of Emerson, who provided philosophical system, and of Thoreau, who became an ideal model of "strenuousness for the spiritual life",[2] was strengthened by Carman's previous knowledge of Plato and other Greek classics, and by his course-work in philosophy at the University of New Brunswick and Edinburgh. Then, in June 1886, Carman recorded a revelation that changed his life.

Fundamental to any understanding of Carman's work and thought is an awareness of the seminal experience incorporated in "Low Tide on Grande Pré". This work, from which Carman dated his poetic career, embodies a moment of revelation which so strongly impressed itself on Carman's mind that he still recalled it forty years later in his second last poem, "Forever and Forever". The insights gained through this experience deeply affected Carman's outlook.

"Low Tide on Grand Pré" is a poem of nostalgic despair; in it, Carman contrasts the joy felt in a previous moment of revelation with the grief he now feels. The poem opens with the setting sun casting such "unelusive glories"[3] over the barren shore that Carman can "almost dream they yet will bide/Until the coming of the tide", can almost visualize the beauty of the scene transcending the temporal limitations of the material world to approach the permanence of perfect beauty. The critical qualifier is "almost"; though the glories of the sunset are not elusive, the dream-vision that nature's beauty can inspire is. Unable to use this beauty in a spiritual aid to vision, the disappointed poet realizes that, in any case, no "escstacy of dream" can change the fact that his companion during a previous vision is absent. In this context, the stream of water is also a "grievous stream" of time which takes the writer wandering through the fields of Acadie in search of that "beloved face". Carried back along this stream of memory, the poet envisions the previous June ("Was it a year or lives ago") when they captured a summer moment,

> ... took the grasses in our hands,
> And caught the summer flying low
> Over the waving meadow lands,
> And held it there between our hands.

That previous summer, though the pair were beside "a drowsy inland meadow stream" rather than by Minas Basin (on the Bay of Fundy), it was a similar beauteous sunset when they launched their canoe. Then, drifting down the stream, they caught and shared a moment of insight into the "secret of some wonder-thing", an instant of illumination that has all the characteristics of a mystic experience. This past moment of insight into ultimate reality and the resultant certainty and joy such insight brought are counterpoised to Carmen's present feelings of uncertainty and grief. Without his companion and unable to repeat his visionary experience, he can only end in nostalgic despair:

> The night has fallen, and the tide . . . .
> Now and again comes drifting home,
> Across these aching barrens wide,
> A sigh like driven wind or foam:
> In grief the flood is bursting home.

The flood of Fundy, imaginatively transformed into a flood of time, finally becomes a flood of tears as Carman grieves over his loss of vision.

In terms of Carman's developing thought, the most important part of the poem is his description of the moment of insight:

> And that we took into our hands
> Spirit of life or subtler thing —
> Breathed on us there, and loosed the bands
> Of death, and taught us, whispering,
> The secret of some wonder-thing.
>
> Then all your face grew light, and seemed
> To hold the shadow of the sun;
> The evening faltered, and I deemed
> That time was ripe, and years had done
> Their wheeling underneath the sun.
>
> So all desire and all regret,
> And fear and memory, were naught;
> One to remember or forget
> The keen delight our hands had caught;
> Morrow and yesterday were naught.

Some mystics describe the "way" to insight; some, the moment of revelation. Carman, in "Low Tide", is one of the latter group and his description evinces all the characteristics — ineffability, noesis, transience, passivity, oneness, timelessness, transcendence of ego and sense of exultation — of the mystical experience.[4] Further, the internal unity and cohesiveness of the three stanzas can only be realized when this identification is understood.

The first essential of the mystical state is ineffability. That Carman's experience has gone so long unexplained probably confirms this quality, as does the vagueness of the phrase "some wonder-thing". The mystical insight is also noetic; in the poet's words, he is "taught . . ./The secret of some wonder-thing". Transience is shown in an earlier stanza which points out that the entire episode occurs in the brief moments of twilight. Passivity, where "the mystic feels as if his own will were in abeyance, and indeed, sometimes as if he were grasped and held by a superior power,"[5] is conveyed by the idea that the "Spirit of life or subtler thing" is the active agent who "breathed", "loosed", and "taught", while the two people are the passive recipients of this experience and of this knowledge. One typical feature of their new knowledge is the consciousness of Oneness and immanence; the statement that "Then all your face grew light, and seemed/To hold the shadow of the sun," indicates a revelation to the poet of the divinity in his companion shining out. It is common in moments of mystical awareness to see this glowing light, not ordinarily apparent, radiating from inside of the object beheld. Another realization characteristic of mysticism is that temporal categories are irrelevant, since all time is contained in the eternal present. This sense of timelessness is specified in the lines:

> The evening faltered, and I deemed
> That time was ripe, and years had done
> Their wheeling underneath the sun
> . . . .
> Morrow and yesterday were naught.

In the mystic moment is the end of flux. As well, to transcend time is to loose "the bands/Of death", for the "real I"[6] is eternally part of the universal Oneness and cannot die. Awareness of this fact is part of what is meant by transcendence of ego, by the general "conviction that the familiar ego is not the real I".[7] This conviction is also indicated in the poem by the abandonment of egocentric drives and feelings:

> So all desire and all regret,
> And fear and memory, were naught; . . .

As for the final characteristic, the exultation felt by the recipient of a mystical insight is evidenced in all three stanzas; the phrase "keen delight" epitomizes this response. The correlation between the illumination described by Carman and the characteristics of mystical experience is total.

Lest misunderstanding ensue, a few further words on mysticism, as it applies to Carman, are in order. He is a mystic in the sense that he has a recognizably mystical experience, thus gaining, in *Webster's* words, knowledge "of spiritual truth, of ultimate reality, or comparable matters . . . through immediate intuition, insight, or illumination and in a way differing from ordinary sense perception or ratiocination". This is not meant to suggest that Carman is a religious contemplative on the order of another Plotinus or St. Teresa or the like. However, as F. C. Happold repeatedly illustrates in *Mysticism: A Study and an Anthology*, to confine "mysticism" only to such adepts as these is inaccurately to apply the term: rather,

> mystical experience is not something confined to those who have risen to the heights of Contemplation, but ... can be present in a less developed form in quite ordinary men and women.... It may happen only once in a lifetime; but, when it does happen, it brings an illumination and a certainty which ... may change the whole tenure of a life.[8]

It is as a person having one or more mystical experiences that Carman is a mystic; the moment of illuminative certainty that is described in "Low Tide" impresses itself so strongly on his mind that he can still recall it over forty years later, in "Forever and Forever".[9]

As for the kind of departure point which gives rise to Carman's insight, it is the contemplation of beauty — "beauty of nature and beauty of people",[10] he says at a later stage of his life, though at this time nature is the only "way" emphasized. Thence proceeds the ascent, which "transcends the physical and becomes mystic",[11] to perception of what Plato calls "absolute beauty". However, where Plato specifies the "right use"[12] of love as the means to insight, the transcendentalists are more comprehensive. They agree that "Beauty, in its largest and profoundest sense, is one expression for the universe,"[13] but feel that it can be perceived both in the external world — nature, art, all other people, and one's own body — and within the soul. Of these, for Carman as well as for Emerson, a major source of inspiration is the beauty of nature.

A last point which should be mentioned is the import of this revelation. As Happold writes:

> True mysticism ... begins in an awakening of the transcendental sense, that sense of something beyond material phenomena which lies at the root of all religious feeling. But it is only the beginning; there must be something more. ...
> One must undergo some sort of experience which is of sufficient intensity to lead to an expansion of normal consciousness and perception, so that there comes to him a new vision of reality which dominates his life and thought.[14]

This statement is applicable to Carman. Previous to his illumination, his writing and comments exhibit a sympathy with the transcendental and a feeling of kinship with nature. But how intensely integral this feeling is to his view of reality is unclear, except that his comments on Emerson and Thoreau confirm an idealistic tendency to see nature's beauty with a spiritual eye. Following his mystical experience, this transcendental kinship is not just intimated but deeply *known*. In and after "Low Tide", the transcendental basis of his poetry is both more evident and more convincing and seems clearly integral to the work. Carman's mystical revelation, as the experiential counterpart to transcendental theory, thus acts as an inspirational spark for his first real creative period. It is no wonder that Carman confides to Lee, "I did not write any poetry of any consequence until I was about 25. . . ."[15]

Between 1886 and 1890, Carman's activities were varied. He read Josiah Royce's *The Religious Aspect of Philosophy* (1885) and was so deeply impressed by Royce's intellectual idealism that he chose, as a preface to his first serious poetry notebook (begun in August 1886), to place a passage from Royce alongside another from his revered Emerson.[16] A similar attestation to the philosopher's impact is provided by Carman's September enrolment at Harvard in a philosophy course taught by Royce. In his book Royce presents a rationally-derived philosophical case for idealism. His systematic "proof that the world is divine and full of spiritual life"[17] could only strengthen Carman's conviction of the truths realized during his mystic experience. Royce gives him a rational as well as an experiential basis for his belief in divine immanence and unity.

During these years spent at Harvard (1886-1888) and back in the Maritimes (1888-1890), Carman wrote over one hundred poems which — frequently manifesting an awareness of the spiritual reality immanent in creation and a feeling of kinship with the divinity behind nature's beauty — generally confirm the mystical nature of his thought. Certain poems — "In Lyric Season" and "In Apple-Time" are two — portray the soul's quest towards absolute beauty, often symbolized by the personification of Nature as a beautiful woman, sometimes unnamed, sometimes called "April", "Spring" or "the Mother". This pursued Beauty is the spirituality infusing all creation; the objective of union with her represents mystic and artistic completion. Using similar symbolism, other poems such as "The Pensioners" provide a significant record of how Carman's mystical transcendentalism sets him apart from other men. The idea underlying the poem is that the coming of "Spring"[18] provides spiritual stimulus to man as well as to Nature, but that, among men, she receives a different response from "overlords of change" as opposed to "pensioners".

Briefly to outline the process of the poem, it begins by including all men in the category of "pensioners of Spring", receiving from her world-wide benefice a spiritual allowance ("the largess [sic] of her hand") which is distributed by the winds, "her seraph almoners" who "unbar/The wintry portals of her land." Most men waste Spring's largesse; her stirring of "the old unrest" (as "In Lyric Season" has it) only impels them to "some fool's idle quest" because they do not fully appreciate their kinship with the rest of creation. Their unrest is "blind unrest". For the mystical transcendentalist, however, there is not blindness but an illuminating awareness of kinship, resulting from the appearance of Spring in her April dress:

> Until her April train goes by,
> And then because we are the kin
> Of every hill flower on the hill
> We must arise and walk therein.
>
> Because her heart as our own heart
> Knowing the same wild upward stir,
> Beats joyward by eternal laws,
> We must arise and go with her; ...

Akin to nature, man is governed by the same "eternal laws" of aspiration and rhythm. Roused by Spring, he partakes in the general striving towards perfection; he shares the "same wild upward stir" towards the joy of universal rhythmic harmony. Understanding his participation in the cosmic concord also means a change in how he thinks of, and responds to, the vagaries of fate; enlightened men, following the upward lead of Spring, must

> Forget we are not where old joys
> Return when dawns and dreams retire;
> Make grief a phantom of regret,
> And fate the henchman of desire;
>
> Divorce unreason from delight;
> Learn how despair is uncontrol,
> Failure the shadow of remorse,
> And death a shudder of the soul.
>
> Yea, must we triumph when she leads.

With a new vision of reality, the attitude to change is not one of pessimism but one of confidence, for spiritual reality transcends material occurrences.

Accordingly, to the initiate of Spring, any April signs — from the "little rain before the sun" to the "First whitethroat's ecstacy unfurled" — are summonses to spiritual insight. Experiencing this insight,

> ... we are overlords of change,
> In the glad morning of the world,
>
> Though we should fare as they whose life
> Time takes between his hands to wring
> Between the winter and the sea,
> The weary pensioners of Spring.

Though the mystic and the ordinary man many undergo equally oppressive hardships, the former, transcending the physical sphere and living in the morning of the spirit, is an overlord of change, while the latter, wasting his spiritual allowance and blindly accepting subjection to the material world, can never be more than a weary pensioner of Spring. The poem emphasizes the effect of Carman's mystical experience on his general outlook.

As time went by, Carman's outward circumstances changed. In February 1890, he left the Maritimes to take an editorial position with the weekly New York *Independent*. Possibly in part because he was cut off from nature by his regular city job,[19] darker notes — though dispersed by the mystic's confidence — begin to appear in his poetry. The best early example is "Pulvis et Umbra" ("dust and shadow"), written July 18. This poem evinces the assurance that mystical insight provides against doubt about the spirituality of creation. More particularly, the poem confronts the annihilation that death suggests, with the confidence born of mystical experience.

"Pulvis et Umbra" opens with a retrospective account of the event which inspires it:

> There is dust upon my fingers,
> Pale gray dust of beaten wings,
> Where a great moth came and settled
> From the night's blown winnowings.[20]

Carman places the moth's arrival in relation to his own autumnal mood; his sense of the forlorn and the mysterious is conveyed through the images of the "lonely hopeless calling/Of the bell-buoy" and the restless "sea with her old secret". In this context, from the "chambers of the twilight", enters the moth,

> One frail waif of beauty fronting
> Immortality and doom.

Marvelling that this child of beauty so fearlessly confronts the possibility of death, the poet attempts to find an adequate metaphorical explanation of its assumed immortality. He considers it as a bird's cry garbed in leaves and dew, as "whimsy Ariel" covered with dust, as the passion in Cleopatra's last breath, as "thistle-drift and sundown" shaped by goblins and infused with spirit by the wind, and as the ghost of Psyche, first searching for Persephone and then returning from Hades with the girl-queen's gift of immortal beauty to Venus.[21] This final comparison leads him to see the moth as "Pilot of the shadow people", come to "hapless port" because there is no one to guide beyond the grave:

> For man walks the world with mourning
> Down to death, and leaves no trace,
> With the dust upon his forehead,
> And the shadow in his face.
>
> Pillared dust and fleeing shadow
> As the roadside wind goes by,
> And the fourscore years that vanish
> In the twinkling of an eye.

Man is seen as totally evanescent, as mere dust and shadow that vanishes in the "twinkling of an eye". In this state of despair even "imperishable" Beauty and Spirit are also transient; "Beauty" is just "the fine frosty trace-work/Of some breath upon the pane", and "Spirit" only "the keen wintry moonlight/Flashed thereon to fade again".

However, in reaching this conclusion the poet finds himself at variance with his own deeply-felt experience; he recalls from his mystical revelation that Beauty and Spirit are more, much more, than ephemeral frost and moonlight:

> Beauty, the white clouds a-building
> When God said and it was done;
> Spirit, the sheer brooding rapture
> Where no mid-day brooks no sun.

"Beauty" manifests the purpose and unity of creation, while "Spirit" indicates the revelatory rapture of mystical insight, transcending the limits of time and physical reality. The erroneous conclusions about Beauty and Spirit, and the argument of evanescence which leads to these incorrect conclusions, are thus overthrown and their antithesis, spiritual life after death, is the only valid alternative:

> What's to hinder but I follow
> This my gypsy guide afar,
> When the bugle rouses slumber
> Sounding taps on Arrochar?

Though spiritual life is the portion of both moth and man, there is still a difference in their lots. Where the moth is "perfect for a day", "faultless as a flower", the man is not. His is "the endless way/ Of the dust and shadow kindred", the way of mutability; his spiritual perfection is deferred:

> Yet from beauty marred and broken,
> Joy and memory and tears,
> I shall crush the clearer honey
> In the harvest of the years.

For the man there is a special compensation for his subjection to "fault and failure". This compensation is the coming of eternal dawn when death shall succumb to the world of the spirit:

> For man walks the world in twilight,
> But the morn shall wipe all trace
> Of the dust from off his forehead,
> And the shadow from his face.

Instead of "mourning", "morn" will reign; instead of the dust and shadow of death, man's end shall be his beginning, his entry into the eternal morning of spiritual existence.

Accordingly, the moth becomes "tidings-bearer" for the poet, taking his greetings and its own beauty down the trail from life through death to "Her whose dark eyes match thy wings", in terms of the Psyche myth a reference to Venus, divine Beauty, to whom Psyche is returning. The Psyche-Cupid allusions function symbolically to represent the beauty and survival of the individual soul, and its eventual union with divine Love. Then, the moth assisted on its journey, the poet exults:

> Pale gray dust upon my fingers;
> And from this my cabined room
> The white soul of eager message
> Racing seaward in the gloom.

This change of mood, from hopelessness to eagerness, is also conveyed by the final stanza's image of the sounding bell-buoy; no longer is it the "lonely hopeless calling" of stanza two, but rather a "sweet low calling":

> Far off shore, the sweet low calling
> Of the bell-buoy on the bar,
> Warning night of dawn and ruin
> Lonelily [*sic*] on Arrochar.

The reason for the change is that, not death, but life-in-the-spirit will triumph, symbolized in the ruin of night by the coming of dawn, heralding this spiritual morning of existence. Carman confronts the annihilation that death and doubt of spirituality suggest with the truths learned through mystical experience.

This poem presents a reasonably unified and consistent poetic statement of Carman's reaction to an incident that befell him. "Pulvis et Umbra" also manifests certain differences in attitude from "Low Tide on Grand Pré" and "The Pensioners". In comparison with the earlier poem, "Pulvis et Umbra" puts a bit more emphasis on philosophical reflection as opposed to purely emotional response, though the leap of mystic faith founded on personal experience is still evident in both works. In comparison with "The Pensioners", the later poem contains some admission that Carman no longer feels the immediate contact with mystic reality evident in that earlier poem; the mystically-based resolution is rooted more in memory than in conviction of instant access to the Oversoul.

Soon after completing "Pulvis et Umbra", Carman received a severe shock in the surprise death of his cousin and close friend, Andrew Straton. Seeking succour, Carman reread Royce's *Religious Aspect of Philosophy*. In reference to Carman's consequent comments about how much the book continued to mean to him, Royce replied:

> The words about my books are among the kindest I ever received, and it is heartily satisfying to know that, many as my faults are, I have been permitted to be of service to one of my fellows in the way that you mention.[22]

Carman's job — he remained an editor for two years — also took its toll of him. In November 1891, he wrote: "I have two passions, poetry and nature. Both are denied me in large measure now. For I must work here among men who do not allow themselves to think of these things."[23] Indeed, between October 1890 and

March 1892, he wrote only five poems; consequently he left his job that spring and spent the summer with Charles G. D. Roberts and Richard Hovey in Windsor, Nova Scotia.

In early autumn of 1892, Carman and Hovey, a Harvard friend just returned from Europe, hiked back to Hovey's home in Washington, where Carman stayed until June 1893. During this period, Carman was exposed to his friend's theory of love. A great advocate of spiritual insight through physicality, Hovey held sensual joy "to be the very health of the soul".[24] A key component in his outlook was sexual love, rising from the physical to the spiritual. In Roberts' words, Hovey exerted "a broadening and emancipating influence"[25] on Carman. At the same time, while staying with Hovey's family, Carman met Jessie Kappeler, a cheerful and beautiful eighteen-year old. They fell in love and, having spent the spring together in Washington, also spent the summer together at Lake Placid. Their romance flourished but eventually, because of strenuous opposition from Miss Kappeler's mother, subsided and was largely ended by April 1895.[26] In the meantime, Carman wrote almost two-thirds of the love poems in *Songs of the Sea Children*, which serve as a record of their relationship.

Inevitably, considering Hovey's emancipating influence on him, the sexual aspect of Carman's relationship with Miss Kappeler appears in the poetry, as this stanza from Song **XXXIV** suggests:

> Thou art the fair seed vessel
> Waiting all day for me,
> Who ache with the golden pollen
> The night will spill for thee.[27]

Explicit though the parallel of the plant imagery to the male and female organs be, the sexual element in the songs is spiritual as well as physical, as lyric **XXXIX** attests:

> The alchemist who throws his worlds
> In the round crucible of the sun
> Has laid our bodies in the forge
> Of love to weld them into one.
>
> The hypnotist who waves his hand
> And the pale streamers walk the night,
> A moment for our souls unbars
> The lost dominions of delight.[28]

These stanzas combine Hovey and Plato. The Hoveian interpretation would be that, through the divine gift of sex used as the expression of love, the two lovers can reach the spiritual height of ecstasy. Use is also made of the Platonic notion (propounded by Aristophanes in the *Symposium*) that Zeus divided each original man into halves and that lovers are people seeking to find and fuse with their other halves. This theory provides additional explanation of why the union of two into one gives such delight — it means the momentary reunion of the divided soul. Platonic theory also accounts for the original fall from delight implied by "lost dominions". Under either interpretation, the sexual union of lovers leads to spiritual insight.

Not only through sexual experience does the body provide a road to the kingdom of the spirit. In reply to a later comment on the *Songs*, Carman explains:

> I don't think 'physical passion in various degrees of intensity' the best phrase to describe the motive of 'Songs of the Sea Children.' They are primarily love poems, of course, but the love passion is sublimated by imagination and meditation, until it transcends the physical and becomes mystic. Raw physical passion (if it could exist without spirit and mind) could not create, it could only procreate. Yet spiritual rapture, love with all its divine attributes, and intellectual elation, cannot divorce themselves wholly from the physical, they must forever be enamoured of outward physical beauty, beauty of nature and beauty of people. The soul must take on substance and form of beauty before it can dwell among men. And physicality must reach up like a mounting wave into the realm of mind and spirit before it can become beautiful.[29]

Carman's emphasis on the application of "imagination and meditation" to the love passion so that it "transcends the physical and becomes mystic," and his stress on physical beauty as an adjunct to states of "spiritual rapture, love with all its divine attributes, and intellectual elation," are essentially a statement of neo-Platonic idealism. Like Plato and the neo-Platonists, Carman here sees the mystic "way" as the right use of love, starting with the appreciation of physical beauty in a particular person and thence ascending by steps to the vision of absolute beauty, or, in Carman's word, "soul".

As well, Carman goes beyond Plato, through Plotinus, to Emerson and his own experience, emphasizing not just bodily beauty but all "outward physical beauty" — "beauty of nature and beauty of people". It is this sense of beauty as the expression of "soul" in the universe that Carman is using both in his comment about the *Songs* and in an 1894 statement that "beauty is only truth made visible, struck into form for these poor eyes to see."[30] His comments on beauty also indicate another reason why he personifies the creating spirit that impels and resides in all nature as a beauteous female; spiritual ecstasy cannot be wholly divorced from the physical and "soul must take on substance and form of beauty" before it can be fully apprehended. Accordingly, the female figure in *Songs* represents both Carman's lover and the Soul that infuses all nature; similarly, the realization of their love represents the poet's attainment of the mystic insight for which he has quested:

> A touch of your hair, and my heart was furled;
> A drift of fragrance, and noon stood still;
> All of a sudden the fountain there
> Had something to whisper the sun on the hill.
>
> Rose of the garden of God's desire,
> Only the passionate years can prove
> With sorrow and rapture and toil and tears
> The right of the soul to the kingdom of love.[31]

The first stanza describes the moment of revelation; its characteristics are ineffability yet noesis ("something to whisper"), transience ("All of a sudden"), passivity (the poet is acted upon, not acting), Oneness (the relationship between fountain and sun is suddenly perceived), timelessness ("noon stood still"), transcendence of ego ("my heart was furled"), and a general sense of joy and love (implicit). The second stanza describes the means to insight; it is to use passion so that it "transcends the physical and becomes mystic", thus proving the individual soul's right to the "kingdom of love" where its oneness with the oversoul is achieved.

D ISCOVERING THAT BODY as well as soul has a spiritual function, and exemplifying the popular Darwinism of his day, Carman was moved to postulate that an evolutionary relationship might exist between the two, that the seeming division between material and ideal worlds might not actually prevail. In "Beyond the Gamut", Carman's philosophical opus, he investigates this and related possibilities.

The situation upon which the poem is based, in Carman's words, is the "meditation of a musician over his violin".[32] As the title implies, this meditation goes beyond the gamut, beyond the lines and spaces upon which the musical notes are written. In other words, the musician is carried away by "Something"[33] in his music, is transported beyond everyday perception into "a new room in the house of knowledge". In this new room, he is given four successive insights into truth.

The first verity that the musician and his violin descry is that

> As all sight is but a finer hearing,
> And all colour but a finer sound,
> Beauty, but the reach of lyric freedom,
> Caught and quivering past all music's bound;
>
> Life, that faint sigh whispered from oblivion;
> Harks and wonders if we may not be
> Five small wits to carry one great rhythmus,
> The vast theme of God's new symphony.
>
> As fine sand spread on a disc of silver,
> At some chord which bids the motes combine,
> Heeding the hidden and reverberant impulse
> Shifts and dances into curve and line,
>
> The round earth, too, haply, like a dust-mote,
> Was set whirling her assigned sure way,
> Round this little orb of her ecliptic
> To some harmony she must obey.

Since sight, colour and beauty are the respective summits of hearing, sound and poetry ("lyric freedom"), transferred into a higher key, the musician thinks that, by analogy and extension, man's "five small wits" may be the lower key from which a loftier summit — "one great rhythmus" — in an even higher key — "The vast theme of God's new symphony" — will be realized. Further, the only difference between all keys, from the five senses to God's rhythmic symphony, is one of degree, not of substance. Consequently, as everything is composed of one substance — a "mass of vibrations" governed by the harmonic "law of rhythm",[34] Carman says elsewhere — there can be no division between physicality and spirituality save in rhythmic period. The visible universe merely vibrates at lower frequencies than the invisible universe; hence, there is a kinship among all that exists.

This last point ("Ah, thought cannot far [sic] without the symbol!"), Carman stresses in a series of stanzas, of which the following is representative:

> Not a bird-song, but it has for fellow
> Some wood-flower, its speechless counterpart,
> Form and color moulded to one cadence,
> To voice something of the wild mute heart.

203

As well as these qualities of sound and colour, things have the attributes of resilience, odour, flavour and soul. All of these attributes vibrate at different frequencies, the first five of which can be perceived through man's "Five small wits". Naturally, just as perceiving rhythm through one sense gives pleasure, so does perceiving it through five result in a correspondingly greater pleasure:

> Peal and flash and thrill and scent and savour
> Pulse through rhythm to rapture, and control, —
> Who shall say how far along or finely? —
> The infinite tectonics of the soul.

The degree to which one perceives the rhythm of the universe affects the development of one's soul. Accordingly, "scarlet and brass" wave-lengths are appreciated by "Low-bred peoples" while blue and purple are preferred by such artists as Monet. Because of his better perception, the artist also acts as a leader in God's symphony of ultimate rhythm; he "Sees not only, but instructs our seeing", in this way augmenting man's ability to perceive the furthest end of the visible spectrum.

Though the first five attributes of things can be perceived through the five senses, what about the attribute of soul, inherent in all creation but on a frequency that cannot be seen even through the highest physical sense, eyesight?

> Red the bass and violet the treble
> Soul may pass out where all colour ends,
> Ends? So we say, meaning where the eyesight
> With some yet unborn perception blends.

Nevertheless, the musician is not depressed; he feels that a sixth sense may be evolved so that soul can be actually perceived, not just intuitively felt:

> I, at my wits' end, may still develop
> Unknown senses in life's larger room.
>
> Superhuman is not supernatural.
> How shall half-way judge of journey done?
> Shall this germ and protoplast of being
> Rest mid-way and say his face is run?

The evolution of spiritual perception is a continuing process.

Reaching this realization the musician consults with his violin and is given his second insight into the harmonic order. Since evolution only results from the full exertion of effort, one should not ascetically deny life and the five existing senses;

rather, "every sense's impulse/Is a means the master soul employs." Thus, on "earth one habitat of spirit", one must "Touch environment" — the whole external world — "with every sense-tip", and "Not for sense sake only, but for soul sake". A common human error is to deny one or the other, to "Soil the goodly feast" or to "Vilify the bounty". The musician, on the other hand, feels that a balance must be struck between the complementary faculties of sense and soul, that the one who is "most man" would venture with Alexander and watch with Buddha. In developing both aspects of himself, he would find "mighty peace possess his spirit".

Accordingly, the musician concludes to his violin:

> Life be neither hermitage nor revel;
> Lent or carnival alone were vain;
> Sin and sainthood — Help me, little brother,
> With your large finder-thought again!

The musician stumbles over the question of "Sin and sainthood", over the problem of evil in a rhythmically-ordered world. Appealing to his violin for a third moment of insight, the answer he gains is that "Good ... shall triumph"; but the problem of evil is not satisfactorily resolved. This time, the musician helps explain evil to the violin. He begins by stating that even when he is long dead, his dreams "Shall be part of all the good that thrills you/In the oversoul's orchestral themes." In other words, the violinist's aspirations will be part of the oversoul's total goodness. However, since the oversoul's goodness can only have its being through the inner victory of the will to goodness over the will to evil, evil is necessary, in Royce's words, "Not indeed to set off the good by any external contrast, but to constitute a moment in the organic unity of the good act."[35] Thus the musician continues:

> What is good? While God's unfinished opus
> Multitudinous harmony obeys,
> Evil is a dissonance not a discord,
> Soon to be resolved to happier phrase, —

Or, in Roycean terms, evil is no more than a momentary dissonance in the organic unity of God's good act, and is soon resolved into God's goodness. The same reasoning applies in the case of the individual's evil impulse; it "forms an element in his realization of goodness".[36] As the musician says, the challenge of evil enables hearts to "know what hearts proclaim".

The musician also argues the alternative: even if evil is someone's "blunder", then it is a minor discord, outweighed by good in the greater harmony. In either instance, evil is not eternal:

> Say I let you, spite of all endeavour
> Mar some nocturne by a single note;
> Is there immortality of discord
> In your failure to preserve the rote?

Instead, after the error is done and gone, it becomes "as fresh clay for the potter" in a parallel to nature's cyclic renewal:

> Blighted rose and perfect shall commingle
> In one excellence of garden mould.
> Soul transfusing comeliness or blemish
> Can alone lend beauty to the old.

The natural cycle and Royce's idea of good and evil's resolution into the good consciousness are both contained in this image. As well, the musician recognizes the necessity of soul to the creation of beauty; without the divine soul, the "garden mould" remains just mould, with no potential for beauty or development. And, having satisfied himself that "Good . . . shall triumph" ultimately and that without the divine gift of soul no beauty or development can occur, the musician can accept whatever fate God, the Master Musician, wills for man.

Man may be different from the rest of Nature in that he cannot lose himself in a merging with all his fellows; he is "sorrow-nurtured" rather than "perfect for a day".[37] Nevertheless, he still has his role to fill in "The vast theme of God's new symphony". Indeed, his role is commensurately different:

> Linked to all his half-accomplished fellows,
> Through unfettered provinces to range,
> Man is but the morning dream of nature
> Roused by some wild cadence weird and strange.

Though linked with the rest of nature, man's task is to transcend the limits of five senses and to range through the "unfettered provinces" of the sixth sense, soul. In this sense he is the "morning dream of nature", hopefully another rung in the ladder of spiritual evolution. These conclusions reached, the musician can return from his exploration of the "new room in the house of knowledge", confidently "Knowing the hereafter will be well".

The musically-inspired meditation then closes with a final insight into three key philosophical truths. The first, a statement about conduct, is that "Love is but the perfect knowledge" which, expressed as "Lovingkindness", "betters loving credence". In other words, not only is the act of loving better than a belief in loving; it also improves belief, makes it better. Carman may be suggesting here the ideas — elaborated upon in "Above the Gaspereau" and "Henry George" soon after — that love is the force motivating evolutionary aspiration towards the spiritual. The second truth is a comment on immortality and beauty:

> Beauty, beauty, beauty, sense and seeming,
> With the soul of truth she calls her lord!
> Stars and men the dust upon her garment;
> Hope and fear the echoes of her word.

The meaning of the quatrain is that, although all else may perish, Beauty and the "soul of truth" she expresses will not. This is, of course, relevant to the artist; his work is a lesser degree of perfect beauty and may transcend ephemerality though he himself will die. As Carman writes two weeks later to Gertrude Burton, "Just to be allowed a few years in this fair encampment, and the pleasure of contriving what-not after our fancies of beauty! That is enough."[38] In this sense, beauty expresses the ultimate aspirations and fears of humankind about immortality. The concluding truth is a summary of the human condition:

> How escape we then, the rainbow's brothers,
> Endless being with each blade and sod?
> Dust and shadow between whence and whither,
> Part of the tranquillity of God.

Though man, as mere "Dust and shadow", is ultimately one with all the rest of perishable nature, he is also part of the tranquillity of God. He is an evolutionary mid-point in the vibratory continuum of the universe, caught between whence and whither, between earth and rainbow. The "morning dream of nature", he is the living proof of evolutionary relationship between the physical and the spiritual. Clearly, the poem as a whole is a philosophically coherent and carefully-considered piece of work.

A brief comparison with "Pulvis et Umbra", similar in certain themes and phrases to "Beyond the Gamut", is useful here as elaboration upon how Carman's thought has developed. The mental process behind the later poem is fairly rational; behind the earlier, comparatively emotional: that is, the conclusions of the later poem have a sounder philosophical basis than the earlier poem's experiential assurance. "Beyond the Gamut" has a cosmological cohesiveness, an emphasis on full enjoyment of the senses as a valid part of life and growth, a rationale for the problem of evil, a general acceptance of one's own individual death, and a carefully-considered belief in spiritual evolution. In all these ways the poem evinces Carman's development since "Pulvis et Umbra".

At this point, then, Carman's outlook can be characterized as evolutionary idealism. The basis of his position is the feeling that sensual joy is an integral aspect of life and growth and that it provides a means of spiritual insight. This insight is achieved partly through the sexual act and partly through the neo-Platonic use of passion as an aid to mystical ascent. In either instance, Carman's discovery that the body has a spiritual function leads him to conclude an evolutionary relationship between physicality and spirituality. Love is seen as the motive force behind such spiritual evolution of nature and man. Compared with his earlier positions — in "Low Tide" an intense awareness of the psycho-emotional revelation that is mystical experience; in "Pulvis et Umbra" an experientially-based (though metaphorically-couched) resolution of spiritual doubt — Carman's philosophy has clearly developed; the problems of evil, evolution, ethics and physicality are now integrated with his mystical insight to form a coherent and consistent philosophy.

As a postscript, Carman's thought continued to develop. In 1899, for example, his work evidences growing interest in the organic harmonizing of body, mind and spirit in everyday life. This new note — apparently deriving from François Delsarte's theory of trinitarian expression, to which Carman is introduced by Richard Hovey and Mary Perry King — appears only in Carman's prose, where he grapples with the wider implications of Delsartean thought. It is not until 1900, when Delsartean theory is augmented by George Santayana's rational idealism and thus is expanded into an unitrinian theology, that trinitarian personal harmonizing appears in Carman's poetry. The impetus behind this expansion is Santayana's *Poetry and Religion* (1900), which challenges Carman as artist and as idealist with its demands for reason in art and religion. The result in each instance is that, though Carman does not accept Santayana's underlying attitude, he does recognize the partial validity of the philosopher's position and adapts his own thought and work accordingly. In terms of art, Santayana's argument causes Carman to give more equitable representation to the rational element, a theoretical third of art's unitrinity; consequently, his poetry becomes less "obscure". In terms of religion, Santayana's book impels Carman to expand personal harmonizing into a full unitrinian theology based on the idealization of Goodness, Truth, Beauty, Love, and Evolution; to this degree Carman accepts the philosopher's rational idealism. As Carman's unitrinian theology unfolds over the next few years, the combined consequences of rationalism and didacticism become increasingly manifested in his writing and he tends to disparage his earlier work. This same point in time (1905) marks the end of Carman's most productive years.

(1974)

NOTES

[1] Bliss Carman to H. D. C. Lee, September 29, 1911. This letter is in the Lorne Pierce Collection of Canadian Manuscripts at Queen's University.

[2] Bliss Carman, "Fresh Fields," *University [of New Brunswick] Monthly*, N.S. 3 (March, 1885), 91.

[3] All quotations from the poem can be found in Bliss Carman, *Low Tide on Grand Pré* (Boston: Lamson Wolffe and Company, 1893 with additions in 1894), pp. 15-18; written June, 1886.

[4] F. C. Happold, *Mysticism: A Study and an Anthology* (Harmondsworth: Penguin Books Ltd., 1963 rev. 1964), pp. 45-48, 53. See also William James, *The Varieties of Religious Experience* (New York: Longmans, Green & Co., 1902), pp. 371-72.

[5] James, *Varieties*, p. 372.

[6] Happold, *Mysticism*, p. 48.

[7] *Ibid.*

[8] *Ibid.*, p. 129.

[9] The most relevant stanzas (from Bliss Carman, *The Music of Earth*, with Foreword and Notes by Lorne Pierce [Toronto: Ryerson Press, 1931], pp. 42-43 are:

> On a day in early June when a young lad was I,
> I was caught in a charm like a wild bird's cry,
> With the sorcery of summer on the marshes by the tide,
> And apple blossoms snowing down by every roadside,
> 'Twas the glory of the world laid a spell on me,
> And I gave my heart away to the Sweetheart of the Sea.
>
> . . . .
>
> And so it came about the years were blown away,
> Light as flying leaves or the fog upon the bay,
> While I must seek my fortune over many lands,
> A follower of dreams with nothing in his hands.
> But always in his mind the cry from the sea
> And the look of Heaven's glory on the face of Acadie.

[10] Carman to Lee.

[11] *Ibid.*

[12] Plato, *The Symposium*, trans. W. Hamilton (Harmondsworth: Penguin Books Ltd., 1951), p. 94.

[13] Ralph Waldo Emerson, "Nature," *Selections From Ralph Waldo Emerson*, ed. Stephen Whicher (Cambridge, Mass.: Riverside Press of Houghton Mifflin Co., 1957), p. 31.

[14] Happold, *Mysticism*, p. 52.

[15] Carman to Lee. Carman turned 25 in April, 1886, two months before "Low Tide" was written.

[16] Carman, "Poetry Notebook: 1886-1888," Pierce Collection.

[17] Josiah Royce, *The Religious Aspect of Philosophy* (Boston: Houghton Mifflin & Co., 1885), p. 481.

[18] *Low Tide on Grand Pré*, pp. 31-34; printed May, 1889.

[19] See note 23.

[20] All quotations are taken from *Low Tide on Grand Pré*, pp. 56-68.

[21] Carman is alluding to the Cupid-Psyche myth, told only by Apuleius. According to Harvey's *Companion to Classical Literature*, the image of Psyche as a butterfly post-dates Apuleius by three centuries.

[22] Royce to Carman, June 1, 1891, Pierce Collection. Carman's previous letter to Royce is unknown; it is not in any collection of Royce letters.

[23] Carman to "Will" (last name unknown), November 18, 1891, Pierce Collection.

[24] Allan H. MacDonald, *Richard Hovey: Man and Craftsman* (Durham, N.C.: Duke University Press, 1957), p. 147. At this time Hovey was engaged in an affair with Mrs. Henrietta Russell, by whom he already had one child.

[25] Charles G. D. Roberts, "More Reminiscences of Bliss Carman," *Dalhousie Review*, 10 (April 1930), 3.

[26] H. Pearson Gundy, "Lorne Pierce, Bliss Carman, and the Ladies," *Douglas Library Notes*, 14 (Autumn 1965), 12-13.

[27] Bliss Carman, *Songs of the Sea Children* (Boston: L. C. Page & Company, 1903), p. 56; written October 10, 1893.

[28] *Ibid.*, p. 61; written in March, 1894.

[29] Carman to Lee.

[30] Carman to Gertrude Burton, October 9, 1894, Pierce Collection.

[31] Carman, "LI," *Songs*, p. 76; written December 1, 1893.

[32] Carman to Burton.

[33] All quotations from "Beyond the Gamut" can be found in Bliss Carman, *Behind the Arras* (Boston: Lamson Wolffe and Company, 1895), pp. 66-80; written September 26, 1894.

[34] Bliss Carman, "Rhythm," *The Kinship of Nature* (Boston: L. C. Page & Company, 1903), p. 115; printed April 6, 1901.

[35] Royce, *Religious*, p. 465.

[36] *Ibid.*, p. 454. The original is italicized.

[37] The phrase is from "Pulvis et Umbra" where a similar contrast of man to other creatures is made.

[38] Carman to Burton.

THE KLONDIKE MUSE

Stanley S. Atherton

THE KLONDIKE TRAIL OF 1898, symbol of the last great gold rush in history, captured the imagination of a continent. By the time Robert Service reached the Yukon in 1904 as a teller for the Canadian Bank of Commerce, public interest in the area was widespread. Well before Service himself began to record his impressions, a "Klondike literature" was already rapidly accumulating from the numerous eye-witness reports, the travellers' accounts, and the books of advice to prospective gold-seekers. For the most part, however, these works emphasized factual events and situations, and only those that were specifically connected with the Gold Rush. While there was plenty of action recorded, little of a meditative or reflective nature could be found in such accounts. The way was open for a writer with talent enough to take advantage of the happy coincidence of event and location to mythologize the north.

Service, stimulated by the recent and contemporary events in his new surroundings, began to produce both poetry and fiction in an imaginative reconstruction of this world. What fame he has achieved continues to rest chiefly on the few volumes his eight years of residence in the Yukon yielded. These include *Songs of a Sourdough* (also published as *The Spell of the Yukon*) (1907), *Ballads of a Cheechako* (1909), *Rhymes of a Rolling Stone* (1912), and the novel, *The Trail of Ninety-Eight* (1910). This body of work, rarely examined critically, deserves attention as one of the earliest attempts in Canadian literary history to mythologize the environment.

In his early poetry Service used the subject matter of the Gold Rush as a point of departure for his comments on man's relationship to the land. In "The Spell of the Yukon", for example, the Gold Rush is dispensed with in the first stanza. From here the poet moves to a description of the physical environment, using the Klondike as a representative northern landscape. The third stanza, and the remaining six, catalogue the varying responses and attitudes the narrator takes towards the North.

A number of these reactions had been articulated a few years earlier by Hamlin Garland. In a *McClure's* article in 1897 he had termed the Yukon "a cruel and relentless land", and a "grim and terrible country". Service made these and similar reactions the subject matter for a number of his best-known poems. The untitled prefatory poem to *Song of a Sourdough* is characteristic.

> The lonely sunsets flare forlorn
> > Down valleys dreadly desolate:
> The lordly mountains soar in scorn,
> > As still as death, as stern as fate.

> > The lonely sunsets flame and die;
> > > The giant valleys gulp the night;
> > The monster mountains scrape the sky,
> > > Where eager stars are diamond-bright.

> So gaunt against the gibbous moon,
> > Piercing the silence velvet-piled,
> A lone wolf howls his ancient rune,
> > The fell arch-spirit of the Wild.

> > O outcast land! O leper land!
> > > Let the lone wolf-cry all express —
> > The hate insensate of thy hand,
> > > Thy heart's abysmal loneliness.

Here one finds a number of key concepts which recur with varying degrees of emphasis in the majority of the Klondike poems: a sense of loneliness, hints of the supernatural, hostile nature, an intense and meaningful silence, and a reminder of man's mortality.

Service is rarely content simply to describe the North. A number of his poems provide effective illustrations of the constant perils to human life in such a desolate area, perils which evoke a continual fear in man of the hostility implicit in the environment. He achieves his effects in various ways, often by utilizing the supernatural element found in indigenous Indian folklore. In "The Ballad of the Black Fox Skin", for instance, he recounts an Indian belief that a particular fox was invested with supernatural powers, and that any who attempted to do it harm would surely suffer. The sceptic who laughs at the superstition and kills the fox is later murdered, and the poem traces a trail of death marked out by all those who possess the cursed skin. By the corpse of the last possessor hoofprints are found, and the skin has mysteriously disappeared.

References such as this to specific supernatural occurrences are set against a wider background of mystery and other-worldliness which often characterizes the North for Service. The narrator of "The Ballad of the Northern Lights" views the aurora "as one bewitched" and describes its mystic beauty as "wild and weird and wan". In "The Ballad of Pious Pete" the presence of witches and frost-tyrants is recorded, adding a further dimension to the supernatural world, and relating it through the image of "cadaverous snows" to human mortality. The language of death abounds in the work, often coupled with Service's characteristic sardonic humour. This pre-occupation with morbidity may account partly for his poetry's continuing appeal. In an age when the threat of violent death is more than ever man's constant companion, the macabre humour of Service takes on a contemporary relevance. Intriguing examples of this "northern gothic" can be found in many of his better-known ballads. Besides those ment-ioned, they include "The Cremation of Sam McGee", "The Ballad of Blas-phemous Bill", and "Clancy of the Mounted Police". In these ballads Service creates a nether world of terror in which men are driven mad or to their deaths. In "Clancy of the Mounted Police" the land terrifies and threatens: "Corpselike and stark was the land, with a quiet that crushed and awed,/ And the stars of the weird Sub-arctic glimmered over its shroud." And in "The Ballad of the Black Fox Skin" the threat is personified in a frightening and archetypal fairy-tale situation: "The Valley's girth was dumb with mirth, the laughter of the wild;/ The still sardonic laughter of an ogre o'er a child."

I F SERVICE HAD continued to react imaginatively to the North in this fashion, he might have created a valuable mythic vision. As it was, he became a magpie, randomly picking up physical or climatic characteristics of the North and using them as they suited his fancy at the time. The result is confusion, with one poem contradicting another; and it is this inconsistency that marks his failure to create a coherent northern myth.

The point is easily illustrated by comparing "The Ballad of the Northern Lights" with the well-known "Call of the Wild". The silent North, a "land that listens", was described by Sir Gilbert Parker as a land where the silence led man to meditate on the divine power that created the universe, and which guided man in his worldly struggles. Service treats this theme in "The Ballad of the Northern Lights", where in a terrifying world "purged of sound" three half-demented men hope to gain brief respite from the elemental forces harrying them by meditating on the things they "ought to think". In the world of the poem, however, the North refuses to allow such meditation; two of the men die, and the third is driven mad.

The ambivalence of Service's responses is seen clearly when the reader moves to "The Call of the Wild", for in this poem the silent North is revealed as the repository of truth: "Have you known the Great White Silence, not a snow-gemmed twig a-quiver?/ (Eternal truths that shame our soothing lies.)/ . . . Have you seen God in His splendours, heard the text that nature renders?/ (You'll never hear it in the family pew.)" Here Service says that only through intimate contact with the natural order can man come to a decision on the values he should use as a guide in life. The contrast with "The Ballad of the Northern Lights" is striking: in that poem the North is judge and executioner, resolutely condemning man to death for his weakness; here the North is teacher, benevolently aiding man to a more meaningful existence.

The conflicting attitudes toward the Canadian North which Service presents in his poetry are echoed in his novel of the Gold Rush, *The Trail of Ninety-Eight*. The novel is first of all a chronicle of a particular time and place, for, as the title indicates, it was the product of a specific historical event. Service, like Ballantyne and other writers on the North, found the subject matter for septentrional fiction in an event which had already stimulated widespread interest in the area. In one sense he was simply exploiting interest which the Gold Rush had created by producing a work of fiction to order, and one for which he could expect to find a favourable reception.

The Trail of Ninety-Eight dramatically retells the story of the struggles of men to reach the Klondike gold fields and their trials after arrival in Dawson. The hero, a romantic Scottish fortune hunter named Athol Meldrum, is introduced to the other characters on the steamer which carries him north to Skagway. Meldrum meets Berna Wilovich, the girl he eventually marries, and he comes into contact with the domineering and greedy Winklesteins, her guardians, and with Jack Locasto, the coarse brute who later intrigues with the Winklesteins to make Berna his mistress.

The terrible crossing of the mountains and the often tragic hardships of the trail from Skagway to Dawson are recounted in a series of illuminating instances which bring the trail to life in a manner reminiscent of Zola.

> It was an endless procession, in which every man was for himself. I can see them now, bent under their burdens, straining at their hand-sleighs, flogging their horses and oxen, their faces crimped and puckered with fatigue, the air acrid with their curses and heavy with their moans. Now a horse stumbles and slips into one of the

sump-holes by the trail side. No one can pass, the army is arrested. Frenzied fingers unhitch the poor brute and drag it from the water. Men, frantic with rage, beat savagely at their beasts of burden to make up the precious lost time.

Service's peculiar sensibility required a complete fidelity to fact, yet at the same time he was striving to realize his world imaginatively. But the conventions of popular fiction demanded a dramatic contrast (and conflict) between a sterling hero and an unregenerate villain. So although Meldrum becomes thoroughly infected with the gold-fever on his arrival in Dawson, he is untouched by the easy virtue of a town where the "good old moralities don't apply". Aware of the mass appeal of exposure, Service made much of the immorality of those in positions of power. When Meldrum is cheated out of a claim he staked, for example, he makes a vehement denunciation of the official corruption which was widespread at the time. While such passages help to make *The Trail of Ninety-Eight* valuable as a social record of the Canadian North seventy years ago, the plot is all too often unduly contrived to admit them.

The intrigues of the evil Locasto with the guardians of the virtuous Berna are melodramatically portrayed in a sequence of incidents which take place while the hero is out mining. Meldrum's return to find that Berna has been forced to become Locasto's mistress, and has since been leading the life of a dance-hall girl, results in his own fall into the world of sin and debauchery about him. At length he is rescued from his self-destroying debauch, and he and Berna live together in a love-sanctified union. The unexpected arrival of Garry, Meldrum's brother, complicates the idyllic existence of the couple. Shocked and disgusted by the common-law union, Garry attempts to seduce Berna to show his brother her true character. The attempt fails, and in a final climactic scene Meldrum and Berna (since quietly married) are caught together in a burning Dawson hotel with Garry and Locasto. Only the lovers escape the blaze.

Although it is obviously a contrived pot-boiler, *The Trail of Ninety-Eight* is nevertheless a significant contribution to literature about the Canadian North. It is one of the earliest attempts to make a myth of the North, to capture the spirit of the land and make it comprehensible. To do this, Service comes back again and again to the idea of the North as battlefield where man tests himself by contesting with the natural environment. While the idea of man and nature in conflict is conventional enough to be a cliché, Service might have used it freshly and effectively in the northern setting. He failed to make it work, however, because he was unable to decide whether such a conflict brings out man's nobler or baser qualities. In a number of passages, of which the following evocation of the spirit of the Gold Trail is typical, the North clearly brings out the worst in man.

> The spirit of the Gold Trail, how shall I describe it? It was based on that primal instinct of self-preservation that underlies our thin veneer of humanity. It was rebellion, anarchy; it was ruthless, aggressive, primitive; it was the man of the stone age in modern garb waging his fierce, incessant warfare with the forces of nature. Spurred on by the fever of the gold-lust, goaded by the fear of losing in the race; maddened by the difficulties and obstacles of the way, men became demons of cruelty and aggression, ruthlessly thrusting down the weaker ones who thwarted their program.

Yet elsewhere, when the North is described as a new frontier, conflict with the environment calls forth nobler instincts. The challenge of untamed nature is met, the battle is joined until "overall . . . triumphed the dauntless spirit of the Pathfinder — the mighty Pioneer."

Similar contradictory reactions to the northern landscape were noted in the poetry, and these are also evident in the novel. On the one hand, the North is repellent to man, its inhospitable nature an unwelcome reminder of his mortality.

> On all sides of the frozen lake over which they were travelling were hills covered with harsh pine, that pricked funereally up to the boulder-broken snows. Above that was a stormy and fantastic sea of mountains baring many a fierce peak-fang to the hollow heavens. The sky was a waxen grey, cold as a corpse-light. The snow was an immaculate shroud, unmarked by track of bird or beast. Death-sealed the land lay in its silent vastitude, in its despairful desolation.

On the other hand it is alluring, a compelling presence which casts its spell on the human imagination: "Who has lived in the North will ever forget the charm, the witchery of those midnight skies. . . . Surely, long after all else is forgotten, will linger the memory of those mystic nights with all their haunting spell of weird, disconsolate solitude." But here, as in the poetry, Service seems incapable of bringing the conflicting views together to create a consistent and meaningful vision of man in the North. The reader leaves his work aware of contradiction rather than ambiguity.

In the Gold Rush and the northern setting two elements for myth-making were ready to hand. The event and the land in which it happened combined to provide the first significant opportunity for mythologizing the North. Unfortunately for Canadian literature the talents of Service were inadequate to cope with the challenge, and the opportunity was lost.

(1971)

216

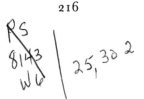

NOTES ON CONTRIBUTORS

ROY DANIELLS is University Professor of English at the University of British Columbia. He is a poet with two published volumes, *Deeper into the Forest* and *The Chequered Shade*; his other books include *Milton, Mannerism and Baroque* and *Alexander Mackenzie and the North West*, and an edition of Thomas Traherne's *A Serious and Pathetical Contemplation*. He is one of the editors of the *Literary History of Canada*, to which he contributed several chapters.

NORMAN NEWTON is a producer of radio drama and music for the Canadian Broadcasting Corporation. He is a poet and the author of several novels, including *The House of Gods, The One True Man* and *The Big Stuffed Hand of Friendship*. He has also published a biography — *Thomas Gage in Spanish America* — and a book on Haida culture, *Fire in the Raven's Nest*.

GEORGE WOODCOCK is editor of *Canadian Literature*. Among his forty published books are several in the field of Canadian studies, including *Canada and the Canadians, The Doukhobors* (with Ivan Avakumovic), *Odysseus Ever Returning, Hugh MacLennan* and *Mordecai Richler*. He is the editor of *Malcolm Lowry: The Man and his Work* and *Wyndham Lewis in Canada*.

DONALD STEPHENS is a member of the English department at the University of British Columbia and has been Associate Editor of *Canadian Literature* since 1960. He is the author of *Bliss Carman*, and his essays have appeared in various Canadian journals. He is editor of *Writers of the Prairies* and of *Contemporary Voices: The Short Story in Canada*.

NORMAN SHRIVE was until recently — and for six years — Head of the Department of English at McMaster University. His *Charles Mair: Literary Nationalist* is the definitive study of Mair both as poet and as political messianist, and his edition of Mair's poems has recently been published by the University of Toronto Press.

JOHN OWER has taught English at many places in Canada, the United States and New Zealand, and has published in literary journals in all these countries and also in France. He is at present teaching at the University of South Carolina.

W. J. KEITH is a Professor of English at University College in Toronto. He is the author of *Charles G. D. Roberts* and the editor of *Charles G. D. Roberts: Selected Poetry and Critical Prose*, but he has also written extensively on English literature, and in this field his books include *Richard Jefferies: A Critical Study* and *The Rural Tradition: A Study of the Non-Fiction Prose Writers of the English Countryside*.

BARRIE DAVIES, a member of the English Department at the University of New Brunswick, has published articles on Canadian and American writers in a number of journals, and is the editor of *The Selected Prose of Archibald Lampman*.

SANDRA DJWA, who teaches English at Simon Fraser University and is a frequent contributor to *Canadian Literature*, is the author of *E. J. Pratt: The Evolutionary Vision* and has recently edited a selection of Heavysege's poetry.

BRUCE NESBITT, also of Simon Fraser University, is the editor of *Earle Birney*, a selection of critical essays, and compiles the annual bibliography of Canadian literature for the *Journal of Canadian Fiction*.

GARY GEDDES, who has recently withdrawn from university teaching to devote himself to writing, is a poet — author of *Rivers Inlet, Snake Root* and *Letter of the Master of Horse*, a critic who has published widely, and editor of *20th Century Poetry and Poetics* and *15 Canadian Poets*.

GLENYS STOW teaches at the University of Guelph, is Associate Editor of *Canadian Children's Literature* and has published reviews of Canadian books in the *Journal of Canadian Fiction*.

JOHN ROBERT SORFLEET is editor of the newly founded *Canadian Children's Literature* and one of the editors of the *Journal of Canadian Fiction*. He has recently completed a book on Bliss Carman and is preparing an edition of the poet's Collected Works.

STANLEY S. ATHERTON teaches at St. Thomas University in Fredericton. He is the author of a book of poems, *Welcome to the Maritimes*, and of articles that have appeared in a number of journals.